Nuns Navigating the Spanish Empire

Diálogos Series

KRIS LANE, SERIES EDITOR

Understanding Latin America demands dialogue, deep exploration, and frank discussion of key topics. Founded by Lyman L. Johnson in 1992 and edited since 2013 by Kris Lane, the Diálogos Series focuses on innovative scholarship in Latin American history and related fields. The series, the most successful of its type, includes specialist works accessible to a wide readership and a variety of thematic titles, all ideally suited for classroom adoption by university and college teachers.

Also available in the Diálogos Series:

Sons of the Mexican Revolution: Miguel Alemán and His Generation
by Ryan M. Alexander

The Pursuit of Ruins: Archaeology, History, and the Making of Modern Mexico
by Christina Bueno

Creating Charismatic Bonds in Argentina: Letters to Juan and Eva Perón
by Donna J. Guy

Gendered Crossings: Women and Migration in the Spanish Empire
by Allyson M. Poska

From Shipmates to Soldiers: Emerging Black Identities in the Río de la Plata
by Alex Borucki

Women Drug Traffickers: Mules, Bosses, and Organized Crime by Elaine Carey

Searching for Madre Matiana: Prophecy and Popular Culture in Modern Mexico
by Edward Wright-Rios

Africans into Creoles: Slavery, Ethnicity, and Identity in Colonial Costa Rica
by Russell Lohse

Native Brazil: Beyond the Convert and the Cannibal, 1500–1900 edited by Hal Langfur

Emotions and Daily Life in Colonial Mexico
edited by Javier Villa-Flores and Sonya Lipsett-Rivera

For additional titles in the Diálogos Series, please visit unmpress.com.

Nuns Navigating the Spanish Empire

SARAH E. OWENS

University of New Mexico Press ❧ Albuquerque

© 2017 by the University of New Mexico Press
All rights reserved. Published 2017
Printed in the United States of America

22   21   20   19   18   17   1   2   3   4   5   6

Library of Congress Cataloging-in-Publication data
is on file at the Library of Congress.

Cover illustration: Diego Velázquez, *Sor Jerónima de la Fuente*, 1620.
The Prado Museum, via Wikimedia Commons.
Composed in Minion Pro 10.25/13.5
Display type is Minion Pro

For my parents, Miriam and Raymond Owens

Contents

Illustrations

✺

Acknowledgments

⊰ I AM HUMBLED AND GRATEFUL FOR ALL THE HELP I HAVE RECEIVED throughout the process of writing this book. Jane Mangan and others at the TePaske Seminar encouraged me to pursue my project as a monograph. Alison Weber and Jodi Bilinkoff read the initial proposal and their letters of support helped me obtain an NEH fellowship. Equally Alison and Jodi have provided continued guidance throughout the project. This book would not have been possible without the NEH fellowship and a sabbatical from the College of Charleston. Thanks to Nuria Salazar, Concepción Amerlinck, Doris Bieñko, and others from the Seminar on Nuns in Mexico City for commenting on the first version of my chapter on Mexico. I am grateful to Tanya Tiffany for sharing information with me about the nuns in Toledo and for her feedback on chapter 1. The nuns themselves in Toledo were extremely helpful. Without their support I would not have obtained access to Sor Ana's manuscript. I need to thank Cayetano Sánchez Fuertes at the Archivo Franciscano Ibero-Oriental in Madrid for his boundless support. Throughout the process Asunción Lavrin has fielded many of my questions on nuns and provided invaluable feedback. A special thanks to Jane Tar for her tips and leads to archival sources. I am especially grateful to Nina Scott and John Crossley, who both read the entire manuscript. In particular, John Crossley has been a wonderful sounding board throughout this whole project. I am very appreciative for the editorial suggestions from Kris Lane, editor of the Diálogos series, and for the guidance from Clark Whitehorn, executive editor of the University of New Mexico Press. I would also like to thank the anonymous reviewer at the press for the thorough review and positive feedback. I owe a debt of gratitude to friends and colleagues from the College of Charleston and community for their support. Thanks to Maricela Villalobos for helping me with the translations, to Danny Jones for his assistance in transcribing the manuscript into contemporary Spanish, to Patrick McCarty for creating the maps, and to Daniel Delgado for taking the photo of the Immaculate Conception in Toledo.

Part of chapter 1 previously appeared as "The First Nunnery in Manila: The Role of Hernando de los Ríos Coronel," *Catholic Historical Review* 102, no. 3 (Summer 2016): 469–91; a special thanks to my coauthor of that article, John Crossley, for allowing me to use part of that article here. Part of chapter 2 previously appeared as "Crossing Mexico (1620–1621): Franciscan Nuns and Their Journey to the Philippines," *The Americas* 72, no. 4 (October 2015): 583–606. I also drew on two of my publications in Spanish for chapter 5: "El legado del rosario milagroso en los escritos de viaje de sor Ana de Cristo hacia Filipinas," *Boletín de Monumentos Históricos* 30 (January–April 2014): 22–35; and "Monjas españolas en Filipinas: La formación de lectura y escritura de sor Ana de Cristo," in *Letras en la celda: Cultura escrita de los conventos femeninos en la España moderna*, ed. Nieves Baranda Leturio and María Carmen Marín Pina (Madrid: Editorial Iberoamericana/Vervuert, 2014): 379–92.

This book would not have been possible without my family. My parents, Miriam and Raymond Owens, have always encouraged me to follow my scholarly pursuits. My dad, who worked full-time until he was seventy-eight years old, proofread every chapter. Lastly I want to give a shout-out to my husband, Barry Hainer, who has been a faithful supporter and travel companion.

Unveiling the Manuscript

⇌

⇌ IN THE MUSEO DEL PRADO HANGS A PORTRAIT OF AN ELDERLY AND austere nun. She is garbed in the traditional habit of the Poor Clares, nuns of the Franciscan order. Although her veined hands and wrinkled face tell us that she has already lived many years, the artist portrays the nun with a penetrating gaze of determination. In her left hand she holds a book—perhaps *The Rule of Saint Clare*—and in her right she clutches a long crucifix. The painter of this captivating portrait is none other than Diego Velázquez. His subject is a Spanish nun from Toledo, Sor Jerónima de la Asunción (1556–1630). She sat for this portrait in 1620 while staying for almost two months in Seville on her way to the Philippines. She had just turned sixty-four at the time, and Velázquez was only twenty-one. She would go on to found the first female convent in the Far East.[1] He would become the most famous Golden Age painter in Spanish history.

Yet there is more behind this story. What most people do not know is that one of the cofounders of the convent of Poor Clares in Manila, Sor Ana de Cristo (1565–1636), wrote a 450-folio biography about Sor Jerónima and their fifteen-month odyssey around the globe. From 1620 to 1621, Sor Jerónima and nine other religious women, including Sor Ana, made a remarkable journey to the Philippines. In brief, the convent's cofounders left Toledo on April 28, 1620, sailed the Atlantic Ocean on the Fleet of New Spain to Mexico, made an overland journey from Veracruz to Mexico City, spent

Figure 1 Diego Velázquez, *Sor Jerónima de la Fuente*, 1620.
Oil on canvas, 63" x 43.3". The Prado Museum, via Wikimedia Commons.

the next five months in the capital, trekked south by mule to the port of Acapulco, sailed on the Manila galleon route across the Pacific to the Philippine Islands, docked at the port of Bolinao on the island of Luzon, and after being carried in litters by native Filipinos finally arrived in Manila on August 5, 1621. The women, accompanied by two friars and two male servants, encountered many obstacles both at sea and on land, perhaps the worst being the death of one of their beloved sisters on a Manila galleon.

I found Sor Ana's manuscript in the convent from which they departed in Toledo, while conducting archival research several years ago in Spain. Since that time I have received a fellowship from the National Endowment for the Humanities and a sabbatical from the College of Charleston that have allowed me to transcribe the entire handwritten manuscript into contemporary Spanish. I have also conducted extensive research in other archives of Spain, Mexico, and the Vatican. Sor Ana's manuscript, research in archives and rare books, and the latest scholarship on early modern history, literacy, monasticism, race, and class all combine to make *Nuns Navigating the Spanish Empire*.

The purpose of this study is to shine a light on Sor Ana de Cristo's narration of the nuns navigating Spain's global empire.[2] Although the jury is still out as to whether this was truly the first global era, I contend that the term *global* is appropriate for my study on this group of Spanish nuns since their travels across oceans and continents exposed them to diverse sets of peoples, cultures, and trade networks. They tasted new foods, heard different languages, and felt the extreme climate change between Spain and the Far East. Sor Ana's devotion to Sor Jerónima and desire to portray her as a future saint is entangled with her navigation of completely new experiences, such as the nuns' encounters with natives in the Caribbean, Mexico, and the Philippines. Over the centuries scholars have focused only on Sor Jerónima. There are many reasons why no one has taken the time to research Sor Ana's life and writings. There is no picture of her hanging in the Prado, she did not miraculously cure the sick, nor did she practice extreme penance. No cleric or nun from past or present has written a biography about her, and there is no ongoing canonization dossier that draws attention to her life. Finally, her 450-folio manuscript has been gathering dust over the centuries, forgotten until recently in the convent archive of Santa Isabel de los Reyes, Toledo. Despite all this, Sor Ana's life is important because she formed part of the group of cofounders who navigated oceans and crossed the borders of two hemispheres. In addition to the physical journey, she also embarked on an intellectual transformation, one that led her to write the lengthy biography of Sor Jerónima. Before leaving Spain, she tells us, she knew how to read but did not know how to write. Lack of the second skill kept her from holding certain offices within the convent, and she certainly could never aspire to become abbess. Yet like the conquistadors who left Spain with the hopes of earning fame and riches, things they could never obtain in the firmly entrenched class system of their homeland, Sor Ana had the opportunity to reinvent herself in the New World.

Nuns Navigating the Spanish Empire highlights Sor Ana's intellectual transformation, one that was sparked by her journey across the Spanish Empire. She went from a semi-illiterate religious woman in her home convent in Toledo to the literate abbess of the first convent in Manila. We know this because she weaves fragments of her own life and perspective into her manuscript. Sor Ana explains how she was taught to write by a Franciscan friar during and after the sea voyage. Although in an assessment of her own writing Sor Ana belittles herself as barely literate, a careful examination of her writing style reveals a literate woman adept in the rhetoric of obedience and humility. Whether she was fully aware of her own subjectivity will never be known. Regardless, an analysis of her manuscript provides a roadmap to her life's journey and, with that, a window offering a gendered perspective of the global early modern world. She treats the reader to descriptions of the Carib natives on the islands of Guadeloupe, the hardships of the China Road in Mexico, and the perilous sea voyage on the Manila galleon route. We learn how the nuns distributed "miraculous" rosary beads to local peoples and used them to ward off deadly illness and stormy weather. The women interacted with recently converted Amerindians and witnessed the cruel beating of a black enslaved woman on a Spanish ship. The fabric of Sor Ana's writing is not seamless. Indeed, many sections are difficult to follow, and we must untangle the threads of her discourse. The complex interplay of post-Tridentine doctrine, clerical rivalries, political maneuvering, and race, class, and gender issues, alongside Sor Ana's own anxiety of authorship, all influenced her retelling of events.

Nuns Navigating the Spanish Empire demonstrates the importance of Sor Ana's writing and the part that she played in positioning Sor Jerónima as a would-be saint. I believe she was well aware of the fact that her own writing would never be published. She also knew, however, that her words would form the basis of future biographies by male clerics. Sor Ana's words carried weight and power. By hiding behind the veil of holy obedience she was able not only to explore her own concept of self but also to actively participate in the promotion of a possible saint. Sor Ana's work forms one of the main building blocks in Sor Jerónima's long road to canonization, a process that is still going on today. In short, Sor Ana also forged a place for herself in Spain's global empire.

The majority of this book follows the linear route of the nuns' journey. The first chapter surveys the steps taken from Spain (and in the Philippines) to acquire the necessary licenses for Sor Jerónima and her cohort to travel to the

Far East. It then traces the itinerary of the nuns from their convent in Toledo south across Andalusia to the port of Cádiz. Sor Ana's retelling of events sheds light on the cultivation of art, music, and theater in Spain's female monastic communities. Chapter 2 is divided into two main sections. First, it explores the transatlantic passage from Cádiz via the island of Guadeloupe to the port of Veracruz. Second, it analyzes the nuns' crossing of Mexico from Veracruz to Acapulco. It highlights the women's encounters with Amerindians, a landmark stop at the Shrine of the Virgin of Guadalupe, life in Mexico City's convents, and the mosquito-ridden China Road to the Pacific coast. In chapter 3 the nuns board an infamous Manila galleon, where they spend the next four months before arriving on the island of Luzon. After exploring Sor Ana's gendered rendition of life at sea, this chapter takes the reader on the women's last leg of the journey as they are carried by Filipino natives in *hamacas* (litters) from the port of Bolinao southeast to the capital, Manila. The fourth chapter analyzes the obstacles that the nuns faced in Manila trying to establish themselves as a discalced convent of Poor Clares. Chapter 4 also explores the lives of some of the other notable nuns who traveled to Manila and their unlikely path to the convent. It concludes with Sor Ana's tenure as abbess and her support of a new convent in Macao, China. Since the first four chapters are dedicated to the nuns' travel story, the final chapter provides an analysis of Sor Ana's text and considers how we should appraise it in light of writings by early modern nuns. Sor Ana's path to literacy highlights the strong literary and auditory culture in early modern Spanish convents, one that exposed nuns to a myriad of religious writings. Not only were nuns exposed to canonical works of the time, such as the lives of saints, but they also found particular inspiration in female religious role models. Chapter 5 emphasizes the importance of several Spanish holy women, such as Mother Juana de la Cruz (also known as Santa Juana, but never canonized, 1481–1534), Saint Teresa of Avila (1515–1582), and Sor Luisa de la Ascensión (1565–1636). In light of these inspirational role models, along with rhetorical strategies and themes common to Franciscan female writers, the final portion of this chapter analyzes Sor Ana's development of her own unique writing style.

Finally, a short epilogue provides information on the struggles that the convent endured over the centuries: from devastating earthquakes, to the British seizure of Manila in 1762, to the Spanish-American War of 1898, to the complete destruction of the convent buildings during Allied bombing in World War II. Despite these major setbacks, the community, now relocated in Quezon City, continues to this day.

Sor Ana de Cristo's Manuscript

I wish to clarify from the outset that this study does not include a full-length translation of Sor Ana's manuscript. There are several reasons for this. The manuscript is quite lengthy: the 450 folios are equivalent to about 365 pages of single-spaced text (216,000 words).[3] Parts of the manuscript follow a linear narrative, but others skip from the narrative present (Manila) to the past (Toledo or during the journey) or vice versa, while some have more of a stream-of-consciousness style, and still others include long sections on visions and prophesies. Instead, my approach has been to mine the text for nuggets of gold, especially regarding the actual journey, and where appropriate I have inserted select English translations throughout this book. Unless otherwise indicated, all the translations are my own.

The manuscript still exists and is held by the nuns at the Convent of Santa Isabel de los Reyes in Toledo, Spain. To the best of my knowledge, the version in Toledo is the only extant manuscript. Through the generosity of the nuns at Santa Isabel, to whom I owe a debt of gratitude, I was allowed to take digital photographs of the entire document, which was written on rice paper from Manila. The narrative is organized into chapters, each with a descriptive title and a number. There are some inconsistencies, however, regarding the chapters. The first forty-seven are written as Roman numerals. Thereafter the text changes to Arabic numbers, but instead of starting with chapter 48, the next chapter commences with 35 and the numbering then continues all the way to chapter 70. The narrative begins with an unnumbered preface (eight folios), but beginning with chapter 1 the folios are numbered. Like the chapters, the folio numbering also has a few inconsistencies: several pages are lacking numbers, or the scribe makes a mistake and skips a number. I have chosen to follow the folio numbers exactly as they are found on the manuscript.

Sor Ana wrote the bulk of her manuscript, that is, the part that is organized into chapters, between 1623 and 1626, after arriving in Manila. The rest of the work continued until 1629, a year before Sor Jerónima's death. She signs the last page of the manuscript "Ana de Cristo, vicaria" (she was vicaress in 1629). The handwriting of her signature appears different from that in the rest of the manuscript, indicating that at least one scribe (perhaps another nun, but we have no way of knowing) worked on the manuscript. We also do not know if the manuscript was copied from one version to another or if Sor Ana dictated sections to scribes. In addition to the

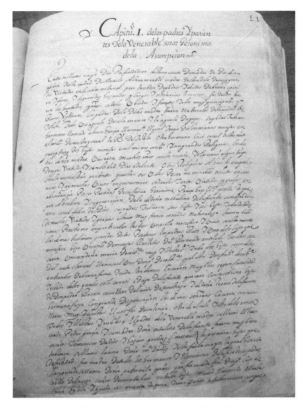

Figure 2 Sample page from Sor Ana de Cristo's manuscript.
The Monasterio de Santa Isabel de los Reyes. Photo by the author.

surviving copy of the manuscript, according to the nineteenth-century
Franciscan historian Félix de Huerta there existed at least one other version, bound in two volumes.[4]

The biography of Sor Jerónima ends after chapter 70. The remaining
folios (about seventy-two thousand words) contain a variety of texts: transcriptions of letters written in 1626 by Fray Alonso de Montemayor, commissary general of the Franciscan Order, to the nuns in Manila; a letter from Sor
Jerónima to the Audiencia or royal court in Manila (1623); several other letters
from male clerics (1626–1629); short biographies of exceptional nuns from
Santa Isabel de los Reyes, Toledo; an account penned by another one of the
cofounders from Toledo, Sor Luisa de Jesús; necrologies, including biographical information about the first novices to profess in Manila—the most notable

Figure 3 Sor Ana de Cristo's signature, last page of manuscript.
The Monasterio de Santa Isabel de los Reyes. Photo by the author.

being a young Christian woman exiled from Japan; and finally an account detailing Sor Jerónima's last year of life, in 1629. Although it is evident that Sor Ana wrote the majority of the work, especially because in the formal chapters she refers to herself in the first person, there are several clues in the document that parts of the manuscript were more of a collective work between several nuns in Manila. This becomes clear in the last section with the biographies written about the exceptional nuns from Toledo. At one point Sor Ana reminds the reader that she was writing from memory "since I never thought I would ever write and I did not pay close attention to anything."[5] Most likely she also drew on the memories of her companions from Spain to fill in blanks about their experiences with Sor Jerónima and others while still in Toledo. Further, the inclusion of Sor Luisa's account helps elucidate Sor Jerónima's relationship to the Third Order laywoman Mariana de Jesús (1577–1620), a pious visionary in Toledo whom the women admired greatly.

Works like Sor Ana's are not always easily categorized into one genre, such as biography or *vida* (spiritual biography), and more frequently than not, they became a blending of two or more genres. To avoid confusion throughout this study, I have chosen to call Sor Ana's text a biography, but I am aware that this is a misnomer. Perhaps Sor Ana never put a title on her manuscript because she herself viewed it not purely as a biography of Sor Jerónima but more as a hybrid text: a combination of biography, autobiography, travel narrative, and convent chronicle. Darcy Donahue's superb study on Discalced Carmelites speaks to the intricate interplay of authorship of vidas and other convent writing. She describes writing within the convent as a communal activity. In one case she examines a coauthored biography signed by five nuns. In another case (very similar to that of Sor Ana), she describes a type of hybrid narrative—both autobiographical and biographical—of one nun retelling the life of another, while at the same time she intersperses her own personal reactions and commentary on her subject's exceptional spirituality.[6] Undoubtedly, the network of exchange that shored up Sor Ana's text not only gave her the confidence to explore Sor Jerónima's agency as the first founder of a convent in the Far East but also added to her own agency as a budding writer and convent chronicler.

It should also be noted that a partial transcription of Sor Ana's biography is included in the *positio* (papers for the process of beatification) that was compiled in 1991 by Pedro Ruano as part of the ongoing beatification process of Sor Jerónima (initiated in 1734).[7] Although there is no title on Sor Ana's manuscript, the Franciscans have taken the liberty of naming the document *Historia de nuestra santa madre Jerónima de la Asunción*. The name is taken from the title of a standalone chapter of the manuscript inserted between chapters 40 and 41 (discussed in chapter 5). I also have used this title to identify Sor Ana's manuscript.

The version in the positio contains less than one-third (approximately sixty-one thousand words) of Sor Ana's entire manuscript. It is incomplete because Ruano selected only sections from the formal seventy chapters, and then only those that he deemed relevant to the promotion of Sor Jerónima as a potential saint. He justifies this selection by relying on another biography about Sor Jerónima, written by the Franciscan friar Ginés de Quesada—who served as Sor Jerónima's confessor during the last few months of her life. Quesada, and subsequent biographers such as Bartolomé de Letona, had access to Sor Ana's manuscript and used it by incorporating whole sections into their own published works.[8] The positio also includes a transcription of Quesada's biography (1713) of Sor Jerónima, which proved invaluable to my research and is the version that I consulted for this book.

The significance of Sor Ana de Cristo's story of the nuns navigating the Spanish Empire should not be underestimated. Her own road to literacy illuminates how she and other religious women negotiated the strict post-Tridentine rules of how nuns should express themselves on paper. Her personal journey and those of her cofounders prove that there were multiple paths to the convent, some of which required transoceanic voyages. Sor Ana's biography of Sor Jerónima enriches our knowledge of the experiences of women who traveled the global trade routes of the Spanish Indies fleet.

The Toledo convent that the nuns left in the spring of 1620 was very different from their future Philippine mission. Toledo had a long and entrenched tradition of female monastic orders. The first convent, Santo Domingo el Antiguo, was founded at the end of the eleventh century. During the time of Sor Jerónima the city was bustling with religious orders, and young women of financial means and "Old Christian" blood could choose to take their vows in any number of orders, from Augustinians and Carmelites to Dominicans, Franciscans, and more. In contrast, Manila was still a remote outpost on the fringe of the Spanish Empire. It had only recently been taken over as a Spanish city, in 1571, and as late as 1619 there had been talk of abandoning the Philippines altogether. The city of Manila itself had a diverse population. In addition to a relatively small community of Spaniards, large

Table 1 Founding nuns from Spain and Mexico

NAME	BIRTH AND DEATH DATES	AGE IN 1620*
Sor Jerónima de la Asunción	1556–1630	64
Sor Ana de Cristo	1565–1636	55
Sor Leonor de San Francisco	1583–1651	37
Sor Juana de San Antonio	1588–1661	32
Sor Luisa de Jesús	1556?–?	64
Sor María Magdalena de la Cruz	1575–1653	45
Sor María Magdalena de Cristo	1594?–?	26
Sor María de la Trinidad	?–1621	—
Sor Leonora de San Buenaventura	—	—
Sor María de los Angeles	—	—

Note: — indicates unknown.

* This was the nuns' approximate age upon departure from Toledo, Spain, in 1620.

numbers of native Tagalogs and Chinese, along with Japanese and imported Asian and African slaves, inhabited the city. Despite the missionary work of Spanish friars and priests, there were no female convents before Sor Jerónima and her cofounders arrived. At the most, the nuns had only heard stories of these distant lands. When the thick gates of their home convent shut behind them, Sor Jerónima and her sisters were about to see with their own eyes the extreme geographical and ethnic diversity within Spain's global empire. *Nuns Navigating the Spanish Empire* brings to the fore the route between these two distinct cities on either side of the world. Simply put, this study offers an important lens through which to view the paths, waterways, and peoples of the Spanish Atlantic and Pacific through the eyes of religious women.

BIRTHPLACE	CONVENT OF ORIGIN	AGE AT DEATH
Toledo, Spain	Santa Isabel de los Reyes, Toledo	74
Getafe, Spain	Santa Isabel de los Reyes, Toledo	71
Corral de Almaguer, La Mancha, Spain	Santa Isabel de los Reyes, Toledo	68
Chozas de Canales, Toledo, Spain	Did not take vows until Manila	73
Sabiote, Andalucía, Spain	Did not take vows until Manila	—
Pinto, Madrid, Spain	Santa María de la Cruz, Cubas	78
—	Santa María de la Cruz, Cubas	—
—	Santa Clara de la Columna, Belalcázar	—
—	La Visitación (Santa Isabel), Mexico City	—
—	La Visitación (Santa Isabel), Mexico City	—

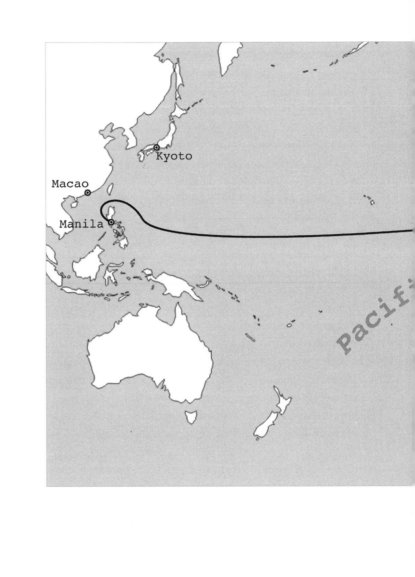

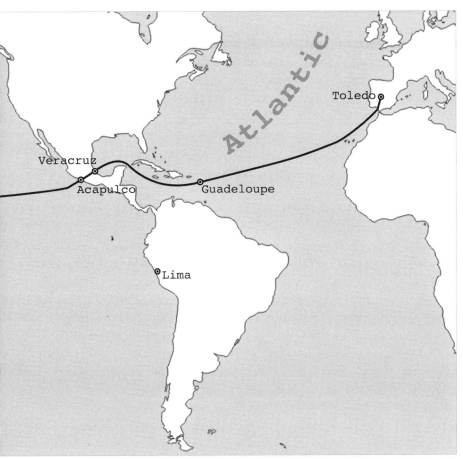

Map 1 The nuns' transoceanic journey from Toledo to Manila.
Map created by Patrick McCarty.

CHAPTER 1

Toledo to Cádiz

⁓⅄

⁓ FEW TRAVELERS WHO HAVE BEEN TO THE SOUTH OF SPAIN IN THE month of May can forget the spectacular show of wildflowers. The expansive pastures, orange groves, and vast tracts of olive trees are bursting with new life. In May 1620, as the small group of nuns made their way from Toledo to Seville and then continued on to the port city of Cádiz, they certainly would have felt the fresh breezes of spring and detected the fragrant scent of jasmine, orange blossoms, and wild roses. Their escort and father confessor, Fray José de Santa María, often told the nuns to open the curtains to their carriage so that they could see the fields of flowers. Sor Jerónima repeatedly denied his requests, saying she preferred the perpetual flowering of his divine presence.[1] It had taken her most of her adult life to finally find herself sitting in that carriage, and she only wanted to continue her lifestyle of permanent enclosure. Nevertheless, she was exhilarated by the grace of God that "there would be convents of nuns in such remote lands."[2] And perhaps it was true that, in the beginning, especially while still on the Iberian Peninsula, Sor Jerónima was able to maintain her austere regimen. Yet, as the paths and waterways became more complicated and she found herself with no other choice than to dine at the table of elite criollos, ride mules on the China Road to Acapulco, or be carried in a primitive hammock through the jungle in the Philippines, controlled moments like that of the carriage would soon become distant memories.

In some ways this constant clash between a desired ideal, that is, living a life of poverty and penance, and the realistic measures needed to secure the funding and permissions for a convent of Poor Clare nuns on the other side of the globe, became the hallmark of the founding of the convent in the Philippines. Sor Jerónima, who hailed from a prosperous family of lower nobility, already had much experience navigating the nexus between piety and patronage. Although she strove to epitomize austerity, living on bread and water, wrapping herself in hair shirts, and tending to beggars, prisoners, and the infirm, Sor Jerónima also had to court some of Spain's most prominent historical individuals, including members of the royal family. Indeed, she needed to strike a careful balance in this complex landscape of religion and politics. She interacted with religious and secular authorities, nobles and merchants, beggars and the destitute, in short, a wide cast of characters. These interactions gave her the experience and the contacts that made it possible for the nuns to receive the necessary licenses and funds, ultimately from the king of Spain, to sail to the Philippines.

After exploring these issues of patronage and piety, my main purpose here is to follow the route of the nuns from Toledo to the Atlantic coast through the eyes of Sor Ana. As the founders pass from convent to convent—from Toledo to Carmona, to Seville, to Jerez, and finally to Cádiz—she treats the reader to penetrating insights into what life was like within these female monasteries. Not only do her words reveal typical expressions of piety through descriptions of the monstrance, images of Saint Clare, and sculptures of the Immaculate Conception, but Sor Ana also introduces us to homegrown theatrical performances and beautiful musical concerts. As with other portions of her manuscript, unraveling meaning is not always easy. As we shall see, one of the main threads that Sor Ana omits in her tapestry of events is mention of Diego Velázquez and the portrait of Sor Jerónima he painted during their time in Seville.

Toledo at the turn of the seventeenth century was filled with monasteries of friars and nuns. In addition to Santa Isabel de los Reyes, there were two other convents of Clarissan nuns in the city.[3] There were many other female convents, too, representing all different religious orders, such as Carmelites, Capuchins, Augustinians, Conceptionists, and Dominicans. Discalced Franciscans congregated in the city at the fifteenth-century Monastery of San Juan de los Reyes that had been founded by the Catholic monarchs Isabel and Ferdinand and was renowned for its gothic architecture and beautiful cloister.[4] Priests, bishops, archbishops, and friars from around Spain

Map 2 The nuns' journey across Spain. Map created by Patrick McCarty.

came to visit the immense and wealthy cathedral of Toledo. During the 1500s it had a staff of over six hundred clerics and "was easily the largest and richest in the peninsula."[5] Many wanted to see the place where the Virgin Mary purportedly presented a chasuble to the Toledan bishop Ildefonsus in the seventh century (he later became the patron saint of Toledo). El Greco painted several works that depict the city and others, such as *The Burial of the Count of Orgaz* that, capture the tremendous religiosity of the local sixteenth-century population and blend it with the legendary spiritual world of a medieval nobleman.[6]

As girls, Jerónima and Ana walked the narrow, twisted alleyways of the medieval city. Remnants of Toledo's diverse past could be seen at every turn: Christian palaces, former synagogues, and Mudéjar architecture. The latter, influenced by the Muslims who lived under Christian rule, left its mark with horseshoe arches and intricately adorned walls with geometric carvings and designs made of plaster, timber, bricks, and tiles. In many ways, the Convent of Santa Isabel represents Toledo's layering of cultures. It had first been a Moorish palace, then the palaces of Casarrubios and Arroyomolinos, and later Queen Isabel I donated the buildings and land to the Franciscans who

Figure 4 Inside patio of the Convent of Santa Isabel, Toledo (geometric carvings).
The Monasterio de Santa Isabel de los Reyes. Photo by the author.

founded the convent of Clarissan nuns in 1447.[7] To this day one can visit
parts of the convent to see the arabesque timber ceilings and archways deco-
rated with elaborate plaster and stuccowork. The Tagus River, far below the
church steeples, cuts a gorge around the city so that the girls could have
looked out from its high banks far over the plains of Castile. They would have
rubbed shoulders with men of the cloth and heard talk of missions in far-off
Peru, Mexico, the Philippines, and even China and Japan. They both grew up
on the same street, the Calle de los Letrados, next to the Church of San
Marcos.[8] Although Jerónima and Ana were separated in age by almost ten
years, Ana knew much about her older companion because she played with
her younger sisters. In contrast to Jerónima's parents, Licenciado Pedro
Yáñez and doña Catalina de la Fuente, who traced their lineage to lower
nobility, we know very little about Ana's family (see chapter 5 for a discussion
of Ana's early years).

Jerónima had two aunts and several cousins who were nuns in the nearby

Convent of Santa Isabel de los Reyes. With her family connections and wealthy background, Jerónima entered the same convent on August 15, 1570. At that time "she became dead to the [secular] world" and changed her name from Jerónima Yáñez de la Fuente to Sor Jerónima de la Asunción.[9] After a yearlong novitiate she took her vows as a black-veiled nun.[10] Once in the convent, Sor Jerónima spent the next five decades behind the thick walls of Santa Isabel. From the very beginning she wanted to profess under the strict First Rule of Saint Clare. As a child she had avidly read the life of Saint Clare, and she already had begun to flagellate herself: "She attached little balls of wax, stuck with pins, to strings and with that she whipped herself until she shed copious amounts of blood."[11] She continued her routine of penance and fasting when she became a nun at Santa Isabel. She became so thin that Sor Ana notes she did not have a menstrual period for over fifteen years.[12] Her lifestyle of abnegation, however, was a problem since the nuns of Santa Isabel followed the Second Rule, which made it a so-called Urbanist convent.

The terminology used in English for these different rules can be confusing, especially because the generic term for Franciscan nuns is often Poor Clares (or *clarisas* in Spanish). Ironically, *poor* does not accurately reflect Urbanist nuns because they often came from well-to-do "Old Christian" families, paid a substantial dowry to profess, brought lands and rents to convents, and in places outside the Iberian Peninsula such as New Spain, had their own living quarters, where they were tended by cooks, servants, and even slaves. The First Rule of Saint Clare that Jerónima yearned to follow was based on a life of poverty and communal living. The First Rule stipulated that communities live off alms (not dowries, land, or rents) and forbade a servant class within the cloister.[13] In addition to the First and Second Rules, widows or married women who did not have the possibility of professing in a convent could take vows of the Third Order. Also known as tertiaries, these lay women professed a life of piety, poverty, and austerity, but they did not always live enclosed.[14] An example, which is explored in chapter 5, is Mariana de Jesús, renowned for her miraculous visions, and her companion Luisa de Jesús, who later traveled with the nuns to Manila. Regardless of the First or Second Rule, after the Council of Trent (1545–1563) all Catholic convents required nuns to live enclosed. Post-Tridentine regulations stipulated very few reasons for which a nun could leave her convent; the only exceptions were natural disasters, imminent warfare, and the establishment of new communities.[15]

Patronage and Piety

Many intersecting factors led up to the promotion of Sor Jerónima as the leader of the expedition to the Philippines. The fact that she had gained a name for herself as the "Saint of Santa Isabel" and the "Saint of Toledo" attracted the attention of male friars from several different orders, especially those who had experience in Asia. With the potential of promoting her as a would-be saint, they saw the spiritual and financial gains as boundless. It was expensive to send missionaries to Asia, but a holy woman such as Sor Jerónima could help obtain financial support from the Crown and wealthy Spaniards. These well-traveled men had already witnessed the success of the Spanish imperial enterprise in establishing religious and charitable organizations in its colonies, especially Mexico (for example, the first convent for women was established in Mexico City in 1540), and they understood that a nunnery in Manila would help secure their missionary expansion in Asia.[16] Sor Jerónima fully embraced the idea, perhaps because she saw this as her last chance to create a community under the First Rule of Saint Clare. Years earlier, in 1584 when she was twenty-eight years old, Sor Jerónima had been named as the founder of a discalced convent in Toledo, but for reasons that we do not know, the convent never came to fruition.[17] Sor Ana does allude to this as a difficult time, full of persecutions in Sor Jerónima's life—some of the nuns "ridiculed her and told her to stay put"—but she never specifies what happened.[18] Despite this setback, Sor Jerónima had been granted the privilege of following the First Rule of Saint Clare while still in Toledo. Still, this was not the same as leading an entire community under the staunch precepts of poverty and penance.

The first male religious to approach Sor Jerónima with the idea of her traveling to the Philippines was not a Franciscan but the Dominican Diego de Soria. In 1599, while visiting a female relative in the Convent of Santa Isabel, Soria had the opportunity to meet and speak with Sor Jerónima.[19] He spoke to her at length about the urgent need to establish a convent in Manila. This first meeting inspired Sor Jerónima to pursue her dream of forming her own convent, but she told Soria that she would prefer to work with friars from her own order.

More than twenty years would pass after that meeting before Sor Jerónima and her small group of cofounders would leave Toledo. During those years, many other highly influential friars met with Sor Jerónima. In 1606 she met the senior ecclesiastical officials Pedro Matías de Andrade, definitor and procurator of the Franciscan Philippine Province of San Gregorio Magno,

Figure 5 *Friar Preaching to Native Americans*, 1700. Engraving by Thomas Doesburgh found in Thomas Gage, *English-American His Travail by Sea and Land*. Courtesy of the John Carter Brown Library at Brown University.

and Francisco de Sosa, minister general of the Franciscans.[20] Friar Luis Sotelo visited Sor Jerónima during his trip to Europe as interpreter for the Japanese embassy (1613–1618) hoping to negotiate direct trade with Spain.[21] He spoke to her at length about his own experiences in Asia and more than likely urged her to expand her missionary goals to China and Japan. He would meet the nuns later in Manila before he returned to Japan and died a martyr there in 1624. Sor Ana reports how Sotelo also animated Sor Jerónima by telling her how he and other friars had told Pope Paul V about the need for a nunnery in Manila. When the pope inquired about what group of nuns would lead the foundation, they informed him about the holy nun from Toledo, "the one who is dressed in *cardas*."[22] Earlier in the manuscript Sor Ana describes Sor Jerónima's hair shirt made with cardas, a sharp-toothed implement used to card (clean and comb) raw wool before spinning. She would peel off the sharp combs from the boards and piece them together to make a spiked garter.[23]

On August 27, 1612, two oceans away in Manila, the main benefactors of the convent, the wealthy married couple of Pedro Chávez and Ana de Vera, drew up a will to sponsor the future community. At the time there were no female monasteries in the Philippines, only the College of Santa Potenciana, first established in 1589 as an institution for poor orphan girls of Spanish descent, some of them daughters of conquistadors.[24] The couple had met with several Franciscan friars, in particular Pedro Matías, who had returned to Manila and extolled Sor Jerónima's remarkable virtues as a holy woman. The following fragment from the will indicates how the perceived sanctity of Sor Jerónima had reached Manila: "The information that we have on doña Jerónima de la Asunción, the nun in the monastery of Santa Isabel, in the City of Toledo, is praiseworthy. Therefore, we would like that she be the founder because we know God is moving her on this project. Should she die on her journey to Manila, a nun from among the ones she had taken along with her should take over. If the said doña Jerónima de la Fuente has died, let this donation be void."[25] As main patrons of the convent, their donation came with several highly coveted benefits. Scholarship on patronage shows that the endowment of convents, chaplaincies, and other charitable institutions could help a person or married couple rise in status among their peers (Chávez and Vera had endowed the first chaplaincy in the Philippines in 1607).[26] Perhaps even more importantly, by founding a convent the patrons would have a guaranteed place to bury their bodies and could expect the nuns to say intercessory prayers for their souls, often in perpetuity.[27] In fact, this was the case with Queen Isabel's daughter, doña

Isabel, queen of Portugal, who was buried beneath the choir of the Convent of Santa Isabel in Toledo.[28] It stands to reason that Chávez and his wife understood all of these potential benefits and eagerly bequeathed their assets to the future convent.

After Chávez's death, Ana de Vera drew up a new will, dated July 1617. By doing so, she reaffirmed her wish to remain as the convent's main patron. Her new will essentially mimicked the first one with the additional donation of houses in Manila and ranches in San Palóc (now Sampaloc). She also reaffirmed her desire to have Sor Jerónima lead the new foundation, but if Sor Jerónima were to die before departure, then she would transfer her bequest to nuns of another order. The language in this document is straightforward and affirms doña Ana's support of the Poor Clares led by Sor Jerónima.[29] Indeed, the words in this will speak to the power and agency of female patrons. Since doña Ana was supplying her land and rents, she wanted a say in the foundation of the first convent and had specific expectations. As we shall see in chapter 4 of this book, however, when the nuns finally arrived in the Philippines, she had second thoughts about her donation, influenced by a nephew recently arrived from Spain.

Convent of Santa Isabel

Perhaps one of the greatest contradictions for Sor Jerónima in her pursuit of poverty was that she had to court wealthy donors and the noble class. Simply put, she was unable to untangle the interplay between her own elite upbringing, the convent's connections to the noble class, and the need to court supporters and patrons of her future convent in Manila. This complex landscape of piety and wealth is very much related to the issues navigated by Teresa of Avila in her quest to reform the Carmelite order. She too understood the contradiction of courting wealthy patrons, especially because they felt entitled to make demands on the running of the convent: for example, by imposing either themselves, family members, or friends as novices.[30]

The Convent of Santa Isabel in Toledo attracted many noblewomen as nuns and others as benefactors: several nuns at Santa Isabel hailed from Toledo's most illustrious families. When Sor Ana cites these women in her account, she does not refer to them as *sor* or *madre* but instead calls them *señora* or *doña*, thus paying tribute to their noble blood. For example, the abbess at the time of Sor Jerónima's departure was doña Estefanía Manrique.

Her brother, don Francisco Tello de Guzmán, had been governor of Manila from 1596 until 1602. Another nun, doña Juana de Toledo, had important ties to the court.[31] Her brother, don Juan Hurtado de Mendoza, served as King Philip III's majordormo and gentleman of the bedchamber.[32] Don Juan, like others close to the king, had the ear of the monarch, especially concerning religious matters, since Philip III was extremely pious. Don Juan's wife, Ana de Mendoza, who held the title of Duchess of the Infantado, had visited Sor Jerónima on several occasions.[33] She looked to the saintly nun for spiritual consultation, prayer, and healing. Sor Ana describes how Sor Jerónima "did the same with many other ladies who came to ask her for Hail Marys; and with these she healed them; such was the devotion and faith that they had in the prayers of the blessed mother."[34] The influence of these women on their husbands, brothers, and other family members became important links in Sor Jerónima's growing network of support.

Sor Jerónima's ties to the royal family certainly helped promote her foundation of the convent in the Philippines. One of her greatest devotees was Queen Margaret of Austria (the wife of Philip III), who had heard about her "fame of sanctity" and visited her at Santa Isabel in 1604. During that visit, the queen asked Sor Jerónima for her intercessory prayers to help her bear a son. She already had given birth to two girls (one had lived only a few weeks) but no male heir to a throne. Evidently Sor Jerónima put her hands on the queen's belly and a few months later, on April 8, 1605, she bore a son, the future king of Spain, Philip IV. This scene is telling for several reasons. First, it underscores the divine powers of Sor Jerónima's touch (a power she would use throughout her life); and second, because Sor Jerónima used her connection with the queen to help promote her travels to the Philippines. She told the queen how Soria had said that "nuns in the Philippines would be even more valuable than friars," at which point Margaret replied that she would support any such endeavor.[35] It is also highly probable that Queen Margaret communicated this conversation to her husband, Philip III.[36]

Sor Jerónima was not the only woman religious with ties to the royal family. During the early modern period a number of other nuns had connections with and held sway over the Spanish kings.[37] King Philip II, his son Philip III, and his grandson Philip IV were all subject to powerful religious female influences. In her study on the influence of royal women on Spanish monarchs, Magdalena S. Sánchez has written, "Royal women did not calmly accept their prescribed political roles but instead found ways to voice their opinions in a fashion that was more acceptable to the male hierarchy. To break male imposed political boundaries, women exploited religious patronage and familial concerns, areas in which men acknowledged and tolerated power."[38] Most notably, Philip II's sister, Juana de Austria, had founded the Poor Clare Convent of the Descalzas Reales in Madrid in 1557. That convent would become a retreat for several female members of the royal family, and they surely wielded some power over their brothers and fathers at court. Some of the royal women who sought refuge in the Descalzas Reales professed vows of the Third Order when they became widows, and others who decided not to marry took the veil as black-veiled nuns.[39] Philip III and his wife, Margaret of Austria, frequently attended mass at the Convent of the Descalzas, and Philip took matters regarding nuns seriously.[40] In regard to Sor Jerónima and the Philippines, although the king was quoted as saying that he objected to "such a saintly woman" leaving Spain, he eventually became amenable to the idea.[41]

As Sor Jerónima's fame of sanctity began to circulate at court, other members of the royal family reached out to the holy nun from Toledo. On one occasion, the Infanta Isabella donated 500 ducats to Sor Jerónima. She had heard about Sor Jerónima through the Franciscan friar Mateo de Sarabia and she wanted to help fund her works.[42] Other members of Spain's elite noble class donated jewels, gold, silver crowns, and fine silks to Sor Jerónima so she could commission paintings, sculptures, reliquaries, and other devotional items for the convent and elsewhere. Some of these donations also were used to adorn magnificent polychrome sculptures of the Virgin.[43] In return, the donors sought her out for advice, prayers, and intercession.

The juxtaposition between these demonstrations of extreme opulence and Sor Jerónima's personal professed poverty underscores the complex social matrix of piety and patronage that permeated life in early modern Spain. On the one hand, Sor Jerónima donated much of the money she accumulated to the poor. She sent pots of chicken and bacon to the prison and local hospitals.[44] She handed out bread and eggs to beggars who frequented the convent *torno* (revolving door). On the other hand, she used a profusion of funds for sacred art and devotional images. To the twenty-first-century reader this might seem like a contradiction to her professed poverty, but this was very acceptable in early modern Spanish society, where faith was often expressed in tangible objects of devotion. In Sor Jerónima's Spain no one saw any contradiction between her own poverty and her spending lavish amounts of money to glorify the Catholic faith. Gift giving was a common way to reinforce patronage networks, especially in convents and at court.[45]

Furthermore, in Counter-Reformation Spain the church supported religious art, and convents filled their walls and altars with paintings and other objects of devotion.[46] The following example of the cult of the Immaculate Conception sheds light on this mind-set.

As discussed in chapter 5, the devotion to the movement of the Immaculate Conception and its importance to the Franciscan order cannot be overemphasized. In the 1600s the male Franciscan monastery of San Juan de los Reyes in Toledo became a center for staunch supporters of the doctrine who believed that Mary was free from original sin at the moment of her own conception and remained so. In 1606 the Monastery of San Juan de los Reyes held the general chapter meeting for the Franciscan Order, which was attended by King Philip III, Cardinal Rojas y Sandoval, and other high-ranking civil and ecclesiastical officials. The procession around the city, with up to one thousand friars, passed by the Convent of Santa Isabel, a milestone that brought prestige to the convent and was documented by Sor Ana.[47] Philip III was a firm believer in the Immaculate Conception and had sent an Immaculist embassy to Rome with a petition to make it official church dogma. In 1617 Pope Paul V responded by issuing a decree forbidding public denial of the doctrine, but it was not until 1854 that Pope Pius IX issued a bull making it official. Nonetheless, not all religious orders understood the Immaculist doctrine in the same way. A fierce debate between Franciscans and Dominicans had been ongoing in Seville and Toledo over the definition of immaculate, that is, when exactly Mary was cleansed of sin (some Dominicans posited that it was only after her conception but before her birth).[48]

Sor Jerónima became an active participant in support of the Franciscan movement by commissioning a magnificent wooden sculpture of the Immaculate Conception for the Monastery of San Juan de los Reyes in Toledo.[49] The Duchess of the Infantado, Ana de Mendoza, donated "precious stones and pearls," and others gave money to richly adorn the sculpture. Although some theologians bemoaned the practice of adorning sculpted virgins with extravagant jewelry and clothing, overall it was common practice in early modern Spain.[50] Sor Ana captures in elaborate detail the excitement and energy of the day that the sculpture was transferred from Santa Isabel to San Juan de los Reyes: "They came for her [the sculpture] with much music and dance; and thus they took her with the emotion of her absence and the joy of seeing the reverence and devotion of the town because everyone was going to swear to defend her conception without original sin."[51] Sor Ana's account of the sculpture is testimony to Sor Jerónima's active role in the Immaculist movement

Figure 6 Polychrome sculpture of the Immaculate Conception, 1616–1617
(anonymous). The sculpture now sits on the high altar of the convent church
of Santa Isabel, Toledo. Photo courtesy of Daniel Delgado.

and her determination to bring this doctrine to the Philippines. It also helps
provide context to her strong connection to Sor Luisa de la Ascensión (the
founder of the Confraternity of the Immaculate Conception). Furthermore,
Sor Jerónima's devotion to the Virgin of the Immaculate Conception helped
form bonds with local peoples on the journey. According to Jaime Cuadriello,
"Images of the *Inmaculada* acquired enormous power to bring people together
both socially and politically within the vast and diverse dominions of the
Spanish monarchy."[52]

Final Preparations

In the year immediately prior to obtaining the necessary licenses to embark on
the journey Sor Jerónima met with two more men who played crucial roles in
the foundation of the nunnery: Hernando de los Ríos Coronel (1559–1623/4)
and Fray José de Santa María (?–1628). The former first visited Sor Jerónima
sometime in the fall of 1619. De los Ríos had arrived one year earlier on the

Iberian Peninsula as the procurator general of the Philippines. In that capacity, he had been appointed by the people of Manila to lobby for their best interests before the king of Spain. He was not a friar affiliated with any regular order, although he had been ordained a secular priest. Having lived on and off in Manila for approximately thirty years, he had extensive knowledge of the Philippines, and his résumé as soldier, captain, sailor, mapmaker, inventor, and diplomat was highly impressive.[53] Over the years he had cultivated many connections while living in Manila. He probably first heard about Sor Jerónima through his Dominican friend Soria, who had served as bishop of Nueva Segovia on his return to the Philippines in 1604.[54] Further, de los Ríos was a staunch supporter of Spain's continued control over the Philippine islands. There had been talk at court about abandoning the Philippines. Among other reasons, the islands did not supply spices as once wished, and it was very costly to maintain the far-off colony. One of de los Rios's main mandates from the people of Manila was to argue for the Crown's continued support. To that effect, he believed that the establishment of a female monastery—the first of its kind—would help cement the king's commitment to the Philippines.

De los Ríos must have been worried when he first met with Sor Jerónima sometime in November 1619. She was so ill that two nuns had to help her walk to the convent's visiting parlor. Nonetheless, de los Ríos told her "he had come for her from Manila, and that she would be taken, even if it were just her bones."[55] He informed Sor Jerónima that he carried letters and news from Manila, in particular, a missive from the convent's main patron, doña Ana de Vera, confirming her bequest.[56] Because he had made the round-trip journey twice before, he knew the route well, and he was to serve as one of her escorts to Asia (but this did not occur). De los Ríos had made a map of the island of Luzon, the first of its kind, and he recommended sailing around the west coast of Luzon instead of going through the dangerous Embocadero (San Bernardino Strait), which had strong currents and rocky coasts.[57] He had written travel logs and memorials with detailed coordinates, wind patterns, and landmarks.[58] Sailing from Cádiz to Veracruz would take approximately two months, and from Acapulco to Manila would take at least three months; it would be especially difficult for the nuns, who had no experience whatsoever with the sea. The women would face seasickness, cramped quarters, contagious diseases, rancid food, typhoons, and potential pirate attacks by Dutch, Chinese, and Japanese ships. In short, during their conversation he most likely explained to Sor Jerónima the real risks of dying on the journey to the Philippines. This did not deter the elderly nun. Instead, she rallied.

It was also during this time that the Discalced Franciscan friar José de Santa María traveled back to Spain in the hope of escorting the nuns to Manila. Like Hernando de los Ríos, Fray José had considerable experience in the Far East. Originally from the Spanish region of Aragon, he had first traveled to the Philippines in 1604, where he took his vows of profession. In 1606 he participated as a missionary in the conquest of the Moluccas (Spice Islands). In that same year he became the guardian of the male Franciscan monastery in Manila, and soon thereafter he founded the Third Order of Saint Francis in the Philippines. He held other high-ranking positions within the order and was the procurator of the Franciscan Philippine province when he returned to Spain in 1619. He also had been appointed head of the mission of the future female convent and would serve as chaplain of the nuns on the journey.[59]

In February or March 1620, de los Ríos was granted an audience with the king. Along with Fray José he traveled to Madrid, where they obtained permission from the king and the Council of the Indies for Sor Jerónima and a small cohort of nuns to travel to the Philippines.[60] Unlike others before them, they achieved this within a remarkably short period of time, "negotiating in one hour [with the president of the Council of the Indies, Alonso Carrillo] what had not been able to be negotiated in more than twenty years."[61] Sor Ana adds that it was also through the "intercession" of Alonso Carrillo's wife that he authorized the necessary permissions.[62] Once again, Sor Ana's description of these events speaks to Sor Jerónima's extensive web of admirers.[63]

Selection of the Nuns

When Fray José de Santa María arrived at the convent on April 19, 1620, announcing that he had finally received the necessary permissions and licenses for the Manila foundation, it took the whole community by surprise. After many years of false starts and false hopes, the nuns could not believe that their beloved Jerónima would be leaving Toledo. Sor Ana describes a scene of utter chaos. Nuns began to weep; others wailed. They called out for the nuns and postulants who had been named: Sor Leonor de San Francisco, Juana de San Antonio, and Luisa de San Francisco (who later changed her name to Sor Luisa de Jesús). They also learned that two nuns from the convent in Cubas (the same convent originally founded by their spiritual predecessor, Juana de la Cruz), Sor María Magdalena de Cristo and Sor María Magdalena de la Cruz, would be joining the expedition. What took Sor Ana completely by surprise, however, is that she was not on the list. Indeed, she describes her personal reaction as "complete shock." Years earlier Sor Jerónima had asked her if she wanted to be part of the foundation, and she had said yes. From that point forward, Sor Ana assumed that she would be part of the mission. In an example that demonstrates her agency, Sor Ana approached Sor Jerónima and reaffirmed her wish to become one of the cofounders. Seeing her intense desire to join the group, Sor Jerónima granted the last spot (she had one more to fill) to Sor Ana.

Although we can piece together the events and reasons why the nuns from Cubas, Spain, were chosen for the difficult journey to the Philippines (in part at least because of their connection to Juana de la Cruz and access to her miraculous rosary beads), it is unclear exactly why or even how the other nuns from Toledo were chosen for the foundation. (Later in this study I will discuss the other founding nuns who joined the group along the journey, first in Seville and then in Mexico.) We can speculate that Sor Jerónima wanted Sor Leonor de San Francisco, Juana de San Antonio, and Luisa de Jesús because they were her closest followers and protégées. She needed like-minded women who truly wanted to follow a life of poverty and austerity. Her cofounders would be role models and teachers of the future postulants in Manila. At age thirty-seven, Sor Leonor de San Francisco (1583–1651) was selected as the novice mistress. Her direct charges were the younger Juana de San Antonio (1588–1661), age thirty-two, and the much older Luisa de Jesús (1556?–?), about sixty-four. Both women were given the habit of novice for the journey and later professed during their first months in Manila. Luisa was a close companion of the esteemed Mariana de Jesús, and by association, highly regarded by the nuns. In fact, Mariana also wanted to join the foundation, but due to her confessor's influence (Luis de la Mesa), she stayed behind and Luisa took her place.[64] This is only conjecture, but perhaps—and ironically since none of the women were that young—Sor Jerónima had doubts about Sor Ana because of her advanced age. Sor Ana was already fifty-five years old at the time and did not know how to write. Whatever the exact reasons, when Sor Jerónima heard Sor Ana's honest desire to join the foundation, she accepted her without reservation.

Toledo to Mora

In addition to Fray José, another friar and two servants would accompany the nuns on the journey.[65] Fray José had obtained permission to use two of the king's carriages, but they had to wait nine extra days in Toledo because the monarch was using them on a trip to Alcalá de Henares. Meanwhile he had collected the two nuns from Cubas. When the two women embraced Sor Jerónima for the first time in Toledo, they detected a flowery fragrance, reminding them of the celestial body of Mother Juana de la Cruz. Sor Ana recalls other instances related to the sense of smell. Some nuns remarked that they detected on Sor Jerónima the scent of the original founder of the convent in Toledo, María la Pobre, while others said that she smelled like flowers.[66] Bearing out the notion that one of the telltale signs of saintliness is odor—usually a pleasant smell of flowers emitting from a body after death— these examples highlight Sor Jerónima's perceived state of sanctity, long before her death.

During these last days in Toledo many local dignitaries, ecclesiastical authorities, friars, priests, bishops, noblemen, counts and countesses, and family members gathered in the city to bid their farewells to the nuns. This extravagant outpouring of support, narrated by Sor Ana, was replicated in all of the larger towns and cities that the nuns visited in Spain and later in the New World. Several high-ranking religious and secular officials, including Hernando de los Ríos, accompanied the group to the small village of Mora outside Toledo. There, at the house of Ana de Mendoza, de los Ríos said goodbye to Sor Jerónima. Although he regretted deeply not being able to escort the nuns to Manila—"he loved our mother very much"—he needed to stay in Spain to finish his business at court.[67] Unbeknown to him, he would never return to the Philippines.[68]

Sor Ana's portrayal of the nuns' first days of the journey negotiates the complex arena of hagiography and historical details. On the one hand she weaves together images of Sor Jerónima starving and abusing her body, but on the other, she reveals hints of realistic everyday occurrences. Since Sor Jerónima was so thin, everyone worried that she did not have the physical stamina to endure such a difficult odyssey. For instance, on the morning that the nuns left Toledo, the abbess of Santa Isabel forced Sor Jerónima to eat a piece of chicken, which she promptly vomited; she was only used to eating bread, a few herbs, bitter oranges, and pomegranates. When the group arrived in Mora, Fray José used holy obedience to require her to eat nutritious meals during the rest of their travels. According to Sor Ana, she accepted his order without complaint.

Sor Ana's description of the road between Mora and Seville is very brief. She compares their crossing of the mountains of Sierra Morena to Saint Teresa's travels to southern Spain, thus equating their future foundation in

Manila to Teresa's Carmelite foundations in Spain. Other than a short visit
to a Conceptionist convent in Carmona she does not describe any of the
places or lodgings where they stayed on their way to Seville.

Seville: Signs of Sanctity

The travel party arrived in Seville sometime in early to mid-May. Their carriages brought them directly to the large Franciscan Convent of Santa Clara
la Real, where they would spend the next six weeks. The convent had its roots
in medieval Spain: in 1289 King Sancho IV and Queen María de Molina
donated the original buildings, land, and funds to start the convent; like
their home community in Toledo, it was filled with the daughters and family
members of Spain's elite and noble class.[69] The Sevillian nuns enthusiasti-
cally greeted the cofounders with a procession while singing the Te Deum.
After visiting the choir, they escorted the women to "a large room," complete
with a large image of the Immaculate Conception and an organ.[70] Sor Ana
explains that the nuns also used this space every Friday to sing La Benedicta
accompanied by organ music.[71] Music was an important part of convent religious ceremonies, and a prestigious convent like this one in Seville would
have attracted nuns who could play instruments and sing. In fact, as in their
home convent in Toledo, some of them could have been given dowry waivers
to become black-veiled nuns in exchange for their musical talents. Some
women sang, while others played instruments such as the organ, violin, harp,
and the bajón or dulcian (an early version of the bassoon).[72]

Sor Jerónima's perceived sanctity spurred a type of cult formation that
began to expand as the women traveled but grew especially during their stay
in Seville. Upon their arrival, word spread quickly that a holy woman from
Toledo was at the Convent of Santa Clara. Attracted by the growing fame sur-
rounding her possible sainthood, many people from all echelons of society
went to "the church's grille as if she had come from heaven."[73] The nuns themselves wanted to speak to Sor Jerónima and touch her. When possible, they
tore off pieces of her habit to keep as relics or snatched pieces of bread from
her plate to cure illnesses. The Sevillian abbess had Sor Jerónima bless a piece
of bread, which she employed to heal a very sick family member. The nuns
followed Sor Jerónima day and night, "watching and taking note of everything she said."[74] Some would distract her with conversation, while others
brushed her back with undergarments; these items were subsequently sent to

female relatives to help treat infertility. The nuns also talked of turning Sor Jerónima's cell into a shrine, especially the area on the floor where she slept.[75]

Notably, these series of episodes add to Sor Jerónima's spiritual résumé. They reflect small miracles related to her divine touch that could be used in a future canonization dossier. Other instances, such as the following example during the Festival of Corpus Christi, shine a light on Sor Jerónima's mystical bonds with celestial beings, especially the Christ Child.

Corpus Christi

The Feast of Corpus Christi was one of the most important religious events in the early modern Catholic world. It was celebrated in early June on the Thursday after Trinity Sunday. The festival in honor of the Eucharist is based on the belief that Christ is embodied in the consecrated host (the doctrine of transubstantiation). In early modern Spain and especially in the Americas, it was an elaborate affair with processions, theater, and feasts.[76] Such was the Corpus Christi celebration put on by the Convent of Santa Clara in Seville, as vividly described by Sor Ana. After mass, the nuns processed around the four inner cloisters with a sculpture of the baby Jesus. Female musicians and singers serenaded the procession as it passed by altars in each of the cloisters. At one point the procession stopped in front of Sor Jerónima so that she could adorn the Christ child with a surplice and a fine cape. For over an hour she processed, trance-like, with the child in her arms, shedding tears while she gazed into the sculpture's eyes in a type of mystical rapture. Because of their familiarity with devotional reading material and portrait images, the nuns who watched Sor Jerónima were not shocked by her experience. Moreover, they had been "primed to receive and understand the cues and gestures belonging to the standardized emotive language of ecstatic visions."[77] Sor Ana's depiction of Sor Jerónima's performance allows the reader to see that her close connection to the child Jesus was not just an interior vision but also one that was perceived by a larger audience.

After the celebration of the Eucharist, one of the Sevillian nuns, Luisa de Bocanegra, told the women about a vision she had of Sor Jerónima and her cofounders. In it, the Lord put his hand on Sor Jerónima's head and looked directly at the nuns from Toledo as he said to the Virgin Mary, Saint Francis, Saint Clare, Saint Teresa, and Madre Luisa de Carrión (de la Ascensión), "You see, here is the captain and these are the soldiers that I have chosen for my work."[78] The foretelling of this divine endorsement of their travels is significant for several reasons. First, the metaphor of the nuns as soldiers fighting in the Lord's name mimics the underlying principle of the festival of Corpus Christi: Christ's triumph (as embodied in the consecrated host) over peoples of non–Roman Catholic beliefs. The militant vision grants the nuns permission to enter the male-dominated realm of missionaries wielding the cross as sword (the Jesuits saw themselves as soldiers of Christ); on their journey they would interact with all types of peoples, at times requiring them to join the ranks of friars in their efforts to battle for the Christian faith. Second, throughout her narrative Sor Ana often recounts visions predicting the foundation of their future convent in Manila. Although this was a common motif in foundation narratives, it certainly served as solace for the women to know that so many people had predicted their journey to Asia. Finally, the vision speaks to the importance of spiritual and missionary role models for these women, including Sor Luisa, who was still alive at the time.

Diego Velázquez's Portraits of Sor Jerónima

Unlike the vivid details that Sor Ana provides in her retelling of the festival of Corpus Christi, she never mentions a word about the portraits that Diego Velázquez painted of Sor Jerónima during their time in Seville. Velázquez painted two full-length portraits of the nun, and both were first recorded as possessions of the nuns of Santa Isabel in Toledo (one now hangs in the Prado and the other in a private collection). There is also a third, half-length version (either by Velázquez or an early follower).[79] Most likely one of the main reasons that the name Velázquez became forgotten to the nuns in Toledo is that neither Sor Ana nor her male biographers, Quesada or Letona, ever made mention of him or of Sor Jerónima posing for the portrait. Despite the later fame of Velázquez, especially as court painter to Philip IV, the attribution of his early work of Sor Jerónima became muddled over the years, and eventually even his signature faded from the canvas.[80] Thereafter the nuns of Santa Isabel in Toledo forgot who painted the portrait of their most famous member. In fact, up until 1927 the portrait was attributed to Luis Tristán.[81]

Why did Sor Ana and the other early biographers decide to omit Velázquez from their narratives? Since Velázquez was still quite young—he was only twenty-one when he painted the portrait—his name would have meant very little to them (later, when he served as a court painter, this would change). Yet this still does not answer the question of why she does not discuss the portrait. I believe that Sor Ana and her contemporaries realized that their own written descriptions of Sor Jerónima were inconsistent with the strong and even healthy looking nun of Velázquez's portrait. Furthermore, sitting for a young male artist who was not a cleric did not agree with their own illustrations of Sor Jerónima as an extremely pious woman. Despite this, it is highly likely that Sor Jerónima sat for Velázquez, since that was common practice for renowned nuns at the time. Most famously, during her visit to Seville, Saint Teresa sat for her portrait, which was painted in 1576 by the Discalced Carmelite Fray Juan de Miseria.[82]

Unlike the distinguished porcelain-colored hands, veined but strong from her advanced age, that Velázquez brushed onto the canvas, Sor Jerónima's biographers portray a nun who lived mainly on bread and water and tortured her body with hair shirts and daily self-flagellation. Sor Ana writes that Sor Jerónima intentionally stained her hands with black ink and took on the harshest of chores so that they would become chafed and ugly. This was exactly the type of representation of the penitent nun that was included as an engraving of Sor Jerónima in Quesada's biography (1713). In that image we see a haggard nun, hunched in prayer next to a crucifix, a skull, an hourglass (representing death), a crown of thorns, a spiked girdle, and other items used for her extreme bodily abuse. Gender discourse in the early modern world inscribed upon a nun's body a narrow definition of religiosity. The print reflects that definition (and should be understood as an allegory), especially when attempting to portray sanctity.[83] It must be said, however, that Velázquez drew on Franciscan iconography when representing Sor Jerónima. He depicted her holding a crucifix in one hand, a reminder of Christ's suffering, and in the other clutching a book, most likely *The Rule of Saint Clare*. Above her head is the Biblical phrase in Latin "It is good to await the salvation of God in silence" and a banderole running from her mouth reads, "I shall be satisfied as long as he is glorified."[84] Regardless of the reasons that the biographers fail to mention the painting, this does not detract from the reality that the Spanish artist painted her portrait and that a patron or patrons compensated him for his services.[85]

Tanya J. Tiffany's excellent study on Sor Jerónima and Velázquez examines the key players who might have been involved in the patronage of this work. She speculates that either the vicar, acting on behalf of the nuns from Santa Isabel, or one of the Franciscan friars traveling with the nuns from Toledo to Seville commissioned and oversaw the work. She also posits that

Figure 7 *Madre Gerónima de Asunción*, 1713. Engraving by José Mota.
The Monasterio de Santa Isabel de los Reyes. Photo by the author.

Francisco Pacheco (Velázquez's father-in-law and teacher) secured the con-
tract for Velázquez because of his own endorsement of the doctrine of the
Immaculate Conception and connection to Franciscan authorities involved
in that campaign.[86] Although we still do not know who paid for the portrait,
the fact that the work ended up back at the Convent of Santa Isabel (until
the twentieth century), essentially for the primary use of the nuns, indicates
that they ardently wanted a keepsake of their most famous sister. The portrait would comfort the nuns, remind them of Sor Jerónima's extreme sac-
rifice and piety, and commemorate her foundation of the first convent in the
Far East.

It still remains unclear, however, why Velázquez was commissioned to
paint Sor Jerónima in Seville instead of an accomplished portrait artist in

Toledo such as Luis Tristán. In fact, Sor Ana states that Sor Jerónima herself had connections to *los maestros*, or masters, in Toledo and had commissioned several paintings during her time at Santa Isabel, including a large altarpiece of Saint John the Baptist.[87] For that work, she compensated the artists (Sor Ana uses the plural) in three installments from money she collected from the nuns who wanted the painting. It was common for Spanish nuns to adorn the walls of their communal areas with large devotional images. Nuns gathered around these paintings because they helped them visualize scenes that they had heard or read about in popular prayer books.[88] Sor Ana's portrayal of these events is fascinating because it sheds light on how religious women interacted with "officials and artists," expediting the process by procuring gifts for them.[89] According to Paula Revenga Domínguez, there were no painter's guilds in seventeenth-century Toledo, so most likely Sor Ana was referring to ecclesiastical officials.[90] The production of an altarpiece such as a polychrome sculpture was a collective endeavor that required specialized craftsmen, sculptors, and painters, and the time taken from conception to completion could be considerable.[91] It appears that Sor Jerónima understood the politics of art production and used gifts to expedite the process. Sor Ana also describes the same scenario when Sor Jerónima commissioned the sculpture of the Immaculate Conception: "There were presents for the maestros and gold jewelry was given to their wives."[92]

Sor Ana's omission of the names of the artists certainly speaks to a culture that did not value the individual artist or those associated with a particular workshop. Unlike Renaissance Italy, where the status of plastic arts was highly regarded, in early modern Spain it was common to equate artists and artisans in large workshops to laborers because they worked with their hands.[93] Yet upon even closer analysis, perhaps the reason that Sor Ana failed to name the artists hinged less on the problem of artists' status (which was, indeed, a problem) but on the fact that the devotional function of the images eclipsed the artists' identity. Regardless, as in Italy, Spain's larger convents did become patrons of the arts, spending large quantities of money on decorative works and portraits.[94]

Excellent scholarship on the visual arts within early modern Spanish convents reveals that some female monasteries did not have to pay for works because they had their own in-house artists. For instance, the Carmelite nuns Cecilia de Nacimiento (1570–1646) and her elder sister María de San Alberto (1568–1640) had been taught by their mother to draw and paint before taking their vows of profession. They brought their artistic abilities to the Convent of

La Concepción in Valladolid, where they painted devotional works. The two women were also gifted musicians, playwrights, and poets.[95] Some talented young artists who did not have the means to pay a costly dowry to enter a convent used their artistic abilities as a dowry waiver to allow them to profess as nuns. Mindy Nancarrow Taggard analyzes two such cases of Spanish nuns from the 1600s. Although both took vows as choir nuns (the highest status in the convent) they felt discriminated against by other nuns who treated them as being of the servant class because they used their hands to produce art instead of dedicating their time to prayer. As a result, those two talented artists preferred to devote their time to spiritual vocations as opposed to artistic ones, ultimately relinquishing their duties as artists and distinguishing themselves as visionaries instead.[96]

Jerez and Cádiz: Theater and Music

Although Sor Ana does not describe any female convent artists, she does portray other manifestations of artistic talent that flourished in religious communities across the Spanish Empire. From studies of early modern theater in Spain, we know that some religious women were talented playwrights.[97] Nuns wrote these works in honor of kings and queens, holy days, religious holidays, and the profession of nuns and for the edification and entertainment of their companions. One of the most famous female playwrights in Spain's Golden Age was Sor Marcela de San Félix (1605–1686), none other than the daughter of the prolific playwright Lope de Vega. Other women, such as the famous Mexican nun Sor Juana Inés de la Cruz, also wrote secular plays that were put on outside the convent.

When the cofounders stopped for the day at the Convent of Santa Clara in Jerez, not far from their departure point at Cádiz, we learn that the art of playwriting was very much alive in southern Spain. Upon their arrival they were immediately taken to the convent choir to admire the monstrance exposing the sacred host. After mass with communion and listening to "an admirable sermon," the nuns were treated to lunch and entertainment. The young novices put on several lively *loas* (short plays) written for Sor Jerónima (and in the name of Saint Francis) about the journey to the Philippines.[98] These types of performances were typical in early modern Spanish female monasteries, and most allegorical plays and such loas were written and acted by nuns within the confines of the convent.[99] As with the plays of the above-mentioned Sor Marcela, members of the nobility, elites, and ecclesiastical authorities sometimes attended these events.[100] On that spring afternoon in the Jerez convent, there is no reason to doubt that these were the types of guests in attendance, all enjoying the creative theatrical production inspired by the nuns' long journey to the Far East.

From Jerez, the small group traveled to their final destination on the Iberian Peninsula. The women from Castile had never seen the sea before, and yet Sor Ana only makes one short reference to their arrival at the coast, noting that the sight of the sea "animated us greatly."[101] Instead, she describes the concourse of dignitaries who came to see the holy nun from Toledo while the nuns spent their last ten days in Spain at a convent of Conceptionist nuns. Since Cádiz was at this time displacing Sanlúcar de Barrameda as Spain's principal port of departure to the Americas, many royal officials and clerics from all orders gathered there before boarding ship themselves. Sor Jerónima also had a cousin in town, Alonso de Herrera, who sent daily provisions to the nuns at the convent. Amid the hubbub of visitors and activity, the Conceptionist abbess ordered some "recreation time" for the cofounders. In this section Sor Ana portrays yet another example of artistic creativity within religious communities.[102] The women were treated to a harp concert accompanied by a singer with "a beautiful voice." The singer later told Sor Jerónima that she was the composer of the piece.[103] This scene reminds us that musical performances, like theatrical productions, were common in early modern Spain.[104]

Like a number of other sections in her account, Sor Ana's short description of Cádiz leaves many gaps. Although we catch a fleeting glimpse into the musical performance, we learn nothing about the Spanish fleet anchored out at sea or the logistical details of the goods Fray José packed for their voyage. Sor Ana is much more interested in depicting Sor Jerónima's characteristic selflessness than illuminating concrete details about their departure. For instance, at one point she asked Sor Jerónima, "What are we going to do with these nuns who never let us alone?" The abbess responded, "We have not come for ourselves."[105] Little by little Sor Ana pieces together examples such as this one to form a larger picture of Sor Jerónima as a future saint. Yet she also inserts her own voice. By asking Sor Jerónima questions about their duty as founders, she explores some of her own doubts, perhaps even regarding her role in the missionary process.

Conclusion

The founding of the first female monastery in the Philippines was no easy feat. It took close to a quarter century for ecclesiastical and civic authorities, friars, nobles, nuns, and female patrons to set up the framework for the future Convent of Santa Clara in Manila. Sor Jerónima's perceived sanctity, her growing cult, and her personal connection to some of Spain's most influential wealthy elites also played vital roles in the creation of the new convent. Despite her advanced age, the wealthy patrons in Manila, Pedro Chávez and Ana de Vera, agreed to bequeath their assets to the future convent only because of their faith in Sor Jerónima. Queen Margaret and other noblewomen who interacted on a personal level with Sor Jerónima communicated their experiences to their husbands at court. Diplomats like Hernando de los Ríos Coronel, who had important contacts in both the Philippines and Spain, coupled with his close connections with the Franciscan friar José de Santa María, finally secured the necessary licenses, permissions, and funds from the king.

Sor Ana's portrayal of the convents along the road from Toledo to Cádiz allows the reader to view not only the hospitality of these communities that opened their arms to the traveling nun—their excitement is palpable—but also the creative atmosphere that permeated these enclaves of women. Catholic nuns throughout the Spanish Empire participated in the creative arts. They painted portraits, composed plays, played musical instruments, and sang solos in convent choirs. In fact, some of these women used their skills to gain access to convents: instead of paying a dowry, they entered monastic communities with the understanding that they would trade their talents for the privilege of professing as a black-veiled nun.[106] One of the noteworthy aspects of Sor Ana's text is that it provides concrete examples of musical and theatrical productions created by nuns for entertainment within the convent. Nonetheless, her narrative is not a comprehensive report, and she leaves gaps about certain events, places, and people that they encountered on their journey.

Because Sor Ana, like Sor Jerónima's other biographers, Quesada and Letona, devotes so many of her chapters to hagiographic details of Sor Jerónima's penitential lifestyle, it is hard at times to really come to understand the true character and personality of Sor Jerónima. If we can find and examine the interstices left open by her biographer, then maybe that will help shed light on the enigmatic life of this saintly woman, and perhaps on Sor Ana too. In reference to Sor Ana's silence regarding Diego Velázquez's portrait of

Sor Jerónima, we can infer that the nuns back in the Convent of Santa Isabel in Toledo wanted a portrait of their beloved sister as a keepsake. Diego Velázquez's lifelike depiction of the abbess could also be used to help foment devotion to her growing cult (although we do not know if it was ever actually used for that purpose) and aid her future canonization process. The nuns also wanted words to paint an intricate picture of their saintly sister. For this reason they turned to one of their own, Sor Ana de Cristo, to write a biography of Sor Jerónima. Unlike the single image of the austere nun painted by Velázquez, Sor Ana's text could piece together a much more complex picture of Sor Jerónima. Copies of her manuscript could be made so that nuns in Manila and back home in Toledo would remember the remarkable aspects of Sor Jerónima and the foundation of the first convent in the Far East. Like the portrait, Sor Ana's words could be used to promote the sanctity of the elderly abbess. Sor Ana mentions by name many of the religious women and men of the cloth who knew Sor Jerónima throughout her lifetime, thus adding a personal touch for her readers. She re-creates the sights, sounds, tastes, and smells that the nuns experienced on their route from Toledo through Andalusia to the Atlantic coast. As we shall see in the next chapter, she also provides a ringside view of the Caribbean islands of Guadeloupe and the nuns' six-month journey across Mexico.

CHAPTER 2

Cádiz to Mexico

⪦ IN SEPTEMBER 1620 SOR JERÓNIMA AND HER COMPANIONS STOPPED for the night at the Hill of Tepeyac in a small village on the outskirts of Mexico City. Like many before and after them, they wanted to pay homage at the shrine of Our Lady of Guadalupe. They visited the chapel, tasted the salty water of an underground spring renowned for its healing properties, and learned from local laywomen about the miraculous appearance of the Virgin to an indigenous man almost one hundred years earlier. Sor Ana's account of this short stopover is the first ever detailed portrayal of the Guadalupe miracle written by a nun. Her description from a gendered perspective sheds new light on this iconic site, previously absent from historical studies.

This short example, discussed later in the chapter, underscores the importance of Sor Ana's narrative. Her perspective provides the reader with a bird's-eye view of the sights, challenges, and dangers that this small entourage faced on their transatlantic voyage: first with their short stopover on the Caribbean islands of Guadeloupe and later during their crossing of New Spain from Veracruz to Acapulco. The focus of this chapter not only is to trace that path but also to analyze how this group of religious women dealt with myriad experiences, including their interactions with local indigenous populations, African slaves, and Mexican nuns in the capital of Mexico. Although the perils were many, especially the nuns' bouts with tropical fevers and severe diarrhea, the women did bring with them a secret weapon: the miraculous beads inherited from their sixteenth-century spiritual predecessor Mother Juana de la Cruz. Those beads supposedly had been blessed by Christ. Throughout this portion of the journey, Sor Ana portrays the widespread devotion in the Americas to Juana de la Cruz, which spanned race and class. As Sor Ana documented the cult of "santa" Juana in the New World, she also laid the groundwork for a similar devotion toward Sor Jerónima.

Atlantic Sea Voyage

The nuns had no choice but to first sail across the Atlantic Ocean to New Spain on their way to the Philippines.[1] A series of papal bulls issued by Alexander VI (1493–1494) that led up to the Treaty of Tordesillas (June 7, 1494) had granted the other feasible route to the East, that is, around the Cape of Good Hope, to the Portuguese.[2] In the Spanish context, these networks of trade routes, known as the Carrera de Indias, used Spanish fleets to link the House of Trade in Seville to ports across the Atlantic such as Veracruz and Cartagena de Indias. Spanish ships also tied together the far-flung voyage across the Pacific from Acapulco to Manila, commonly known as the Manila galleon route (discussed in the next chapter).[3] Travel on the currents of the Atlantic and Pacific Oceans was a precarious endeavor. On the one hand, unknown coastlines with reefs and sandbars wrecked galleons, storms and gale-force winds battered vessels, and tossing seas caused horrific seasickness; on the other, Dutch, British, and Moorish ships attacked Spanish fleets, hoping to capture treasure and merchandise. For protection, Spanish mercantile vessels sailed together with military ships in convoys. In the early years the fleet made two annual sailings from Spain: one to Panama and another to Mexico. The voyage from Cádiz to Veracruz covered a distance of 4,860 miles and took approximately two and a half months.[4]

The eight nuns did not travel alone on their transoceanic journey. They were accompanied all the way to Manila by their father confessor, Fray José de Santa María, another friar, Francisco de Granada, and two male servants, Jerónimo Fortuno de Lovera and Blas de Valencia.[5] While in Seville, Fray José made all of the logistical arrangements for the sea voyage. The king had initially granted him 179,680 *maravedís* (equivalent to about 661 silver pesos or 8 *reales*) for the journey but later added 41,160 (151 pesos) to that amount.[6] He also gave them a daily allowance. The friar was permitted to bring "five tons of books and clothing" for the whole party.[7] According to González Zymla, the five *toneladas* translates into approximately 1,457 kilos, which, divided among twelve, equals about 121 kilos per passenger. He explains that this might sound excessive, but the weight accounts for much more than books and clothes. It includes liturgical items, mattresses, bedding, cooking utensils, and all of the food for the sea voyage.[8] Among other things, Fray José purchased 150 live hens, three hen coops, eight sheep, twenty-four hams, twelve *quintales* (544 kilos) of hardtack biscuits, dried fish, crates of preserves, rice, olives, vats of cooking oil, earthenware jars of wine, bolts of wool cloth for friars' and nuns' habits, and white linen for sheets and household articles.[9] Of the total of 7,270 reales that Fray José spent, the most expensive items were the biscuits (924 reales), the linen (794 reales), and the wool for habits (700 reales).[10] Spanish vessels did not provide any of these items for their passengers. Paying passengers did receive water, salt, firewood for cooking, and access to one or two communal cooking stoves called *fogones*. The very real threat of fire loomed large on ships, and passengers were forbidden to light their own stoves.[11]

The small group sailed on a mercantile ship called *Nuestra Señora del Rosario*, owned and captained by Diego Meléndez.[12] It traveled as part of the fleet destined for New Spain, commanded by General don Juan de Benavides.[13] According to varying sources, the convoy of ships set sail in July or early August 1620.[14] The summer heat must have been oppressive for the nuns, especially because they were dressed in their long woolen habits, with a cloth wimple covering the head, neck, and sides of their faces. As they boarded the ship, they would have donned veils to conceal their faces. The nuns waited three days aboard the ship before it left port. During that time, Sor Jerónima's cousin Alonso de Herrera visited the group daily. He brought them "prepared foods, warm bread, wine, gifts, and other things." Nuns from Cádiz sent the women baskets filled with even more provisions. According to Sor Ana, they were so well stocked that Jerónima, through a Third Order religious—whom she playfully called her *mayordomo* (butler)—gave out rations to passengers, priests, sailors, and cabin boys alike.[15]

Throughout their transatlantic voyage the nuns tried to keep themselves enclosed. Sor Jerónima had already instructed the sisters to close the carriage curtains during their travels on the Iberian Peninsula, and while staying in convents they received visitors only at the torno (revolving door) or in the convent parlor. Despite these precautions, they would have been exposed to a wide variety of seamen, passengers, servants, and slaves, especially when boarding

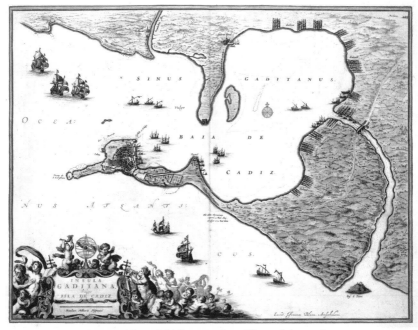

Figure 8 Map of Cádiz, 1662. Joan Blaeu, *Atlas maior.*
Dutch National Library, via Wikimedia Commons.

and disembarking the ships. We know that several different nationalities crewed the Spanish fleets (especially Portuguese), with the only stipulation that they profess the Roman Catholic faith.[16]

All of the information that we have about the nuns' passage on the fleet of New Spain stems from archival research and secondary sources. Sor Ana's manuscript reveals almost nothing about life on board ship during their crossing of the Atlantic Ocean. She only mentions that they all fared well during the sailing, expect for Sor Jerónima, who suffered from intermittent fevers. We will never know why Sor Ana left this portion of the journey blank, but perhaps in retrospect, years later when writing her narrative in Manila, this sea voyage seemed relatively tame compared to the rest of the odyssey. For a better understanding of what it must have been like for the women to set foot on a Spanish galleon and to then spend the next six weeks out to sea, we can turn to another group of nuns who crossed the Atlantic, though they traveled somewhat later.[17]

Like the Franciscans who wanted to expand their order in the Philippines, the Capuchins also sought to spread their communities in the Indies. In 1665

Figure 9 Cornelis Verbeeck, *Spanish Galleon Firing Its Cannons*, ca. 1618/1620. Oil on panel. National Gallery of Art, via Wikimedia Commons.

a group of six Capuchin nuns, also from Toledo, left Spain to establish the first Capuchin convent in the capital of New Spain. Instead of documenting their new foundation in a convent chronicle, the nuns wrote about their experiences in letters back home to their beloved spiritual sisters and confessor in Toledo. Their missives provide a window on the extremely difficult conditions on board the Indies fleets. The women slept cheek to jowl in a small cabin at the stern of the ship. In general, the stern was reserved for senior officers and members of religious orders.[18] (We do know that the Franciscan nuns were given a cabin in the stern on the Manila galleon.) In the seventeenth century, five friars generally occupied a full cabin, ten feet long by eight feet wide. Yet the six Capuchin nuns were allocated only half a cabin. Their cramped quarters, combined with the summer heat and humidity and the stench produced by a lack of general hygiene, proved very difficult for the nuns.[19]

The Capuchin nuns complained bitterly of extreme seasickness. They were not alone in their suffering. Experts in maritime history note that almost everyone, even seasoned mariners, suffered from this ailment.[20] Due to their nausea, the women had trouble eating and had to forego their daily communion for twenty days. In a letter written from Puerto Rico, one nun, Sor María Toledo, explains graphically "that we have all been very sick, that no one could do anything, and that we would all vomit in unison."[21] She concludes by saying that the nausea was nothing, however, in comparison to her constant fear of shipwreck. The nuns' letters describe severe storms and tempestuous seas. One storm in particular battered the ships to such an extent that their cabin filled with water and several bunks were drenched.[22] Seasickness, malnourishment, and fear of drowning all took a toll on the Capuchin nuns. In subsequent letters from their new convent in Mexico City they often mentioned the hardships endured during their time at sea and even began to refer to themselves as *las navegantas* (the navigators).[23]

While the Capuchin nuns stopped on the island of Puerto Rico before continuing on to Veracruz, we know that the Franciscan nuns spent the night on the more easterly islands of Guadeloupe. The stopover on these islands made a stark impression on the nuns, and it is here that Sor Ana resumes her narrative of their transatlantic journey.

From the Islands of Guadeloupe to the Capital of New Spain

The Spanish fleet generally stopped in the Caribbean to take on firewood for cooking, foodstuffs, clean drinking water, and other supplies. In this case, the ships carrying Sor Jerónima and her cofounders made a port of call on a small group of islands of the Lesser Antilles belonging to France, and thus the French spelling of Guadeloupe. Christopher Columbus visited these islands on his second voyage in 1493, and at that time he named them Guadalupe in honor of the Spanish Our Lady of Guadalupe from Extremadura (not to be confused with the Mexican Guadalupe).[24] The imperial fleet utilized the islands until 1630, when French colonists began to invade the Antilles, taking over Guadeloupe and Martinique.[25] After that, Spanish ships visited other islands, such as Cuba or Puerto Rico, for fresh supplies and trade.

Sor Ana's description of the short stop on Guadeloupe helps shed light on the mentality of the Spanish nuns, not only as reformers of the order of Poor Clares in the Americas but as missionaries to its native peoples. The nuns were mortified that the ships sailed through the Caribbean islands without any concern for the spiritual well-being of their inhabitants. Sor Ana writes, "The Indians of Guadalupe shed many a tear seeing that the armada of Christians passes them by every year."[26] Her narrative affirms that women had direct contact with the local population (the infamous Island Caribs who had taken over the islands centuries earlier). This is corroborated by Quesada's biography of Sor Jerónima. He explains that the natives approached the ships in canoes, offering fresh fruit, chickens, and other items in exchange for knives and steel. Several of the men and women were brought to the stern of the ship so they could converse with the nuns.[27] Sor Ana implies that the Caribs had some rudimentary knowledge of Christianity. For example, when shown a crucifix, one man said he did not know who it represented, but another said it was Christ and that his name was Juan and his wife's, María. Another man named Nicolás asked one of the nuns for a rosary. Spanish was evidently spoken.

Overall, these brief observations reveal the nuns' desire to actively participate in missionary work, something normally reserved for friars. On the one hand, the women were impressed that the Amerindians wanted to learn more about the Catholic faith, but on the other, they were saddened by their nakedness: "They brought the women and children to us, all naked, and our souls loathed to see them condemned, unless God helped them."[28] This theme of nakedness and the innocent savage echoes a common trope in early Spanish chronicles of the New World. Sor Ana and her sisters feared that these people would be condemned to hell, but at the same time she equates their nakedness with their innocence. Their docile nature made them perfect candidates for evangelization. Her view, like that espoused by many Spaniards, was that these native peoples of the Americas had the intelligence of children and needed guidance.[29]

Sor Ana knew that their time on the islands of Guadeloupe was limited, but she still tried to find a practical solution to bringing Christianity to these islands, one that would also benefit the Spanish fleet. In order to achieve their missionary goals, she portrays the islands as an ideal place for a Spanish settlement: "There are said to be fourteen islands with beautiful land. There is a river, which is really welcome as the ships are in dire need of fresh water. They are also well supplied with poultry, swine, fruit, and firewood. Since there is Christianity and beautiful tree-covered mountains, they say it would be a good place to build ships. We saw it at sunrise and it seemed to be an earthly paradise."[30] Sor Ana must have also known that the Spanish navy desperately needed large trees for shipbuilding. As Europe depleted its forests for agriculture, fuel, and construction, countries like Spain, Portugal, Holland, and England began to look abroad for alternative sources of timber. In the early modern period, for example, it took between fourteen hundred

Figure 10 Famiglia Indiana Caraiba, 1818. John Gabriel Stedman,
Narrative of a Five Years' Expedition against the Revolted Negroes of Surinam.
Courtesy of the John Carter Brown Library at Brown University.

and two thousand trees to build one large warship.[31] Sor Ana employs her
description of the landscape, filled with tree-covered mountains, as an
enticement to the Crown to settle the islands. As for the souls of the indigenous inhabitants, Sor Jerónima wrote a letter to the king to remedy the situation: "Thus, she wrote a letter to the king so that he would give an order to
send missionaries to the island to instruct the natives in the [Catholic] faith
and that he do this on a yearly basis."[32] In a brief aside, the Englishman
Thomas Gage, who traveled extensively throughout Mexico and Guatemala,
also stopped on the islands on Guadeloupe a few years later, in 1625. Unlike
the nuns' encounter with docile Caribs, his expedition came across an "army
of treacherous Indians."[33] Sadly, as was the case in all of the Caribbean, the

native Amerindians were nearly wiped out by disease and warfare and, by the mid-1600s, European settlers had deforested much of the islands to make way for large-scale sugar plantations.[34]

The native Caribs of Guadeloupe were just the first in a series of indigenous populations with whom the nuns interacted on their long journey to the Philippines. Like the local peoples of Guadeloupe who had some basic experience with the Christian faith (indicated by their Catholic names), the other Amerindians whom the women encountered in New Spain had long since been converted, most of them living in Franciscan or Dominican *doctrinas* (segregated parishes).[35]

When the nuns set foot in New Spain, the population of Native Americans had already suffered a major decline. The ravages of smallpox, other epidemics, warfare, and hard labor from the *encomienda* system had decimated the population. Estimates vary, but there were at least 10–12 million people in central Mexico before the Conquest, and by the early 1620s only 750,000 remained.[36] Due to their smaller numbers and because there were not enough friars to cover vast tracts of lands, many native populations were forced to relocate into doctrinas so that friars could teach them the Catholic faith. Driven by the epidemic of 1576–81 and pushed by secular Spaniards who wanted to take over native lands, more forced resettlement occurred between 1593 and 1605.[37]

Despite the forced cultural assimilation of Christianity and deliberate anti-idolatry measures of the sixteenth century, Nahua populations of central Mexico were able to integrate and hold on to many of their pre-Conquest beliefs. David Tavárez contends that ritual practices such as the use of hallucinogenic plants, bathing and naming ceremonies for infants, and the use of the oral genres to disguise deities remained imbedded in Nahua cultural memory through the first half of the 1600s.[38] As we shall see, the nuns interacted with these small settlements of Native Americans, but because Sor Ana (and most Spaniards) lumped all of the natives into the single category of Indians, she never names any of their different ethnicities or languages. Furthermore, since their interactions were brief, she did not scrutinize their practices. Nevertheless, we catch glimpses of these cultures, especially when natives came to greet the nuns during their short stays at the doctrinas.

During their movement across New Spain the nuns came into even closer contact with people of African descent, some slaves, some free innkeepers, and others servants or Third Order religious in convents, but all of them Christians (at least to some extent). It must be said, however, that most enslaved Africans, especially those who were brought over on slave ships, received only minimal instruction in the Catholic faith. Slaves of African descent also brought with them many of their own religious beliefs and rituals that they incorporated into a syncretic form of Christianity. In his recent study David Wheat has noted, "The acquisition of Iberian languages and appropriation of Iberian religious practices did not necessarily signify the loss of African identities, loyalties, beliefs, or memories."[39] The majority of Africans originally came from west and central Africa. Unlike the declining numbers of indigenous peoples during the time of the nuns, the population of Africans and mulattos was on the rise in the 1620s.[40] Africans also came into close contact with Amerindians, at times intermarrying. Their offspring, known as *zambos*, became more integrated into Spanish society than their African parents, but they still held on to vestiges of their African heritage.

Indigenous Mexicans and Africans alike embraced the Spaniards' faith in saints, relics, apparitions, and miraculous occurrences, but they also made them their own. The fusion of their own beliefs in the spiritual world and the power of amulets and healing through touch and herbs, along with the supernatural elements of Christianity, created a unique syncretism of beliefs and cultural behavior common to popular Catholic religion in New Spain. In the words of one scholar, "By 1600, popular Catholicism in Mexico was a fascinating combination of African, native, and Spanish traditions."[41] Sor Ana introduces us to this world through her depiction of the cult of "santa" Juana's rosary beads.

We first learn about one such black woman (Sor Ana refers to her as a "negra"), a slave called Margarita, when the small entourage spent three nights at the house of Captain Alonso de Mújica and his wife, doña Juliana, in Veracruz. Unfortunately we do not know anything more about Margarita's background. We do know that Margarita worked for the nuns, because Sor Ana states she did needlework for them. When Margarita suffered from heart pain, Sor Jerónima made the sign of the cross over her chest with one of the miraculous rosary beads from Juana de la Cruz. Later, in a letter written to the nuns, doña Juliana claimed that Margarita never suffered from the ailment again. It is extremely difficult to know exactly what Margarita thought about the beads or to what extent she believed in their miraculous powers, but Sor Ana's narrative hints at the power of icons across the lines of race and class. Margarita was not the first woman of African descent whom the nuns encountered in the New World. As we shall see in the next section, on the trail from Veracruz to the capital, the nuns also came into contact with female black innkeepers.

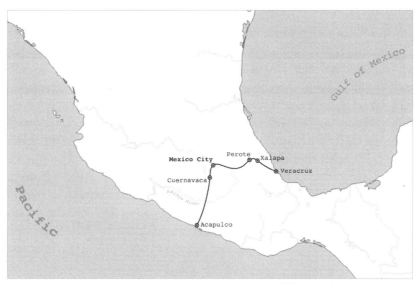

Map 3 The nuns' journey across Mexico. Map created by Patrick McCarty.

Veracruz to the Capital

During the colonial period, there were two main trails from Veracruz to Mexico City. The first, used by Hernán Cortés, went by way of the snowcapped Orizaba volcano. After the Conquest this route was less transited because of difficult terrain and lack of villages for supplies. Accompanied by friars; servants; the ship's captain, Diego Meléndez; and several indigenous guides, the nuns took the more common route to the capital (255 miles), known as the Camino de Ventas or the Path of Inns, since it catered to most travelers: merchants, soldiers, friars, priests, viceroys, and their retinues journeying to Mexico City. The first part of the trail required travelers to either walk or ride mules. It passed through the Spanish settlement of Xalapa and continued on to Perote—now a small city, but at the time a way station with an inn. From Perote, the trail greatly improved, and carriages were used the rest of the way to the capital. On the outskirts of the city, the trail merged into a cobblestone road, "the calzada de Guadalupe," enabling visitors to pay their respects at the shrine of Our Lady of Guadalupe.[42]

Despite the welcome presence of some rustic inns, the path from Veracruz to the capital was still wild when the nuns set foot on Mexican soil in early September 1620. They faced torrential downpours, which filled the tracks with mud and debris. Rivers swelled and swift currents required them to wait several days before making necessary river crossings. In this inclement weather, the women mounted mules for the first time in their lives, and with their long habits they must have ridden sidesaddle, an awkward position that would have thrown them off balance. Riding was made even more difficult because the first section of the trail outside Veracruz rose up steeply from the coast toward the high plains of the interior. Sor Ana describes two major falls: in the first, she fell off her own mule into the mud, and in the second, the nuns witnessed Sor Jerónima and her mule tumble down a ravine. The group believed that the elderly abbess had met her death, but they all rejoiced when Fray José "found her tranquil and calm, hanging from a small branch."[43] Sor Ana's fantastic portrayal of this event plays nicely into her overall narrative, that is, highlighting the abbess's powers to overcome all types of adversity.

While traversing New Spain, the nuns slept in roadside inns, huts, local homes, Franciscan monasteries and churches, and the open air. Sor Ana's descriptions of the rustic inns paint a picture of the diverse milieu of those who lived and worked in these places. Most of the innkeepers were women and in some cases are depicted as *negras*. The treatment of the nuns ranged from a cold reception—one woman gave the group only green wood to light a fire and hid a basket of bread under her bed—to just the opposite: another innkeeper welcomed the women with open arms and provided them with a warm meal. In the latter inn, the nuns rewarded the woman by letting her touch her rosary with one of Juana de la Cruz's original beads. The beads repeatedly served as a nexus with the local population. In another inn, Sor Jerónima cured a local Spanish farmer of a strange illness by having him hold a bead in his mouth all night long. Sor Ana affirms that many people came to touch their rosaries to one of the original beads because there was a great devotion to Juana de la Cruz everywhere they went.

On the other hand, the culture shock of sleeping beneath the stars must have been extreme for the group of nuns, since they had spent the vast majority of their lives behind the thick walls of their convent (fifty years in the case of Sor Jerónima). Nevertheless, Sor Ana always views these experiences from a positive angle and at times with a sense of humor. Shortly before they arrived in Xalapa, she writes, "We felt tremendous joy seeing ourselves in that countryside. It was Thursday evening and because of the trees and river we felt ourselves accompanying the Lord in his garden and so we said psalms together." She then explains how a late-night shower had drenched the group and the next day "we rode the mules like wet chickens, but all in a good mood as we crossed the river, our mother in the lead like a flagship."[44]

Soon thereafter, as the nuns approached Xalapa, they came across their first Franciscan doctrina. In this section of the manuscript, Sor Ana's discourse again weaves in threads of Sor Jerónima's missionary efforts. As she portrays reactions of the local indigenous to the saintly nun from Toledo, her descriptions show how the nuns transcended the limits of agency typically assigned to women religious. In this case, she writes, "The whole village processed with cross and banners. They held bouquets of flowers, which they presented to us and they gave our blessed mother a crown of flowers, and they put a garland around her neck. They asked for her in their language, causing great devotion in everyone. This lifted her spirits; she kept saying, 'Blessed be God.'"[45] These moments of Sor Jerónima's contact with the native Mexicans provide salient instances of the Spanish nun's effect on indigenous and Spanish populations alike, and, albeit briefly, the native people's inspirational effect on her, as depicted in the preceding excerpt.

According to Sor Ana's account, Sor Jerónima caused awe wherever she went, especially in remote outposts among converted Amerindians: "And since in those lands they had never seen nuns before, they thought they had come down from heaven. They beat their chests, saying, 'How could it be possible for us to see such things in our lifetime?'"[46] Although female convents had long been common in Mexico, with the first foundation in 1540, nuns rarely, if ever, left their enclosed monasteries, and they certainly would not be found in remote regions. Sor Ana's descriptions of the trail between Veracruz and Mexico City throw into sharp relief the utter incongruity of women dressed in dark habits, with veils covering their faces, traversing the trade routes of New Spain. Again, she captures the astonishment of the local people:

> An innkeeper sent one of her sons to another innkeeper to see if the nuns had arrived. She told him that they had not come, but instead some priests dressed in robes and black headdresses. The mother raced across the countryside on horseback so she could see this. She brought us some eggs and bread to eat and she relaxed with us. She said that her son had called us priests but did not know anything else, and others were saying that we were the priests' wives that they had brought from Castile, that we were not nuns. And so we traveled with such confusion among the Indians as if one had come from another world.[47]

Sor Ana also addresses the issue of the scarcity of ordained friars and diocesan priests in the rural areas along the trail.[48] She writes, "We came across several doctrinas where the Indians serve as *curas* (priests) since there are so few ministers other than those who come from Spain, and they are spread thin throughout these places."[49] Most likely Sor Ana was referring to indigenous lay brothers and not to ordained clergy, since the Mexican provincial councils of 1555, 1565, and 1585 had prohibited such ordinations. The Third Council of 1585, however, was later revised with vague language from the Holy See and could have allowed for a few exceptions.[50] Regardless, Sor Ana's description of the men leaves open the possibility that these indigenous priests did take on duties outside their official purview, perhaps even administering the sacraments, or at the very least helping friars with proselytization.[51]

We also see how Sor Jerónima served as holy inspiration to the local Spanish and criollo populations. In an intriguing instance while in Xalapa, several Spanish women from high society (*gente principal*) approached the abbess from Toledo to tell her that they played cards. First she chastised them for this life of immorality, warning them of people who had lost their haciendas and souls to the vice. She then conjured up the image of "saint" Gregorio López (1542–1596; never canonized), a Spaniard who had lived his life as a hermit in New Spain and who, like Jerónima, was sought out for his advice and intercessory prayers. Sor Jerónima told the women that she hoped they would not end up condemned for gambling like the woman she had read about in López's life story.[52] After listening to these cautionary tales, the Spanish ladies promised to give up the practice.[53] Beyond the anecdote about Sor Jerónima's ability to touch people's lives far outside the enclosure of a convent, two facts resonate: all types of gambling, including cards, dice, and board games, were ubiquitous in New Spain; and although an ordinance from the *cabildo* of Mexico City in 1583 forbade women to partake in such games, this did not deter them from playing cards.[54]

The nuns rested for three nights at a Franciscan monastery in Xalapa. The commissary general of all the Franciscan friaries in New Spain had sent out an order to the guardians (head friars) to personally take care of the nuns, and Sor Ana frequently mentions their hospitality. One guardian later accompanied the nuns six leagues, or about eighteen miles, along the difficult path to the inn of Perote. He assigned indigenous men to hold the reins of each mule so they could lead the nuns on dangerous bluffs overlooking rivers and streams. The entourage spent the night at the historic inn of Perote, which had been built in the 1520s.[55] The next day the nuns left their mules behind and were driven in two carriages the rest of the way to Mexico City.

The Shrine of Our Lady of Guadalupe

Sor Ana's vivid descriptions of the road between Veracruz and Mexico City not only provide insight into the dynamic interplay between the Spanish nuns and the local inhabitants but also cast new light on one of the sites most visited in Mexico today. As we have seen, Catholicism in the New World, much like its counterpart in Spain, revolved around belief in miracles, visions, and intercessions for the dead. It emphasized public displays of devotion to the Virgin Mary, saints, and holy relics. When possible, early modern Catholics embarked on pilgrimages and visited shrines. The most important shrine in New Spain (at least by the 1620s) was located on the main thoroughfare leading into Mexico City. Like many other travelers at the time, the small group of nuns from Spain made a stop to pay homage at the Chapel of Our Lady of Guadalupe.[56] Sor Ana describes their visit:

> The next day's journey in New Spain was to a chapel that they call Our Lady of Guadalupe; we spent the night there. It is a paradise and the image is one of much devotion. It was manifested when Mexico was won and dust was being thrown in the eyes of the enemies. She appeared to an Indian in that place where [the chapel] is now, that is, between two boulders, and she told him to have a church built for her. A little fresh water sprang from the ground where her feet had touched. We saw it when we passed by the spot and it is boiling as if over a very large fire. We were given a jug and it tasted salty. Also, some laywomen (*beatas*) who were taking care of the chapel told us that the Virgin herself asked the Indian for his cloak made of cloth, which measured from head to toe. Her image was imprinted on it and then she gave it back to the Indian, telling him to put it in that place, where it would make many miracles. There are more than forty silver lamps [in the chapel] and there are rooms for people who go there to pray novenas.[57]

There is much to say about this short description of Guadalupe and her miraculous image. Foremost, it is one of the earliest accounts written in

Spanish by a woman. It not only describes the site of the apparition of the Virgin Mary but also provides a description of the miraculous imprint of the Virgin on Juan Diego's cloak (although his name is omitted). Notably, Sor Ana's account of the site has never been studied as such and is absent from historical studies on the cult of the Virgin of Guadalupe.[58] We do know that other texts penned by women in the sixteenth century mention Guadalupe, but those references are in last wills and testaments. For example, Elvira Ramírez's will of 1557 briefly mentions her request for masses to be said at the Church of the Virgin of Guadalupe.[59] Sor Ana's account has very little in common with these Spanish wills but can be better compared to other travel narratives, such as the autobiographical account by the Englishman Miles Philips, who survived the botched John Hawkins slave-trading expedition at San Juan de Ulúa in 1568. Later, as a Spanish prisoner, Philips visited the Guadalupe shrine on his way to Mexico City. He writes,

> The next morning we departed from thence on our journey towards Mexico, and so travelled till we came within two leagues of it, where there was built by the Spaniards a very fair Church, called our Lady's Church, in which there is an image of our Lady of silver and gilt, being as high and as large as a tall woman, in which Church, and before this image, there are as many lamps of silver as there be days in the year, which upon high days are all lighted. Whensoever any Spaniards pass by this Church, although they be on horseback, they will alight, and come into the Church, and kneel before the image, and pray to our Lady to defend them from all evil, so that whether he be horseman or footman he will not pass by, but first go into the Church, and pray as aforesaid, which if they do not, they think and believe that they shall never prosper; which image they call in the Spanish tongue, Nuestra Senora de Guadalupe. At this place there are certain cold baths, which arise, springing up as though the water did seethe; the water whereof is somewhat brackish in taste, but very good for any that have any sore or wound, to wash themselves therewith, for as they say, it healeth many. And every year once, upon our Lady Day [March 25, the Feast of the Annunciation] the people use to repair thither to offer, and to pray in that Church before the image; and they say that Our Lady of Guadalupe doth work a number of miracles. About this Church there is not any town of Spaniards that is inhabited, but certain Indians do dwell there in houses of their own country building.[60]

In comparing Sor Ana's and Miles Philips's descriptions, we see that both were amazed by the numerous silver lanterns hanging in the church (now the old basilica). They also partook of the healing waters at the sanctuary, mostly likely the site of the modern-day Chapel of the Pocito.[61] Yet their observations of essentially the same place are subtly different. Philips does not mention the role of Juan Diego; he emphasizes instead the silver statue of the Virgin.[62] In contrast, Sor Ana specifically describes the Virgin's apparition to an Indian and the imprint on his cloak. This difference is not a surprise; as Barbara Fuchs has pointed out, Philips's description of "the chief Catholic icon of New Spain—oscillates between detached skepticism and less critical acceptance."[63] Sor Ana, on the other hand, never wavers.

Sor Ana's matter-of-fact description of the site underscores the Spanish belief in the superiority of the Catholic faith in the conquest of indigenous peoples.[64] She does not, however, cite any connection between the Catholic Virgin of Guadalupe and the Aztec goddess Tonantzin, a correlation that had been made earlier by another Franciscan, Fray Bernardino de Sahagún.[65] Moreover, Sor Ana omits any reference to the tension prevalent between Franciscans and Dominicans during the mid-sixteenth century regarding the Virgin and her relationship to Tonantzin.[66] It is not surprising that she ignores the power struggles between the orders, especially those regarding any relationship to an Aztec goddess. Her worldview, although expanded by her travels, did not accommodate other belief systems. She firmly believed in the superiority of the Catholic faith as the only true religion. When describing the local Amerindians, she reduced them to naked primitives, in need of evangelization. Unlike some of her male Franciscan counterparts (most famously those from the previous century, such as Fray Toribio de Benavente "Motolinía" and Fray Bernardino de Sahagún), she shows no indication that Sor Jerónima and her companions had any wish to learn indigenous languages or understand native belief systems.[67] Sor Ana's portrayal of Juan Diego and his encounter with the Virgin speaks more to the influence of the Council of Trent in the Americas, which promoted devotion to the Virgin and other saints, than to any interest in native peoples in their own right. At the same time, Sor Ana had to tread lightly in the complex religious landscape, where women's writing was already viewed with skepticism.

Sor Ana's account provides the modern reader with some fascinating clues about the shrine in the early 1620s. Her allusion to the beatas is particularly intriguing. We know very little about these women who took care of the chapel, although at least one testimony describes how indigenous peoples of

THE TOWN OF GUADALUPE,   LA VILLA DE GUADALUPE,   LA VILLE DE GUADALUPE,
   Taken from a balloon   Tomada en globo   Prise en ballon

Figure 11 *The Villa de Guadalupe*, 1855–1859. Casimiro Castro, lithography, via Wikimedia Commons. This image from the mid-1800s, taken from the perspective of a
hot-air balloon, provides a good overview of the old basilica and the Hill of Tepeyac.

Cuauhtitlan would visit the shrine to clean and repair it.[68] Miles Philips also
mentions the indigenous people who lived in the vicinity of Tepeyac and
took care of the chapel. It is noteworthy that the beatas, rather than the local
friars or priests, assumed the role of cultural informants; it was they who told
the group about the miraculous encounter between the indigenous man and
the Virgin of Guadalupe. It is possible that Sor Ana was referring also to a
group of local Spanish orphan girls sponsored by a *cofradía*, or confraternity,
that paid for their dowries. Yet according to Gustavo Watson Marrón, the
documentation for the orphans' dowries covers only the period between 1576
and 1593, so the practice probably ended around that time.[69] It is doubtful
also that the beatas were precursors to the Capuchin nuns, who founded
their community much later, in the 1780s. This section of Sor Ana's record
might well lend itself to more study.

The Capital of New Spain

After paying homage to the Virgin of Guadalupe, the nuns continued on to the capital of New Spain. Sor Jerónima's wealthy cousin Gonzalo Sánchez de Herrera wanted the group to stay at his house, but she insisted on staying in a convent, although they later stayed with him when they left the city. She also wanted to arrive in secret to evade the pomp created by such a visit. Sor Jerónima had already rejected the opportunity to stop in Puebla, and she had "asked our father [Santa María] to take another route to avoid ostentation."[70] Things did not occur as planned, however, and many high-ranking officials, including the archbishop of Mexico, accompanied the group to the Convent of La Visitación.

In contrast to their experience on the deserted trail from Veracruz, the nuns must have been amazed to enter Mexico City. Upon their arrival, the capital boasted 150,000 residents and matched many European cities in size and grandeur. Mexico City had a cathedral (1573), a university (1553), and a printing press (1539).[71] There were a myriad of religious institutions. The Inquisition was established in Mexico City in 1570. Its jurisdiction covered the entire territory of New Spain and the Philippines, but it did not persecute Amerindians, who as neophytes—and viewed as childlike in their understanding of Christianity—were exempt from the harsh punishments meted out by the Holy Office. The same was not true for people of African descent, enslaved or free. Mendicant orders of Franciscans, Dominicans, Augustinians, and Capuchins and an abundance of Jesuits priests lived and preached in the city. Many Jesuits served as confessors to female religious regardless of their own monastic order. As mentioned earlier, the first female convent was established in 1540, and from that point onward, the city was filled with nuns. In the words of Thomas Gage, "There are not above fifty churches and chapels, cloisters and nunneries, and parish churches in that city, but those that are there are the fairest that ever my eyes beheld."[72]

Despite the proliferation of nunneries, there were no Discalced Franciscan convents in the city at this time. La Visitación had been founded in 1601 under the First Rule of Poor Clares, but shortly thereafter the community adopted the less strict Second Rule.[73] We can surmise that Sor Jerónima opted for La Visitación because of a letter penned by Fray José to the Duke of Lerma, the king's favorite, in 1612. In his campaign to acquire the necessary licenses to found the convent in the Philippines, Fray José strengthened his argument by implying that the nuns could reform the convent in Mexico City while on their way to Manila, "as they [the Mexico City nuns] lacked someone to teach them how to follow their original constitution and ceremonies."[74]

During their five-month sojourn at La Visitación, the Spaniards accepted two Mexican nuns to join their new foundation in Manila: Leonora de San Buenaventura, the vicaress of the Mexican convent, and María de los Angeles, a nurse. Sor Ana does not explain why they chose these particular women. We can only speculate that as vicaress in Mexico, Sor Leonora had the necessary leadership skills to become an abbess in Manila (a post she would later hold) and that as a nurse Sor María possessed healing skills that would prove useful on the rest of the long voyage.[75] Sor Ana remarked that many other nuns offered to accompany the group, but since there was not enough space on the ship and they lacked the appropriate documentation, the group could accept only the two women from La Visitación.

Many wealthy visitors showered the women with gifts, but Sor Jerónima gave strict orders to accept none of them. She made only two exceptions: a crucifix given to the nuns by the commissary general of New Spain, Alonso Montemayor, and what Sor Ana calls a "large image" of the Immaculate Conception. It is not completely clear whether the latter was a painting or a sculpture, but Sor Ana does say that it was placed on the altarpiece in Manila. Once again Sor Ana emphasizes Sor Jerónima's determination to follow the austere precepts of the First Rule of Saint Clare. She refused monetary donations, gold, silver, and reliquaries. Most likely, however, Sor Jerónima accepted the image of the Immaculate Conception because that was going to be the name of their future convent in Manila: Convento de la Madre de Dios de Concepción (although to this day it is most commonly known as "el convento de Santa Clara").[76] Moreover, Sor Jerónima's acceptance of the image would also serve as a reminder of the aforementioned Franciscan campaign of the Immaculate Conception.

While at La Visitación, the women lived in a diverse social milieu, including indigenous servants and African slaves, common in large nunneries of New Spain. The Spanish nuns encountered an indigenous servant woman who worked in the infirmary and cared for their travel companion, Sor María de la Trinidad, after she fell down a flight of stairs. Sor Ana narrates how "an upright Indian called Inés" professed great devotion to the nun from Cubas, praying to an image of Juana de la Cruz, kept in the convent.[77] Both Quesada and Sor Ana also point out how Inés was greatly admired for her ability to communicate with souls in purgatory. Further, we learn from Quesada's biography that Inés was a *donada* (servant class) originally from the distant Caribbean city of Cartagena de Indias.[78] How she made it from Cartagena to Mexico City is unknown, but evidently her story was not so uncommon. In 1542 Charles V officially prohibited the enslavement of indigenous peoples, but many slave traders found loopholes in these laws. Nancy van Deusen's recent study focusing on the sixteenth century shines a light on how "hundreds of thousands of [indigenous] slaves and servants were deracinated from their homelands and shipped to disparate sites."[79]

This section of the account is notable for several reasons. On the one hand it speaks to the legacy of Juana de la Cruz outside of Spain, making patent her influence on different ethnic groups and social classes in Mexican convents. On the other hand, it serves as a window into the different circumstances of all types of women within these large convents. In this case, we encounter an Indian woman from the distant city of Cartagena de Indias. Although as an indigenous woman Inés could never profess as a black-veiled nun, she navigated the system, finding a place for herself in the convent as a visionary. Perhaps because of their gratitude toward Inés or to the nuns in general for their hospitality, it appears that Sor Jerónima left two of the miraculous rosary beads at the Convent of La Visitación, and according to a late seventeenth-century chronicle, other beads were left in churches like that of Santa Clara.[80]

Shortly before departing from the capital the nuns paid a visit to the two other Franciscan convents in the city. They spent three days at Santa Clara and another three at San Juan de la Penitencia, itself an offshoot of the convent at Santa Clara. The nuns in those two convents had a lavish lifestyle, and as a member of the same order, Sor Jerónima probably felt obligated to visit them to encourage them to adopt a stricter observance of Saint Clare's precepts of poverty. Sor Ana relates the impression that Sor Jerónima made on New Spanish convents when she summarizes a letter that they received from a friar: "He wrote to our mother, saying how her example had benefitted those convents of nuns."[81]

The nuns from Santa Clara welcomed the Spaniards with open arms. At the convent, they came into contact and established bonds with the disparate classes and races who inhabited this large calced or less austere nunnery. Although their home convent in Toledo did have servants who helped the nuns, there was no comparison to Mexico's large convents that adhered to a strict hierarchy based on skin color, wealth, proof of "Old Christian" blood, and parental legitimacy. At the apex, the choir nuns were upper-class white Spanish women and criollas (Spaniards born in the New World); they were followed by a secondary class of mestizas (women of mixed Spanish-indigenous parentage) and then by a servant class of mulatas, Africans, and indigenous women. Interestingly, sometimes women of color became extremely pious and were at times revered as holy women, thus transcending the secondary status bestowed them by their skin color. The most famous example is Catarina de San Juan (ca. 1600–1688), known as the "China Poblana." Originally from India, she was captured by Portuguese slave traders and eventually brought to the city of Puebla, where she was revered as holy woman.[82]

Sor Ana describes one such holy woman: "We especially enjoyed Madre Leonor de los Ángeles, who is greatly venerated in the convent and in town."[83] We know that Leonor de los Ángeles, originally from Oaxaca, was a donada, "donated" to the convent by her father at a young age; that is, she took the habit as part of the servant class. Over the years she became greatly revered as a visionary, but as a mulata she could not profess as a black-veiled nun.[84] She might, however, have taken the vows of the Third Order, thus her title of madre. Madre Leonor told the women about a vision she had of the Spanish nun Sor Luisa de la Ascensión, who supported the sisters' travels to the Philippines.

During their time at the convent in Mexico City, the Spanish women received several letters from Sor Luisa encouraging them to found the discalced convent in Manila. Sor Ana cites a short fragment from one letter: "Do not give up this undertaking that will result in boundless glory for my sweet Jesus."[85] Sor Luisa's words must have provided encouragement to the small group of founders, especially because the most difficult portion of their journey still lay ahead of them. Madre Leonor's vision of Sor Luisa also attests to the network of female Franciscan role models in New Spain's convents. Armed with her words of encouragement, the nuns set out on the last leg of the land journey. After spending several days at the house of Gonzalo Sánchez de Herrera, Sor Jerónima's cousin, just outside Mexico City, the entourage mounted mules again at the end of February 1621.[86]

The China Road: From Mexico City to Acapulco

Known by many as the Camino de China, or China Road, the trail from Mexico City to the Pacific coast covered approximately 285 miles.[87] It was aptly named because it served as the main thoroughfare for the transport of Asian commerce—in exchange for vast quantities of Spanish silver—from Manila via Acapulco to the capital of New Spain. Unlike the Path of Inns from Veracruz to Mexico City, this route was sparsely populated, especially the section from Cuernavaca to the coast. Because the difficult terrain did not allow for carriages, most travelers either walked or rode mules. Formidable obstacles included dense tropical forests, steep mountain passes, and several river crossings. These obstacles were bearable in comparison to the swarms of mosquitos that gave no respite to humans. Priests, merchants, and adventurers penned descriptions of the trail during the seventeenth and eighteenth centuries. They all attest to the extremely harsh conditions of the China Road. For instance, we can turn to an account written by don Juan de Herrera y Montemayor, a Spanish merchant, who journeyed to the coast in late summer 1617 to board a ship bound for Callao, Peru (one of the few other ports of call from Acapulco). He states that he stopped at "La Venta de la Viuda" (the Widow's Inn), three leagues, or nine miles, from the coast: "Here we experienced Acapulco's poor climate, which is the grave of Spaniards, paradise of mulatas. We martyred ourselves with the incredible amount of mosquitos and bats."[88] Don Juan also spent most of his time in Acapulco weak from high fevers, the same ailments that afflicted the Spanish nuns.

During the nuns' difficult trek to the coast, we soon learn that the women relied on their miraculous rosaries to cure physical ailments; they ground up the beads and mixed them with water to use as medicine. The substance of the actual beads is never clarified, but in Antonio Daza's description of Juana de la Cruz's rosaries, he says they could have consisted of jet, wood, coral, or glass.[89] The nuns, unaccustomed to riding mules, now suffered from saddle sores. To cure her horrible bout of *almorranas* (hemorrhoids) and fearing that she might be overcome by colic, Sor Leonora de San Buenaventura was given "a ground-up bead from Saint Juana with a sip of water. After this was done she was completely cured."[90] At first glance it might seem strange, or even impossible, to the contemporary reader that the ground-up beads could have cured the nuns, but some of the beads, particularly those made of coral, were believed to have medicinal effects.[91] Furthermore, recent studies on the "placebo effect" lend credence to the nuns' belief in the beneficial powers attributed to the medicinal beads. Modern science teaches us that although the medicine itself might be a sham, belief itself at times can trigger chemical changes in the body, such as immune responses that can benefit the patient.[92] Moreover, the nuns used the beads as medicine sparingly, only in rare instances, when all other options seemed to have failed. Sor Jerónima and her sisters truly believed that ingesting Juana's rosary bead as a remedy would help Sor Leonora, and it did.

Sor Leonora's bout of hemorrhoids and colic did not compare to the intermittent fevers that plagued everyone in the travel party. These were most likely caused by swarms of mosquitos carrying malaria or other tropical diseases. Sor Ana writes,

> We arrived at another place where a priest was saying mass. He had two sacristans on either side of him fanning away a myriad of mosquitos. We made confession, received communion, and right there in the church we had dinner. Then he went with us as far as the River Balsas, which we crossed in dugout canoes [*calabazas*], each one tied to the other and rowed by Indians. We then crossed the River Papagayo, which was the roughest part of the journey due to its ups and downs and rocky cliffs. God saved us from great dangers because there were jaguars [*tigres*] and other wild beasts in this area.[93]

Nevertheless, the beauty of the landscape astounded Sor Ana, especially the cultivated native fields and orchards near Cuernavaca: "There were many rivers and streams with lovely water and wooded springs. There were fruit trees, coconut palms, orange groves, banana plants, and a type of plant that they use to make pita thread.[94] . . . There were vineyards and trees where cotton grows; reeds so tall and thick that they are used to build houses and churches; sturdy pines and solid hardwoods. There were such pleasant fields, flowers, fruits, and trees that it seemed like paradise. Indeed, we were told that we were very close to it and to the River Jordan."[95]

Sor Ana's description of these native lands as a type of earthly paradise echoes the common trope used first by early explorers, conquistadores, and missionaries and later by poets and authors such as Bernardo de Balbuena and Carlos de Sigüenza y Góngora.[96] Jorge Cañizares-Esguerra affirms that this mentality evolved into the notion that God resided in his garden while the devil lurked in the wilderness.[97] For Sor Ana, the comparison of the cultivated fields and orchards to paradise provided a metaphor for the triumph of Christian evangelization in the area. Indeed, on the trail from Veracruz to Acapulco, the travel party faced real dangers from wild animals, airborne pests, and raging rivers, but Sor Ana mostly highlights their positive encounters with converted natives at the Franciscan and Dominican doctrinas.

The Port of Acapulco

For most of the year, the port of Acapulco was a sparsely populated, remote outpost of the Spanish Empire. Hot temperatures and humidity prevailed during springtime, and other than a few buildings such as the Franciscan monastery, very little permanent construction marked the town. Yet once a year, with the arrival of the Manila galleons, the town grew from a mere five hundred inhabitants to two thousand. The annual Feria de Acapulco attracted thousands of different types of people involved in the buying and selling of Chinese and other Asian goods. Spaniards, criollos, mestizos, mulattos, Indians, Chinese, Filipinos, and more converged for these few short weeks every year, making the normally desolate port of Acapulco a melting pot of cultures.[98]

The nuns arrived in Acapulco around mid-March but had to wait until April 6, 1621, for the departure of the only ship that year, the *San Andrés*.[99] The galleons generally arrived and then left Acapulco between the months of January and March. There was only a short window, due to the monsoon season, for the ships to safely make the round-trip journey from Manila to Acapulco.[100]

After stopping at the Franciscan monastery in the port, the nuns went directly to their housing. Sor Ana describes their accommodation as a rustic posada where they fashioned a room into a visiting parlor with a cane grille. The nuns enclosed themselves in this lodging for close to a month.[101] Fevers afflicted all of the women, but no one as severely as Sor Jerónima. She fell so ill that she was administered the Viaticum and there was talk of leaving her at the port. Shortly before departure, she rallied and insisted on walking to the ship of her own accord. Later in her narrative, Sor Ana makes reference to her recovery and attributes it to one of Juana de la Cruz's original beads, which Jerónima had ingested as medicine. Something that Sor Ana never mentions, however, perhaps because they never left their cloistered room, was the tremendous commerce and activity generated by the arrival of the Manila galleon. Although this is disappointing to present-day readers, it should come as no surprise. Sor Ana's own subjectivity as an early modern nun guided her choice of the details that she believed pertinent to her story. In her worldview, Sor Jerónima's astounding recovery took precedence over the Acapulco fair.

Conclusion

Sor Ana's narration of their passage across New Spain highlights the agency of early modern women religious. I contend that if we interpret writings like Sor Ana's by contextualizing them within their historical framework, we can come closer to the mind-set of the early modern nun who lived within a complex and fluid religious climate. Indeed, following the development of Sor Ana's own subjectivity is paramount to understanding her account of their travels. We cannot take all of her descriptions at face value, such as her depiction of passive and friendly natives, since she embeds many of her cultural prejudices in her observations. Clearly, her representation of these peoples, open to evangelization, tells us more about Sor Ana than it does about the Amerindians. At the same time, we should be careful in comparing the nuns' experience in Mexico with that of Franciscan friars with their role as missionaries to the natives. The Spanish women wanted to see indigenous people converted to Christianity, but their mission did not include any mandate to learn about indigenous culture or language.

As Sor Ana's words trace their path across Mexico, describing each new experience, her rhetorical negotiation of Sor Jerónima's missionary agenda gradually begins to dovetail with her own role in shedding light on the saintly qualities of the abbess. Not only does Sor Ana portray Sor Jerónima's wherewithal to survive the transatlantic crossing, her near-deadly mule accident, and her bouts with high fevers, but she also presents her as an inspiration to Amerindians and Spaniards alike. To accomplish this, she frames part of her narrative with support from highly regarded religious women of their Franciscan order. She mentions the letters from Luisa de la Ascensión encouraging Sor Jerónima not to give up on her quest to establish the new convent under the strict auspices of the First Order of Saint Clare. Even more, she draws on their predecessor, Juana de la Cruz, and the widespread devotion toward her miraculous beads. Sor Ana writes that Sor Jerónima widely distributed these beads to the local population. She astutely realizes that the beads are a type of spiritual currency, highly coveted by many people in New Spain regardless of race or class.[102] It is at this moment that we catch a rare glimpse of tension between the sisters, when Sor Ana states that the two nuns from the convent in Cubas—Sor María Magdalena de Cristo and Sor María Magdalena de la Cruz (who had inherited the beads from Juana de la Cruz)—should be more generous with their large supply of beads and give them out to travelers in the Philippines as protection against storms and other perils at sea.

Sor Ana's positioning of Sor Jerónima as a future saint should not detract from the novelty of the nuns' experience nor from the unique perspective she provides us of their journey. Her words paint a picture of the diverse cultural milieu that unfolded as the nuns arrived at different sites, from the Franciscan doctrinas near Xalapa to the shrine of Guadalupe, from the large female convents of Mexico City to the entrepôt of Acapulco.

In the next chapter Sor Ana offers yet again a gendered perspective of their global odyssey. She and her sisters leave terra firma and embark on one of the longest and most dangerous sea voyages in the world.

CHAPTER 3

The Manila Galleon

～❦

❦ THE IMAGE OF A MANILA GALLEON CONJURES UP ROMANTIC VISIONS of adventure, sunken treasure, pieces of eight, one-eyed pirates, and wind-blown sailors. One can almost smell the salty air, see the clear blue waters of the Pacific, taste the exotic fruits of some far-off tropical island, and hear the chattering of parrots. In reality the voyage from Acapulco to Manila took about three months, with passengers and crew in crowded quarters. The return trip, which could last between six and nine months, has been described by the seventeenth-century Italian globetrotter Gemelli Careri as "[the] most dreadful of any in the world."[1] Ships departing from Acapulco had to navigate over six thousand miles of open ocean before reaching the Mariana Islands, let alone the easternmost islands of the Philippine archipelago.[2] Crossing the Pacific Ocean exposed passengers to many potential perils, such as typhoons, scurvy, dysentery, and enemy attacks. At times heavy seas could cause rig-gings to break, masts to snap, and decks to flood. Storms, along with poor navigational skills, could shipwreck a vessel on reefs and strand sailors on desert islands.[3]

"El galeón de Manila," or the Manila galleon, was a generic name for the small flotilla, usually one to two ships, that made the yearly round-trip voyage from Acapulco to Manila between 1565 and 1815.[4] Due to favorable currents and the northeast trade winds, the Carrera de Poniente or westward run from Acapulco to Manila was relatively quicker, taking approximately three months, in contrast to the longer eastward voyage.[5] Although the galleons usually carried some form of armaments, these were not frigates (warships) but large merchant vessels made of sturdy hardwood to carry large loads of cargo. Many galleons were built in the yards of Cavite, located across the bay from Manila.[6] From the Philippines to Mexico the ships' holds were bursting with silks, cotton, porcelain, lacquer-ware, furniture, jewelry, precious gems, and spices.[7] Until the early 1700s the galleons also carried human cargo to Mexico, that is, slaves from all over Asia, all grouped under the general term of *chinos*.[8] On the trip to Manila, the ships stocked some European and Mexican goods for their colonists, but they mostly filled their hulls with Spanish silver, most of which would go to satisfy China's insatiable demand for the metal.[9] The silver came from the Mexican mines of San Luis Potosí, Guanajuato, and Zacatecas, but also from the huge silver mountain of Potosí located in modern-day Bolivia. The galleons traveling to Manila also carried a host of passengers: missionaries, priests, soldiers, prisoners, political officials, and to a lesser degree, colonists. There were also some slaves on the westward voyage, but they were personal property belonging to passengers and crew.

While some recent scholarship is beginning to fill the gap, there is still a lacuna of critical studies dealing with the lives of women on the Manila galleons.[10] The story of Sor Jerónima and her sisters on the ship to the Philippines provides the first known account of nuns crossing the Pacific. Unlike Sor Ana's sparse description of the fleet of New Spain and crossing the Atlantic, in this section of her account she provides ample detail of the voyage from Acapulco to Manila. The nuns spent 110 days (April 6–July 24) on the Pacific Ocean, and the death of one of her spiritual sisters certainly left a mark on Sor Ana's psyche. Exactly how Sor Ana and the other nuns dealt with death and dying is a topic explored later in this chapter. Additionally, I turn to Ginés de Quesada's biography of Sor Jerónima to fill in some small gaps left open by Sor Ana's account. He tells us, for example, the name of the ship, the *San Andrés*, stating that it was the only galleon to leave Acapulco at that time.[11] On the other hand, he omits important details of the nuns' experiences with other women, most notably their interactions with an enslaved woman on board the ship and their stay with a pious native woman from Pampanga on the island of Luzon. It is worth repeating that such omissions remind us of the uniqueness of Sor Ana's gendered narrative, one that permits the modern reader to see the lives of other women on the way to Manila.

This chapter follows the nuns' transpacific route: it traces the sea voyage from Acapulco to the port of Bolinao on the island of Luzon and the overland and fluvial journey from Bolinao southeast to Manila. Through the eyes of Sor Ana we see what life was like on the ship for the nuns: from their daily prayers and interactions with clerics, naval officers, and common mariners to illness, death at sea, the harsh treatment of a black woman, and the perils of storms and slack winds. Notably, she frames her narrative around the power of Madre Juana's rosary beads, a theme evident in the crossing of Mexico. The last part of the chapter analyzes the nuns' journey from Bolinao to Manila. Through the prism of Sor Ana's account, we are treated to a rare glimpse of the path from the port of Bolinao on the west coast of the island, southeast to the fertile rice fields of Pampanga, and then into the large marshy delta of the Pasig River emptying into Manila Bay. Likewise, we are presented with the nuns' interactions with native peoples, some recently converted to Christianity but others hostile to the Spanish presence on the island.

History of the Transpacific Route

The Spaniards were not the first Europeans in the Far East. At the turn of the sixteenth century the Portuguese, in search of precious spices, began to look for routes other than the Silk Road to the Moluccas, now part of Indonesia. In 1498 Vasco da Gama sailed around the Cape of Good Hope and then continued all the way to the coast of India, to Calicut. As early as 1512 Francisco Serrão had landed on Mindanao, the largest Muslim-dominated island of the southern Philippines. After these early expeditions, the Portuguese began to set up trading posts and small colonies in Malacca, the Moluccas, Macao, and Goa. They made a fortune in the export of cloves, nutmeg, and cinnamon, spices that were widely coveted in Europe.

The Spaniards did not want to leave the lucrative spice trade solely in the hands of the Portuguese. They turned to the imaginary line of demarcation—which divided new lands claimed by Spain and Portugal—to justify their own expeditions to the Spice Islands.[12] At first Spain laid claim to the Moluccas, but after a series of disastrous attempts to secure them, in 1529 Charles V sold the islands to the Portuguese for 350,000 ducats under the Treaty of Zaragoza.[13] As part of the treaty, a new line of demarcation was fixed, and Spain redirected its attention to another group of islands, later named Las Islas Filipinas in honor of Charles's son, who became King Philip II. The Portuguese explorer

Ferdinand Magellan had already discovered a new passage for the Spanish Crown to the Philippines in 1521, around the tip of South America, but the strait now named after him was a dangerous maze and took too long to serve as a trade route. Magellan's voyage prompted other explorers to look for better routes from the American continent across the Pacific to the Philippines. Several navigators attempted different maritime crossings, including from Peru, but it was not until November 1564 that Miguel López de Legazpi left Acapulco to make his maiden voyage to the Philippines. His trip would not have been possible without the aid of his experienced pilot, Andrés de Urdaneta, who had sailed to the Molucca Islands as a young man. A year later, in 1565, the galleon *San Pablo*, guided by Urdaneta, returned to Mexico to commence trade with New Spain.[14] For the next 250 years, until 1815, the Spanish galleons plied the vast waters of the Pacific.

For the typical westward voyage from Acapulco to the Philippines, most ships would sail a relatively straight course across the Pacific, first arriving at the Mariana Islands and then sailing to the Strait of San Bernardino, then known as the Embocadero, on the outermost eastern edge of the archipelago. The expertise of the ship's pilots would then be essential to navigate the vessels through the Embocadero and around many islands before arriving on the western coast of Luzon and finally reaching Manila. Ships' captains were repeatedly advised to leave the port of Acapulco by the end of March so as to enter the Embocadero before monsoon season, which typically started sometime in June or early July. If it were deemed too dangerous to enter the passageway between the islands, then the galleons would remain at the entrance to the Embocadero or find another port before returning to Acapulco.[15] In such cases, passengers were required to make an overland journey across Luzon to Manila.[16] A similar scenario affected the galleon *San Andrés*, carrying the founders of the convent, as we shall see later in this chapter.

Daily Life on the Manila Galleons

On April 6, 1621, the *San Andrés* left the port of Acapulco. Although Sor Jerónima had rallied enough to board the ship of her own accord, she was feverish and very weak. According to Sor Ana, "Our mother was so thin that we put her in a bed and she did not leave it, suffering incredible pain, until we disembarked."[17] The nuns had been given a large cabin at the stern with "a beautiful corridor with a small toilet," right next to their Franciscan escorts.

The ten women quickly converted their living space into a type of enclosed convent, with Sor María Magdalena de la Cruz and Sor Luisa de Jesús assigned as two doorkeepers. They gave the post of *provisora* to Sor Magdalena de Cristo. It was her job to prepare the food in the cabin and then hand it over to the two servants—the same men who had traveled with the group from Spain—so that they could cook it in the communal stove (fogón) in the forecastle. We know very little about the actual food that the nuns ate on the galleon, because no ship's manifest has been located, but the main provisions for the Pacific voyages were similar to those on the Atlantic runs: live chickens, swine, salted meats, dried fish, and hardtack.[18] Sor Ana does mention a gift of three hundred hens: "The Father Guardian gave us about one hundred hens and the mother of our sister María de los Angeles sent more than two hundred with many other gifts."[19] Sor Ana also refers to the scarcity of water on the vessel, especially toward the end of the long voyage, when, according to the friars, "there were soldiers who would give a peso for a jug of water."[20]

Upon enclosing themselves in the cabin, the nuns ate their meals and took care of their bodily necessities in close proximity. Since Sor Ana tells us that the nuns had their own toilet in the corridor we know that they did not use "the gardens," a euphemistic term for the latrines reserved for officers and passengers, located on the poop deck, much less the latrines for the mariners, at the prow of the ship.[21] Most likely they used bedpans for Sor María de la Trinidad and Sor Jerónima since they were too weak to leave their bunks. Simply put, the lack of hygiene for the ten women must have made conditions atrocious.

The women quickly became acquainted with high-ranking secular and ecclesiastical officials who made it a point to visit the nuns in their cabin. Notably, the "general de la armada," don Jerónimo de Valenzuela, paid special attention to the nuns' comfort, "as if it were his only duty."[22] (Throughout her narration Sor Ana refers to don Jerónimo as the general of the armada, despite the fact that only one ship was sailing to the Philippines. Since *general* is the title that Sor Ana uses to address don Jerónimo, I have also adopted it for this study. Technically, he probably held the highest position on the ship, that of captain general, with Diego de Rivera as second-in-command, or master of the ship [*maestre*]).[23] As was typical for the voyage to Manila, the ship was filled with missionaries and secular clergy. All twenty-four friars on board were Franciscans, with the addition of one Jesuit and one Dominican; those two had been chosen to carry correspondence to their respective orders. With the large quantity of soldiers traveling to the islands to take up posts at different presidios, there was not enough room that year to take members of other religious orders.[24]

The friars and nuns prayed together on a daily basis, singing the "Salve Regina" to the Virgin, while the priests said prayers and also sang the litany responsively in four voices in the choir. The nuns heard many sermons on Sundays, since there were "many great preachers," including Juan de Rentería, the newly appointed bishop of Nueva Segovia (a diocese in the north of Luzon). According to Quesada, on many days of the week the friars gave spiritual lessons to everyone on board the ship. In his opinion this developed a well-behaved group of seafarers, so much so "that it seemed more like a convent of nuns, rather than a squadron of soldiers and sailors."[25] Sailors had notoriously bad reputations in the early modern world, and Quesada's commentary speaks to his effort to portray an atmosphere that was becoming to the pious nuns.[26] Both Quesada and Sor Ana imbue the ship with a sacred quality. In essence, their words portray a sacralization of space and objects. The ship becomes a floating convent worthy of enclosed nuns and the water of the ocean is converted into sacred ground where they will have to "bury" one of their own.[27]

Similar to other religious writers of the period, Sor Ana (and Quesada) often kept track of time by way of the liturgical calendar, especially for important religious holidays such as Holy Week, which they celebrated during their first days on the vessel. In this way, Sor Ana marked the mortal illness that afflicted Sor María de la Trinidad, the white-veiled nun who had joined the group in Seville (and was originally from the convent in Belalcázar). Sor María fell deathly ill on the Octave of the Ascension, approximately forty days after the celebrations of Easter Week (Easter Sunday fell on April 11). Within five days she was dead.

Death at Sea

Illness and death often struck the Spanish fleets of the Indies. In addition to wounds sustained in warfare, there were many dangers on the high seas: accidents, drownings, diseases, and epidemics took countless lives. Some galleons, especially the *capitana* (flagship) and *almiranta* (second ship), employed a physician, or at the very least, a barber-surgeon for bloodletting.[28] Sanitary conditions were almost nonexistent on seafaring vessels, and the treatment of bloodletting often did more harm than good. Scurvy, a disease resulting from a lack of vitamin C, afflicted passengers and crew alike, but it was much more common on longer runs such as the return voyage to Acapulco, since the typical symptoms of fatigue, weakness, and bleeding from the gums do not commence until after three months. Contagion could spread rapidly on any vessel, and those with weakened immune systems, often the young and elderly, or those who had no natural immunity from exposure in childhood, quickly succumbed to diseases such as smallpox and measles. As transoceanic travel increased on a global scale, more and more diseases were introduced to different ports, and epidemics such as smallpox raged through local populations.[29] Ship's logs also recorded outbreaks of what the English called "the bloody flux," or dysentery, which weakened and killed seafarers.[30]

Sor María de la Trinidad suffered from a high fever and *cámaras* (diarrhea). She also did not respond to "any remedies," which could have included bloodletting and purges. The severity of Sor María's condition took the entire group by surprise, since they had been much more worried about Sor Jerónima, who was suffering from the same symptoms. Sor María may have been weakened by some sort of malaria-type illness from the hordes of mosquitos on the China Road from Mexico City to Acapulco, or maybe the poor quality of water, first in Mexico and later on the galleon, led to her diarrhea. Did Sor Jerónima have dysentery and then pass it on to Sor María, or vice-versa? But why didn't the other women, who shared such close quarters, exhibit the same symptoms?

Although it is difficult to diagnose the exact cause of Sor María's illness, we do know some of her symptoms and the environmental factors, many of which coincide with both types of dysentery, amoebic and bacillary, the first caused by pathogenic amoebas that invade the intestines and the second by bacteria. Both types of disease flourish in places with poor sanitary conditions and are spread by the feces-oral route. Throughout history outbreaks of dysentery typically have occurred in close quarters: on ships, in prisons, and in military garrisons. The main symptoms of amoebic and bacillary dysentery are diarrhea, at times with bloody stools, emaciation, fever, and weakness. In mild cases a patient will have no or only transient diarrhea, while acute dysentery can lead to death.[31]

Sor Ana's and Quesada's retellings of the nuns' experience in Acapulco and the death of Sor María on the high seas correlate closely with the above description of dysentery. During the nuns' month-long stay in Acapulco the women never left their enclosed posada. Most likely their accommodations were similar to those of the Dominican friar Domingo Navarrete, who wrote about his short stay in 1647: "The houses are all low, without any upper floor at all; the best of them are mud-wall'd and all thatch'd."[32] During their stay in the hot and humid climate of the Pacific, all the nuns began to exhibit fevers. Everyone recovered, including Sor Jerónima, but some of the sisters probably carried the disease on board the ship. While on the vessel, they again enclosed themselves in one room: the same place where they prepared their food, ate their meals, and took care of the two sick nuns. It must have been very difficult to avoid any contamination during the patients' extreme bouts of diarrhea, especially because a typical cabin measured about ten feet long by eight feet wide.[33] After less than two months at sea both Sor María and Sor Jerónima began to suffer from high fevers and diarrhea. One died, and the other, gaunt and emaciated (also typical of chronic dysentery), survived the ordeal.

It was always preferable to bring a body ashore for a proper burial in sanctified ground near a church; however, this was not always possible since bodies decay rapidly in hot weather.[34] For this reason, burial at sea was common on Spanish ships. After a solemn funeral ceremony a body was typically thrown overboard tied with a heavy object like a cannonball, or it was wrapped in a hefty piece of discarded sail. In his voyage on a Manila galleon, Gemelli Careri notes that an earthen vessel was tied to the feet of a diseased sailor to help sink the body.[35] Wooden boxes that served as coffins were reserved only for high-ranking officials.[36] In the case of Sor María, the bishop and Franciscan friars celebrated her funeral service. Instead of the traditional ringing of the church bells, three farewell salutes were fired in her honor. The nuns and clergy "sang *responsos* [prayers for the dead] as she was thrown into the sea, dressed in her habit and clutching a crucifix."[37]

Nuns as Healers

For a fruitful comparison of the emotions felt by the nuns at the loss of Sor María, we can turn to another group of traveling religious women. Almost a century later, in the early 1700s, a small cohort of nuns journeyed from Madrid to Lima to establish the first Capuchin convent in South America. Instead of making a land crossing of the Isthmus of Panama and then sailing south to Peru, the women boarded a ship that navigated the eastern coast of South America down to Buenos Aires. From there, the group made their way across the vast Pampas and the high Andes before boarding another ship north to Peru. The mother abbess of that foundation, Madre María Rosa, documented their travels and the subsequent foundation of the community in a convent chronicle. Her account describes the illness of one of the nuns, Sor Estefanía, who developed a large *zaratán*, or cancerous breast tumor, on the sea voyage to Buenos Aires.[38] While still on board the vessel, the nuns did their best to comfort the nun. In addition to giving her a medicinal cordial, they held vigils, never leaving her side. Sadly, by the time they reached the port of Buenos Aires the tumor had metastasized and Sor Estefanía died shortly thereafter. Madre María Rosa succinctly describes their pain: "Our grief and that of our father confessor was beyond words since we had witnessed her leave the cloister only later to die in a foreign land."[39] Notably, the case of Sor Estefanía's passing highlights the communal support felt by dying nuns who were surrounded by their sisters and friars of the same order.

Certainly Sor María must have also felt this kind of support on the Manila galleon. Although she was very far from her home convent in Andalusia, her spiritual sisters would have tried their best to comfort her by saying prayers, and friars would have guided her final moments in the prescribed steps of "the good death." In short, if followed properly, the tenets of the good death helped a soul spend as little time as possible in purgatory before ascending into heaven. Important steps in the process included a final confession, viaticum (communion), extreme unction, and suffrages or funeral prayers said after death.[40]

In general, Catholic nuns had much experience in caring for fellow convent members. Nuns alternated working in the convent infirmary, aided by servants and slaves. While convent nurses consulted with physicians, they ultimately spent the majority of the time with ill patients. Sick nuns were excused from their regular duties and ordered bed rest and a nutritious diet (one high in animal protein, especially poultry). In Mexico City some of the larger nunneries had their own apothecaries, stocking remedies that they sold to the local community. Such convents took advantage of the healing knowledge of their indigenous servants, who often worked alongside nuns in the infirmary.[41] One of the two nuns who had joined the Spanish founders during their stay at the Convent of La Visitación in Mexico City was a nurse. As noted in the previous chapter, Sor María de los Angeles's nursing experience would become invaluable to the group on the Manila galleon. Interestingly, she also was the one who supplied the group with two hundred chickens—often considered medicinal food in those years—for the transpacific voyage.

Since Sor Jerónima exhibited the same symptoms as Sor María de la Trinidad, everyone feared she would not survive the passage to Manila. Don Jerónimo asked about Sor Jerónima constantly, and everyone on board the ship said a daily communal prayer for her recovery. The abbess's condition worsened to such an extreme that "sixty attacks of the deadly diarrhea left her weak and only a shell of herself."[42] Sor Jerónima's situation had become so grave that Fray José de Santa María, the bishop, and the general held a secret meeting to discuss her imminent death, especially what to do with her body. The bishop resolved the matter by saying "there was no reason for her to be fish food and she would be brought to Manila in a box."[43] When the vicaress, Sor María Magdalena de la Cruz, was informed of this decision she cried out to Saint Juana for intercession. The nuns then gave Sor Jerónima a ground-up rosary bead to drink and her health began to improve.

Years later, while established safely in Manila, the nuns told Sor Jerónima about how they had used two of their "original" beads from Mother Juana to cure her: one at the port of Acapulco and then another while on the *San Andrés*. Sor Jerónima responded that she could have just touched the beads because the originals "would have been more valuable to cure two kingdoms."[44] Even though Sor Jerónima believed the nuns could have used the original beads to better effect, perhaps those same beads were made of a substance, like coral, that could have helped with her diarrhea.[45] Moreover, since the original beads were so precious, they had not given them as medicine to Sor María de la Trinidad (at least Sor Ana does not mention this). It may be a coincidence, but after ingesting the bead the abbess regained her appetite. From that moment onward she began to eat chicken broth cooked in the fogón for the afternoon meal and at night more broth with a "ground up chicken breast and *almidón* or farina, which was heated up with a candle since no other fire was allowed for fear of fire in our wooden cabin."[46]

Slavery on the Manila Galleon

In the eyes of the Spanish nuns, the rosary beads not only cured physical maladies, but they also had the power to soothe the destitute. One poignant example from Sor Ana's narrative offers a new angle of vision from which to view the chilling cruelty of slavery and servitude aboard these seafaring vessels. In this scene Sor Ana describes how a negra, or black woman, named María tried to commit suicide by throwing herself overboard. After several witnesses had thwarted her attempt by grabbing the hem of her skirt, the ship's captain ordered María to be tied to the mast and whipped. In response to María's cries, Sor Jerónima sent a friar with a bead from Saint Juana to bless her, at which point, trembling and sweating profusely, María fainted at the friar's feet. Later María spoke of a black man who wanted to take her to hell, but the moment she felt the bead's touch, he released her from his clutches.[47] From her cabin Sor Jerónima then asked María, "Did you know you were going hell?" She said yes but explained that since she had been robbed of some *cuartos* (copper coins) and beads, the black man had said, "You have no other alternative than to throw yourself into the sea."[48] Instead of denouncing the cruelty inflicted on María or inquiring about the circumstances that drove her to such desperate measures, the Spanish nuns were much more concerned with her spiritual well-being. In the end, they calmed her by giving her "many beads."

This episode reminds us that these Spanish religious women, although very interested in following the First Rule of Saint Clare (prohibiting slaves and servants in the convent), still brought a rigid class system with them to the Philippines. It is also likely that they were accustomed to seeing this type of physical abuse. They may have witnessed the ill treatment of indigenous and black slaves in the convents of Mexico City. Whipping was a punishment commonly accepted for slaves and also used by the Inquisition.[49]

Although we know very little about the exact circumstances of María on this particular voyage, Sor Ana's depiction of the black woman gives a human face to female slaves. Ample scholarship on the Atlantic slave trade, and to a lesser extent the Pacific slave trade, also can help us better understand her fate and that of others. As already noted, the majority of slaves traveling on the Manila galleons back to Acapulco were part of the transpacific slave trade that imported chinos as slaves from Asia to Mexico. Seijas estimates that roughly eighty-one hundred captives were brought to Acapulco between 1565 and 1700. Even though this quantity is relatively small in comparison to the number of African slaves brought across the Atlantic to Spanish America— an estimated 450,000 slaves disembarked in Spanish American ports between 1580 and 1640—it does not diminish the horrors endured by enslaved chinos, especially during the transpacific crossing to Acapulco.[50] The Pacific slave trade to Mexico officially ended in 1672 when the Crown treated chinos under law as Indians: as vassals of the Spanish monarchs, they could not be held legally as slaves.[51]

Other types of enslaved people also traveled on the Manila galleons, albeit smaller in number. Some black slaves worked on ships as common sailors, while even a few freed mulattos served as pilots. These sailors of African descent had come via the Iberian Peninsula and were Christians by acculturation—as opposed to those "converted" by the ineffectual mass baptisms inflicted on enslaved Africans in trading ports before sending them to the New World.[52] Most slaves traveling west were on board Manila galleons as personal servants to passengers and crew. Royal decrees limited these numbers to one slave per person, but high-ranking officials could apply for a special license to take more. No one was allowed to transport slaves for sale in Asia, so the slaves brought to Manila were few in number. Hernando de los Ríos Coronel, the Philippine procurator general who had helped the nuns receive the necessary licenses to travel to the Philippines, traveled to Acapulco in 1618 with two of his personal slaves.[53]

María's possession of money points to the hypothesis that sailors used her for sex. Pablo Pérez-Mallaína has uncovered several cases of mulatas, although not necessarily slaves, serving as sexual partners for Spanish sailors. Despite the fact that men of the sea were forbidden to engage in sexual activity—they faced reprimands, fines, and even abandonment ashore for such crimes—such rules did little to deter this behavior.[54] De los Ríos firmly condemned female slavery in the galleon trade for moral reasons, petitioning the king to prohibit female slaves. He decried the fact that some sailors used their slaves as concubines and even shared them with passengers.[55] The Crown already had issued a royal decree in 1608 banning female slaves on galleons, but as evidenced here with the case of María, that decree was widely ignored. Further, Tatiana Seijas estimates that "approximately one-quarter of the slaves who crossed the Pacific were women."[56] Although the testimonies are sparse, as is common even today in the silencing of rape victims, the Manila galleons must have been very dangerous for enslaved women. The account of the Asian slave Catarina de San Juan, better known as the China Poblana, bears witness to these dangers, since in 1619 the trader who transported her from Manila to Acapulco dressed her as a boy for her own protection.[57]

Other Dangers on the Transpacific Crossing

Unlike the precarious situation María faced, the nuns had the Franciscan friars to guard against any unwanted advances from drunken sailors or ruthless soldiers. It was impossible, however, for them to protect the women from the other perils of the high seas. For example, the nuns witnessed firsthand the fear instilled by hostile warships. While Sor Jerónima was just beginning to recover, the general decided to hold a live drill to see how his soldiers would respond to an enemy attack. Keeping the drill a secret, he had a cabin boy climb up to the crow's nest. Apparently he played the part well, calling out with conviction that he had spotted three Dutch warships on the horizon. According to Sor Ana, there was great commotion while "the captains and soldiers" prepared for battle. In fact, they put a loaded cannon next to the nuns' cabin and said they were going to hide the women down the hatch (*escotilla*), which was dark "like a cave." When the friars told Sor Jerónima the plan, she sat up in her bed, thin as a rail, saying, "Me, in the hatchway? I will do no such thing. Before that I'll help throw *piezas* [cannonballs] if necessary and I'll tell those heretics a thousand things."[58] Not only does this quote demonstrate Sor Jerónima's strong personality—she is afraid of nothing—but it also alludes to the very reason that the Spaniards were preparing for enemy attack: they needed to protect the large quantities of silver transported on the Manila galleons on the return trip to the Philippines.

Statistically, Spain's enemies rarely succeeded in capturing the galleons on the westward run to Manila. During the entire era of the galleon trade, between 1565 and 1815, there were dozens of skirmishes, but only one galleon, the nine-hundred-ton *Covadonga*, was captured, and that was not until 1742. In that instance the British commodore George Anson carried away 1,313,843 silver pesos, 35,862 ounces of silver bullion, and some cochineal dye. On the return run to Acapulco, galleons heavily laden with valuable Asian goods, not to mention chests of gold coins and pearls, were captured three times by the British, in 1587, 1709, and 1762 (the last also by Anson).[59] The same construction that allowed the ships to hold large quantities of goods made them very difficult to capture. The galleons were massive vessels, some of them displacing more than two thousand tons. Although they could not outrun British and Dutch warships, they were built of solid teak, *molave*, and flexible *laguan* that absorbed cannon fire, and the very high freeboard deterred soldiers from entering the ships.[60] As we have seen with the *San Andrés*, contingents of soldiers traveled on the galleons for protection, but during battle all hands were to be called on deck, including every member of the crew, which averaged around one hundred men in the seventeenth century.[61]

In reality, the natural elements, in contrast to enemy attack, posed a much more serious threat to the galleon trade. Just to name one tragic example, a year earlier, in August 1620, the *San Nicolás*, carrying three hundred people, was wrecked by a major typhoon near Samar. But it must be said, too, that the western run was much less dangerous because it usually could reach the Philippine archipelago before the onset of typhoon season.[62] Nonetheless, the *San Andrés* weathered several squalls on the high seas. One night, a helmsman in charge of the tiller steered the ship in such a way that he swamped the cabins, almost tipping over the galleon. Sor Ana explains how everyone quickly said confessions, even some seamen who had not confessed in ten years.[63] Anxiously, they all looked to Sor Jerónima for refuge. She then ordered "one of Saint Juana's beads to be thrown into the sea," which instantly calmed the stormy waters. The mariners told similar stories about past sailing trips when they had utilized Saint Juana's beads, often tying them directly to the ship's mast to calm tempests.[64]

In addition to wrecks caused by violent storms, the exact opposite could happen: slack winds could have ships drifting onto shoals or into enemy lands. Sor Ana describes a similar scenario when the winds stopped blowing for ten days straight. The friars also worried that the ship might have to land in Japan, in which case "they did not want to let their beards grow so they could slip onto the island as laymen, and as for us, they were going to build a hut with branches in the countryside until they could inform Manila to send a ship."[65] Their fears were not unfounded (although such an event was unlikely on the Manila-bound leg). In 1596 a typhoon shipwrecked the *San Felipe* off the Nipponese coast on its return voyage to Acapulco. Due to Japanese ill will toward Catholic missionaries, especially Discalced Franciscans, a group of twenty-six Christians, some Franciscan friars from the ship, and other Japanese Christian converts died by martyrdom in Nagasaki on February 5, 1597.[66]

The Nagasaki martyrs were not the only Christians to be persecuted by the Japanese. Since the end of the sixteenth century the Japanese had become extremely skeptical of Christian missionaries. Although the Jesuits did wield some power in Japan due to their connection to powerful Portuguese trading networks, they too began to feel the effects of the anti-Christian edicts of 1612 issued by the Tokugawa shogunate, especially in 1614 when all missionaries were expelled from the islands. The risk of martyrdom, however, did not deter the Franciscan missionaries. They had begun their fledgling mission in Japan in 1593 with a handful of friars scattered around Kyoto, Osaka, and Nagasaki. Within a few years they, along with other religious clergy, had succeeded in converting approximately three hundred thousand Japanese to Christianity, out of a total population of about twenty million.[67]

Sor Jerónima and her sisters came in direct contact with some of those converts who later fled to the Philippines.[68] One in particular, Lucía de San Juan, originally from Kyoto, became a novice at their Franciscan convent. The nuns also knew personally several of the friars who yearned to spread Christianity in Japan. Luis Sotelo, for example, who had met the nuns in Toledo, was now in Manila, biding his time before he could slip back into Japan to continue his goal to spread Christianity. He had recently returned from Spain and Rome with a Japanese embassy that sought to increase trade with Spain in exchange for allowing some Christian missionaries on the islands (not all shoguns opposed Christianity).[69] Those efforts did not succeed, and although Japan did still allow some limited trade, namely with the Dutch, it essentially closed off its borders in 1639 and did not reopen them until the mid-1800s. Sotelo and several others, like Ginés de Quesada, Sor Jerónima's future confessor in Manila, disregarded Japan's severe anti-Christian edicts and would eventually die as martyrs.[70]

The friars on board the galleon were not the only ones worried about landing on the Nipponese coast. The general of the armada, don Jerónimo, approached the abbess for help, since he and his men had been throwing rosary beads into the sea but to no avail. Sor Jerónima did her best to console him, and before long a wind filled the sails, blowing the ship away from enemy territory. Again, Sor Jerónima prayed to Saint Juana, this time asking for a quick landfall since their food rations and water supply had dwindled to dangerously low levels.

The *San Andrés* finally pulled into the port of Bolinao on the western coast of the island of Luzon on July 24, 1621. Under normal circumstances the ship would have sailed directly to the port of Cavite by Manila, but the winds were deemed too dangerous. (Months later the *San Andrés* eventually sailed to Manila, arriving on October 26, 1621.)[71] When the galleon reached land, the sailors built a *chalupilla* (small skiff) so a small expedition could hug the coast and arrive in Manila before the land party. The steward, along with four sailors, then did something unique. Instead of asking for more rosary beads from Saint Juana, the men approached Sor Jerónima for her blessing and asked her to touch their rosaries. She complied, and they tied the beads to the mast of their small skiff. Notably, this scene represents a changing of the guard. Up until this point Sor Ana has underscored the powers of Saint Juana, but now she transfers the focus of devotion from Juana to Jerónima. Most importantly, the sailors' faith in Sor Jerónima's beads provided an important reference in the abbess's burgeoning résumé of sanctity.

Crossing Luzon

The Philippines consists of over seven thousand islands, with the two largest being Luzon at the north and Mindanao in the south. When Legazpi arrived in 1565 the archipelago contained kinship units called *barangay*, with no centralized government, making it relatively easy for the Spaniards to establish bases for trade and conquest on several islands. By the time of the arrival of the Spanish nuns, most of Luzon (with the exception of the northwestern mountainous province) had accepted Spanish authority, while Muslim-dominated Mindanao and the Sulu archipelago did not submit to Spanish rule until the late nineteenth century. As in most parts of the Spanish Empire, the first missionaries were friars and not secular clergy. In 1594 Philip II had given each religious order geographical regions for their missions on Luzon: the Dominicans were in the north, Bataan, and Zambales; the Augustinians claimed the fertile center and south; and the Franciscans worked in the area around Laguna de Bay and the Camarines Peninsula.[72] Friars set up doctrinas (parishes of converted indigenous) in their provinces, learned native languages, and began to proselytize. As early as 1593 the first bilingual catechism in Spanish and Tagalog was published in Manila.[73] By the 1590s friars had baptized between two hundred thousand and three hundred thousand individuals.[74] Nonetheless, these mass baptisms did not always mean complete conversion. As Giraldez notes, "A syncretic Christianity emerged in which, despite friars' efforts, pre-Spanish beliefs and customs were still very much present."[75] It should be noted, too, that because the lowland indigenous peoples of Luzon lived mostly apart from the Spaniards, surrounded by kin, they learned very little Spanish.[76] In exchange for evangelization (and peace), native Filipinos were expected to pay tribute, mostly in the form of rice and beans, and all able-bodied men had to work forty days a year on roads, shipbuilding, and in militias, among other types of forced labor.[77] As we shall see in the following section, Sor Ana's depictions of the indigenous peoples of Luzon oscillate from reluctant acceptance of semi-naked native bearers to horror at heathen natives to admiration for a pious Kapampangan woman.

After resting three days at the regional magistrate or alcalde's house at the port of Bolinao (he had invited the nuns to stay with him while they were together on the ship), they began the arduous five-day trek south to Manila. With the exception of a handful of friars whom the nuns met in the doctrinas of Augustinians and Dominicans, the areas outside of Manila were largely

Map 4 The final leg of the nuns' journey to Manila. Map created by Patrick McCarty.

devoid of Spaniards.[78] Sor Ana describes how she and her sisters were carried for several days across swamps in litters (hamacas) "on the shoulders of four Indians" (native Filipinos were often called *indios*). With colorful language she explains that it felt like being on "a [funeral bier] and the only thing missing was the pall [cloth covering a coffin]; when it rained we made a kind of tarp with our veils."[79] There were no pack animals at that time in the rural Philippines, and it was not uncommon for indigenous men—some paid, others forced into domestic labor—to bear the loads of supplies and missionaries on their shoulders.[80]

Not only do Sor Ana's remarks shed light on missionaries' exploitation of native labor, but she also comments on the Spaniards' fear of the Negritos, the indomitable indigenous people from the mountainous areas of Luzon.[81] She explains how during the first days they had to be very careful because "pagan *negrillos*" hid in trees and would shoot at unsuspecting travelers. In order to scare them off, armed escorts periodically shot their harquebuses into the air. Although the native bearers must have unnerved Sor Ana, she appears to have accepted the men as vassals of the Crown. On the other hand, her depiction of the Negritos as hostile pagan savages hanging from trees echoes the politics of Spaniards who viewed them as infidels.[82] Sor Ana does not comment directly on the issue of indigenous slavery, but her comments on the Negritos allude to the complex landscape of human bondage on the archipelago. By emphasizing their barbarian nature, dark skin, and actions as marauders against unsuspecting travelers, she frames the Negritos as natural enemies of Christianity and, as such, worthy of slavery. Sor Ana further emphasizes their "otherness" by juxtaposing them with the "native Indians," whom she describes as humble and not interested in wealth. Ironically, these very same lowland "native Indians" were the ones who pressured the king to allow for some exceptions to the royal decree issued in 1574 outlawing indigenous slavery in the Philippines.[83] These lowland native peoples had owned slaves as part of a system of debt peonage before the arrival of the Spaniards, and they did not want to give up this part of their culture.

In light of the previous analysis, Sor Ana's subsequent portrayal of western Luzon's indigenous elite highlights the nuns' complex and fluid views toward the native population. In a town near the Pampanga River the small group stayed two or three days "at the house of *una india muy principal* [an elite native woman], very devout, and wearing a habit."[84] Vicente Rafael's nuanced study of the Tagalog people during the colonial period can help us contextualize the nuns' encounter with the Pampanga woman. By the end of the sixteenth century Spanish authorities had begun to single out ruling elites, calling them *principales*. The principales were exempt from the payment of tribute and could be men and women alike. Rafael notes, "Through them the Spaniards sought to extend the bureaucratic reach of the state to the local level."[85] Since Spaniards relied on the elite class to help govern the new colony, they were allowed to keep servants and slaves, which was part of their pre-Hispanic culture.[86] Moreover, some indigenous elites associated closely with Catholic clergy helped to spread church doctrine, as evidenced by the native woman that the nuns encountered.[87] In fact, Sor Ana directly states that the woman already lived like a nun: she dressed in a habit, got up at midnight to pray matins with her servants, and recited holy prayers. She treated the group of nuns very well, showing them affection and giving them gifts. Sor Ana emphasizes how she did all this despite the fact that "we did not understand a word she said nor she us."[88] Sor Ana's depiction of this devout indigenous woman would have given them evidence that indigenous Filipinas, regardless of their proficiency in Spanish, had the right qualifications to become nuns.

After leaving this elite woman's house the nuns left behind the litters and then boarded a typical sampan, a type of flat-bottomed riverboat used in Asia. Sor Ana describes the scene: "After finishing the journey of the hamacas we rode in a sampan the rest of the way to Manila. We traveled on the river; there are several leagues of beautiful greenery and the countryside is a mangrove that leads to the sea. As such, the river narrows in an area that enters the city and it wraps around the wall. Our convent is next to the sea and the river, with only one street between it and the wall."[89] In sum, Sor Ana's narration takes the reader from the wild countryside of Luzon—with fierce "Indians" hanging from the trees—to a picturesque riverboat ride into the city, home of their future convent.[90]

Conclusion

Transoceanic sailing has been described as "a space of personal transformation," and the transpacific voyage must have been just such an experience for the founding nuns.[91] Certainly the desperate conditions on board ship, especially the loss of Sor María de la Trinidad, left their mark on Sor Ana. And yet, unlike other portions of the manuscript where Sor Ana inserts her own personal commentary, on the Manila galleon and later during the crossing of Luzon, her voice recedes into the background. In some ways, however, her selection of events speaks just as loudly as her commentaries. Her gendered perspective, one that prioritizes the experiences of women, is revealed when we compare her account to Quesada's version of events. Unlike Quesada, Sor Ana focuses on the reality of female slaves on the Manila galleon. Although her rendering of the harsh situation might not meet the expectations of the modern observer—she does not condemn the beating—she and her sisters do their best to console María by giving her some of their precious beads. Further, Sor Ana offers enough detail to paint a broad picture of the desperate conditions on seaborne vessels. Perhaps without her knowing it, her portrayal of the scene speaks to slaves' resistance to bondage and cruelty. In the words of one scholar, "slaves did resist, their opposition to bondage and ill-treatment running the gamut from individual work slowdowns to escape, blasphemy, suicide, abortion, infanticide, conspiracy, and violent rebellion."[92] When María's drastic attempt to throw herself overboard fails, she resigns herself to her fate by exhibiting a remorseful and submissive attitude; in other words, she turns to another coping mechanism as opposed to suicide. Quesada, on the other hand, silences María's plight by omitting any reference to her situation.

Sor Ana is also extremely interested in shining a light on the miraculous recovery of Sor Jerónima. Despite her severe illness, similar to one that took the life of Sor María de la Trinidad, Sor Jerónima rallies. Every person on board the galleon, from the captain general of the ship to the common sailor, is astounded by her Lazarus-like recovery. With their own eyes they had seen her waste away, becoming nothing more than skin and bones, but when they approached the Philippine archipelago she began to regain her strength, a fact they could only assign to divine intervention. Up until this point in her narrative, Sor Ana emphasizes the powers of Saint Juana's rosaries, especially the healing power of the beads as medicine, but from this moment on she switches her focus to Sor Jerónima's miraculous touch. She had already done this to some extent earlier in the manuscript, especially during her description of their stay in Seville, when the local nuns tried to touch Sor Jerónima or tear off pieces of her habit, but now her survival marks a critical shift in the narrative. Here, instead of coveting beads from Saint Juana, the sailors ask Sor Jerónima to bless their rosaries.

Sor Ana's narration of the crossing of Luzon from the port of Bolinao southeast to the city of Manila provides other vivid examples of Sor Jerónima's saintly qualities, at the same time that it exposes the women's perception of different indigenous groups on the island. Overall, in the eyes of Sor Ana the "Eastern Other" is even more foreign than the Amerindians whom the group encountered in Mexico. It may be tempting to judge Sor Ana's commentaries on the Negritos as racist, but we need carefully to contextualize the worldview of these seventeenth-century nuns, especially in relationship to the Crown's endeavor to use men and *women* to expand imperial policies.

While on Luzon, Sor Ana demonstrates how Sor Jerónima began to cultivate a group of followers outside Manila, such as the native woman from Pampanga. Sor Ana's depiction of this elite indigenous woman speaks to missionaries' efforts to use local women (and not just men) to help spread the faith. Although the pious head woman had not learned a word of Spanish, she may have been exposed aurally to translations of devotional manuals in order to lead a life of a religious laywoman.[93] Even more important, this type of native Kapampangan and others would later visit the abbess in Manila and, after her death, become witnesses in her beatification case. Nevertheless, their devotion to Sor Jerónima could not dispel the many harsh trials that awaited the nuns upon their arrival in Manila, as we shall see in the next chapter.

CHAPTER 4

The Convent in Manila

⁓ WHEN SOR JERÓNIMA AND HER SISTERS FIRST SET FOOT IN MANILA on August 5, 1621, they were treated like royalty. Governor don Alonso Fajardo and his entourage, military officers and soldiers, Franciscan friars, judges and their wives, and other leading families greeted the nuns. After the governor ordered his captains to fire a salvo in their honor, he accompanied the women to the house of their patron, doña Ana de Vera. While there the women met their main benefactor for the first time and were visited throughout the day by the archbishop, friars from different orders, members of the Holy Office of the Inquisition, and other dignitaries. Many who greeted the nuns that day thanked Sor Jerónima "for her bravery at traveling such a long and dangerous route," as every Spaniard in the city born outside the Philippines knew firsthand the perils of the Manila galleons.[1] They also could relate to any culture shock that the women might soon experience. They were about to begin their new lives in a tropical city about fifteen thousand miles from the Iberian Peninsula. The weather in Manila was extremely hot and humid and late afternoon thunderstorms routinely battered the city. Residents complained of the continual onslaught of mosquitoes, which forced them to sleep under nets at night.[2] The weather, so extremely different from the parched plains of Castile, was nevertheless a relative nuisance in comparison to the hardships that the nuns would endure during their first years in the Philippines.

The city of Manila that the nuns encountered in 1621 was bustling and diverse. There were Spaniards, Portuguese, local Tagalogs, Chinese, Japanese, Indians, Africans, and more, all living under a hierarchal system imposed by the Spaniards. During the early years of the Conquest religious orders had established roots in this nascent outpost of the Spanish Empire: first the Augustinians (1565), followed by the Discalced Franciscans (1578), the Jesuits (1581), the Dominicans (1587), and the Augustinian Recollects (1606).[3] A few years after the Spanish foundation of Manila in 1571, the city had about forty-three thousand residents; the population was diverse, in part due to slavery. Tatiana Seijas notes that "a full quarter of this population were enslaved."[4] Slavery and forced labor drafts were common in the early modern Philippines, and on the backs of local Tagalog peoples, together with foreign and Muslim slaves, the Spaniards built churches, municipal buildings, palaces for the governor and archbishop, and even hospitals. The first conquistadors and settlers founded their city at the mouth of the Pasig River that flows into the Manila harbor.[5] To protect themselves from foreign attack, especially from Dutch and Chinese naval forces, the colonists erected a wall around their buildings; most Spaniards and criollos (their descendants) lived within a walled area, or Intramuros. While this area protected Spanish citizens from foreign incursions, it also was meant to keep out undesirables, who were relegated to other parts of the city. Most notably, the Chinese merchant population known as Sangleys, connected to the galleon trade, were constrained to living in another area outside the walls called the Parian.

Several scholars agree that the age of globalization was born with the opening of transoceanic trade networks, first with the Portuguese route around the Cape of Good Hope to Goa, which was then linked by the Manila galleon route across the Pacific. As such, Manila became "the world's first global city."[6] Indeed, since Manila's foundation in 1571 the wealth of the city had depended on the yearly galleon trade, and without the diverse ethnic milieux that converged in this entrepôt, this never would have been possible. Yearly an average of twenty to thirty Chinese junks would sail into Manila in order to trade goods, mostly silks and porcelain in exchange for silver, and without the Sangleys this would have been nearly impossible.[7] Nonetheless, the Spaniards severely discriminated against the Sangleys; the repercussions were several violent revolts resulting in massacres of thousands of ethnic Chinese. For example, some twenty-four thousand people were slaughtered in 1603 and another twenty-three thousand in 1639.[8] Native Tagalogs made

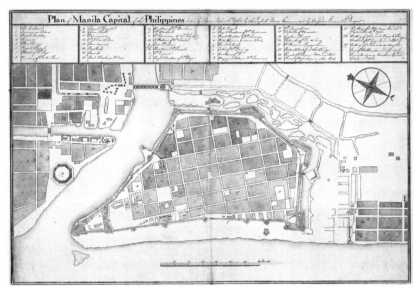

Figure 12 Plan of Manila, capital of the Philippines, 1762. Although this map is from a later date than when the nuns lived there, it provides a good image of the walled city. Author: English Army Brigadier General Draper. Biblioteca Nacional of Spain, via Wikimedia Commons.

up the majority of the population outside Intramuros, but other ethnic groups populated the city. Portuguese traders brought slaves from diverse parts of Asia such as Malacca (Melaka) and Goa and also as far away as East Africa.[9] A small population of Japanese Christian exiles also lived in their own segregated area of the city known as Dilao. Unlike their dealings with the Chinese, the Spaniards respected the Japanese because they had been forced to flee their homeland due to religious persecution.

As the small Spanish colony began to slowly expand, it still lacked a nunnery. In 1589–1594 the College of Santa Potenciana had been established for orphan girls. The well-heeled residents of Manila saw that institution as a charitable organization, more for the lower classes—illegitimate girls, unmarried widows, and women of ill repute—and not as a suitable place for their own daughters. Driven by the need to find a place to put unmarried offspring of descendants of the original conquistadors, preparations were made to open the first convent in the Far East. The Discalced Franciscans who sponsored the endeavor needed to find someone who would serve as a compelling role model to postulants. The friars in Manila also were trying to strengthen this strict branch of the Franciscan order (also known as Franciscan Alcantarines), and they hoped to establish a female convent to mirror their own ideals of poverty. As discussed in chapter 1, Sor Jerónima de la Asunción, already revered in Toledo as a popular saint, was chosen for this task.

This chapter investigates convent life during the nuns' first decade in Manila. It analyzes the many competing factors in the running of the new community: secular interests, ecclesiastical rivalries, patrons, race, and class. Unrest among the nuns also played a part in the instability of the convent during this time period.[10] In her narration of these events Sor Ana does her best to continue to underscore Sor Jerónima's extreme piety while she navigates the dangerous minefields concerning self-governance and Sor Jerónima's steadfast will to implement the strict First Rule of Saint Clare. The last part of Sor Ana's manuscript brings to the fore some of the other nuns who formed part of this first convent in the Far East. Included in these pages are letters from the commissary general of the Franciscan Order, Fray Alonso de Montemayor. Writing from Mexico, not only do his letters offer words of support to Sor Jerónima and her followers but they also encourage the nuns to write about themselves and the first novices.

After being officially sanctioned by Montemayor, other nuns wrote about themselves and their spiritual journeys. The main focus of this chapter is to show how the nuns, through their own writings, navigated their lives in the Spanish Empire. Through archival documents outside of Sor Ana's manuscript, we hear the voices of Sor Juana de San Antonio and Sor María Magdalena de la Cruz. Sor Jerónima saw Sor Juana de San Antonio as a visionary and future spiritual leader of the nuns. Sor María Magdalena would later travel with a small group of nuns to establish the first convent in Macao, China. Sor Ana also served in the position of scribe for one of her cofounders: Sor Luisa de Jesús, the pious laywoman who took the place of Mariana de Jesús days before their departure from Toledo.

Sor Ana's text serves also as a type of necrology for the convent, documenting the pious lives and deaths of the first nuns to profess in Manila, among them, the first and only Japanese novice, Sor Lucía de San Juan. An analysis of the lives of all these women has much to say about the varied paths that early modern female religious took to reach the convent. After Sor Jerónima's death, Sor Ana became the next abbess of the convent in Manila and oversaw the launching of the new foundation in Macao. Sor Ana did not document these final years in her manuscript, for which reason we must rely on other archival and rare printed book sources to piece together her final years as abbess.

Convent Life in Manila

Within a day of their arrival, the nuns learned that Ana de Vera already was having second thoughts about her donation. Her nephew Antonio de Vera, recently arrived from Spain, had convinced his aunt that she should not give away her estate. In fact, after spending only one night at her mansion in Intramuros, the nuns found themselves living on her ranch outside the city in an area called Sampaloc. The women were heartbroken after having traveled so far only to find resistance from their patron, and this new lodging was a primitive shelter fashioned from bamboo and boards so that it "rained on us only a little less than on the journey." Understanding the seriousness of the situation, and seeing the nuns tired and deflated, several Franciscan friars visited the women during their four-day stay on the ranch. Fray Sotelo brought the cofounders gifts and encouraged them by saying, "Well, dear sisters, let's go now as pilgrims to Japan."[11] Although his words were spoken somewhat in jest, at the same time he had been encouraging Sor Jerónima for years to spread the order of Saint Clare into China and Japan. Without a doubt the abbess shared this desire, but first she still needed to fight for her convent in Manila.

It took over a month before the nuns finally returned to Ana de Vera's large house located in Intramuros. In the meantime the group had been transported to a nearby Franciscan monastery in Sampaloc—primarily used to minister to the local indigenous population—called Nuestra Señora de Loreto. Their own patron, doña Ana, also had donated this small building, run by Franciscan friars. While there, on September 8, 1621, the cofounders Juana de San Antonio and Luisa de Jesús took the habit as black-veiled nuns (they had traveled as novices). But the small structure often flooded, and several nuns began to fall ill. Their precarious living situation was not resolved until the *oidor* (judge) Jerónimo de Legaspi and his wife, doña Mariana de Velasco, intervened on behalf of the nuns. On September 13, 1621, the nuns boarded sampans one last time; accompanied by the governor and Franciscan prelates, the small entourage navigated the Pasig River back to Intramuros. In short, Legaspi forced doña Ana to make good on her promise and hand over her estate to Jerónima and her cohort. Once they returned to the city, they converted doña Ana's mansion into their convent—she had donated two houses, a place that would stand (despite having to rebuild after several devastating earthquakes) until World War II, when the convent was completely destroyed by Allied bombing.

The first decade in Manila was extremely volatile for the nuns. In the beginning the group found support in the Franciscan provincial Friar Pedro de San Pablo, and the small convent began to grow. On October 31, 1621, the community received their first three novices, local criolla women from well-to-do families.[12] Later, on November 18, Sor Jerónima and all the nuns professed the First Rule of Saint Clare under the provincial San Pablo and their vicar Fray José de Santa María. Soon thereafter, however, Fray José was sent outside Manila and a new provincial took the place of San Pablo. Suddenly Sor Jerónima lost much-needed support in her desire to lead the convent under the First Rule of Saint Clare. Undeterred, the abbess felt empowered by a license from the Franciscan commissary general of New Spain, Fray Diego de Otalora, to follow the First Rule, and she proceeded with the management of the strict convent.[13] As a guide she used the book of the First Rule, sent to her by the Royal Discalced nuns from Madrid. In essence, she wanted to run the convent only with alms, prohibiting dowries and rents from novices or patrons. Further, she wanted the destitute heiresses of the conquistadors to be able to profess (without a dowry), and she also envisioned permitting local mestiza and indigenous women into the community. As daughters of Poor Clares, the nuns would perform their own chores—cooking, cleaning, washing clothes, and caring for the sick—and not allow any servants or slaves. At first sympathetic friars went around Manila collecting money and food for the nuns, but later, when other friars refused, Sor Jerónima assigned two Third Order laywomen affiliated with the convent to collect alms.

Sor Jerónima's vision soon began to clash with that of local elites and the next generation of Franciscan provincials who oversaw the convent. Many leading families did not want to see their daughters on the same level as poor Spanish women, much less share their status as brides of Christ with mestizas. They pushed for the convent to accept only criollas with dowries as black-veiled nuns (along with servants and slaves), and they believed mestizas should be admitted only as donadas (essentially servants). This angered Sor Jerónima—"as if they were not Christians"—and she referred to two black saints within the Franciscan order as precedents.[14] Others complained that Sor Jerónima was accepting too many novices, and they feared that there would be a shortage of Spanish women eligible for marriage. Indeed, the

Figure 13 (left) Justiniano Asunción, *A Spanish Mestiza of Manila*, 1841.
Although this painting is from a later time period than when Sor Jerónima
and her cofounders lived, it provides a good image of a Spanish mestiza. Wa-
tercolor plate mounted in scrapbook. The Miriam and Ira D. Wallach Division of Art, Prints and Photographs: Art & Architecture Collection. Courtesy
of the New York Public Library. New York Public Library Digital Collections.

Figure 14 (right) Justiniano Asunción, *Una Yndia Natural de Filipina*, 1841.
This painting belongs to the same time period and collection as figure 13.
Despite its later date it provides a good perspective of a native Filipina. Water-
color plate mounted in scrapbook. The Miriam and Ira D. Wallach Division
of Art, Prints and Photographs: Art & Architecture Collection. Courtesy of
the New York Public Library. New York Public Library Digital Collections.

population of Spaniards in Manila during 1621 was only around three thousand people, about a third of them women.[15]

Voicing these concerns, Governor Fajardo went to see Sor Jerónima in an attempt to persuade her not to accept women from elite families. Although we do not know specific names, some of the nuns within the convent itself also joined in the campaign against Sor Jerónima. Sor Ana reveals these underlying tensions when she quotes Sor Jerónima as saying, "What hurts her most is that some of them [the nuns] whom she brought with her, not only have they not been a help to her, but they have become instruments for major fighting, used by the same friars, against her and with them."[16] Specifically, Sor Jerónima's unwillingness to relax any aspects of the First Rule angered the Franciscan provincial Fray Juan Bautista. He did not think Sor Jerónima's goals were realistic, especially from a financial standpoint, since Manila depended almost solely on the unpredictable galleon trade. The convent did, however, receive substantial donations during these early years, especially from Sor Jerónima's growing cult of admirers. Sor Ana, for example, describes the wealthy Portuguese captain Gaspar Méndez, who sent them money, candles, wine (for mass), rice, vinegar, sugar, chickens, bacon from Mexico, linen, thread, and more.[17]

Nevertheless, the atmosphere within the newly established convent became very heated when Sor Jerónima did not back down before the governor or the provincial. As a result the provincial Bautista took extreme measures in his effort to impose dowries and servants (and also to punish Sor Jerónima). First, he ordered the *descomunión*, or excommunication, of the abbess by posting a notice on the convent's main door. When that did not work, on May 10, 1623, he deposed her from her position as abbess. This came as a complete shock to the nuns, since they believed Sor Jerónima had the right, as the original founder, to govern the convent for twenty years. Bautista, however, claimed that her three-year term, dating from the time she left Toledo, was finished. In her place he put another one of the cofounders, Sor Leonor de San Francisco. Although Sor Jerónima had no choice but to accept the demotion from her superior, she was not deterred from her ultimate mission.[18]

As a savvy leader, Sor Jerónima knew that she had the proper licenses and documentation to govern the convent under the First Rule. She also knew that this would not be possible without intervention from authorities in Mexico and Spain. To this end, Sor Jerónima and her followers began a letter-writing campaign. She penned missives to the highest authorities possible: the king of Spain (Philip IV), the Real Audiencia (high court) of Manila, the Franciscan commissary general of the Indies (Fray Juan Venido), and the commissary general of the Franciscan Order (Fray Alonso de Montemayor).[19] These letters elicited a firestorm of responses.[20] Ultimately, all agreed that Sor Jerónima did have the proper documentation to run the convent under the First Rule, but she was told to accept only criollas as novices. There could be exceptions in extraordinary cases, as we shall see with the first Japanese novice. Interestingly, Sor Jerónima's fight to allow native women to profess mirrors some of the same obstacles encountered by pious indigenous women of New Spain. It was not until 1724 that the first convent for native women was established in Mexico City.[21]

After Sor Leonor de San Francisco's three-year term, Sor Jerónima was reinstated as abbess in 1626 and remained in that position until her death in 1630. Despite the fact that she returned to her position, Sor Jerónima's final years as abbess were no calmer than the first. She encountered continued opposition from her superiors, and some insisted that the nuns break the community into two convents: a larger one that would follow the Second Rule and allow dowries and a smaller one with only twelve nuns that would subsist solely on alms. In sum, Sor Jerónima never acceded to these demands. Indeed, during her tenure as abbess she expanded the convent under the First Rule. In her letter to King Philip IV of July 31, 1626, Sor Jerónima asks him for a special decree *not* to limit the number of nuns in the convent. In that missive she places their current number at thirty-three sisters (most likely referring to the total number of women, including postulants, novices, and nuns).[22]

Fray Alonso de Montemayor: A Mandate to Write

Despite the turbulence of Sor Jerónima's years as abbess, she must have felt solace from the responses that she received from Franciscan authorities outside Manila. We know this because Sor Ana makes it a point to include copies of some of these letters in the last part of her manuscript. Between January and February 1626 Fray Alonso de Montemayor, commissary general of the Franciscan Order of the Indies, sent a bundle of four letters: two addressed to Sor Jerónima, one to Sor Ana, and the last to Sor María Magdalena de la Cruz.[23] He had met the cofounders when they passed through Mexico City, and this personal connection may have helped their case. Although Montemayor was still across the ocean in Mexico, through his letters he demonstrated his support of Sor Jerónima's desire to follow the First Rule of

Saint Clare. After reviewing her case, he was sure that she would soon be reinstated as abbess since the commissary general of the Indies, Fray Juan Venido, had written a memo to that effect.[24] Furthermore, he encouraged the nuns to develop their plan to send a new seed group of founders to set up another convent in Macao, China. In the manuscript his four letters are placed directly after Sor Ana's more formal biography of Sor Jerónima ending with chapter 70.[25]

At first glance, it might appear that the last part of Sor Ana's manuscript is a hodgepodge of documents tacked on to the end of the biography. Nevertheless, on closer reading, Montemayor's letters frame much of the content of this last section, and these documents also help fill in some of the gaps regarding the other nuns who associated themselves with Sor Jerónima. Sor Ana also inserts her own commentary between the copied letters, shedding light on how they were received by Sor Jerónima and later used as evidence against her detractors: "I put the letters here so that one can see how the prelates treat her [Sor Jerónima] with esteem. . . . Being present the eight *discretas*, the provincial father, and five nuns, there was no lack of people who said she was lying, and not telling the truth, and she was not a founder but a destroyer."[26] Sor Ana's positioning of these letters, along with her own commentary on these events, reveals her adept use of a rhetorical strategy common in conventual foundation narratives: overcoming immense obstacles. Here Sor Ana recounts all of the obstacles put before Sor Jerónima, in this case the dissent between nuns and ecclesiastical authorities, and how she manages to overcome their opposition in her quest to lead the new convent.[27]

These letters also shed light on how Montemayor pushed the nuns to write about themselves and others. In two of the letters he orders under holy obedience that Sor Jerónima write an account about her spiritual life and the foundation of the new convent in Manila. Likewise, he requests that she document the lives of her cofounders. Since this was such a monumental task, in his letter to Sor María Magdalena from January 8, 1626, he asks her to help Sor Jerónima (later we will see how she served as scribe for Sor Juana de San Antonio). In his last letter, from February 6, 1626, Montemayor acknowledges receipt of Sor Jerónima's work *Carta de marear en el mar del mundo* (Chart for navigating the worldly sea), which, unfortunately, like almost everything else written by Sor Jerónima, has now been lost.[28] After reminding Sor Jerónima to document her own life and the foundation of the convent, he states that each of the founding nuns should also write about themselves.

Sor Juana de San Antonio (1588–1661)

When given this opening by Montemayor to document their own lives, several of the nuns seized the opportunity. One of the most prolific, Sor Juana de San Antonio, would soon become, at least in the eyes of Sor Jerónima, the next spiritual leader of the nuns in Manila. Over a period of fourteen months between 1628 and 1629 Sor Juana dictated three volumes (770 folios), the bulk of her spiritual autobiography, to Sor María Magdalena de la Cruz. Later, from 1636 to 1641, she dictated a fourth volume (662 folios) to Fray Lucas de la Concepción. Her monumental work, titled *Noticias de la verdad* (News of the truth), fills more than fourteen hundred folios.[29]

The first section of volume 1 narrates how Sor Juana carved out her own course in finding her way to the convent. Born in Chozas de Canales (a village near Toledo) to a well-to-do family, Juana felt repulsed by the idea of marriage and instead dreamed of becoming a nun.[30] Since her parents were opposed to her desire to take the habit, and they denied her a dowry for profession, at a young age she ran away to work as a servant in Toledo. After working in a posada (inn) for the poor and later interning in the Colegio de Silíceo, Juana finally entered the Convent of Santa Isabel as a *familiar*, or part of the servant class.[31] Sor Jerónima, impressed with Juana's desire to live a life of poverty, invited her to become part of the mission to Manila. Juana was already thirty-two years old at the time and seized this unique pathway to become a nun. Both she and Luisa de Jesús never would have been able to profess as black-veiled nuns if they had remained in Spain.

Overall, Sor Juana de San Antonio's lengthy four-volume set, *Noticias de la verdad*, contains very little autobiographical material but mainly describes "news and attributes of Christ and his Mother," which she claimed came directly from the Lord and the Virgin Mary. The style of her text resembles that of her spiritual predecessor Juana de la Cruz, author of *El libro del conorte*, spiritual sermons dictated to her directly from Christ himself. Like her foremother, Sor Juana de San Antonio saw herself as the mouthpiece of the Holy Spirit because she received miraculous revelations about the magnificence of the Immaculate Conception; also like Juana de la Cruz, she dictated her supernatural revelations to a scribe. But, unique to her circumstances as a nun who had traveled halfway around the world, Sor Juana de San Antonio's writings also embark on missionary themes such as God's ultimate plan to extend the Catholic faith into Japan and China.

At the beginning of volume 1 Sor María Magdalena included a two-and-a-half-page prologue of her own. In it she makes direct reference to Montemayor's mandate to document the lives of the cofounders. She states that Sor Jerónima ordered her, under holy obedience, to serve as Sor Juana's scribe since Sor Jerónima was too occupied to complete this task herself. Sor María Magdalena explains that Sor Juana was also extremely busy. Among other duties she worked as the convent turn-keeper (*tornera*), she oversaw the purchasing and dispensing of provisions as the *provisora de gasto*, she cooked for friars and sick nuns, and she washed the chalice cloths brought to her by friars. Because of her busy schedule Sor Juana could only dictate her work to Sor Magdalena between 3:30 a.m. and 5:30 a.m. while she plucked five to six chickens. She spoke at such a rapid pace that in less than fourteen months her scribe had written over seven hundred folios. What is unclear is whether Sor Juana lacked the literary skills to pen her own work or whether she felt more confident dictating than writing.[32] (As we shall see, the questionable literacy of Sor Juana is a theme addressed in her Inquisition case at the end of her life.)

The sheer volume of Sor Juana's manuscript must have preoccupied Sor Magdalena, because she specifies that she did not have a chance to edit or correct any of her writing. Thus it appears that she wanted to protect herself, either from vindictive friars or from the long arm of the Inquisition, by citing Sor Jerónima's endorsement of the text: "She has read it and authorized it with incredible joy in her soul." Further, Sor Magdalena hopes the "saintly order" of Saint Francis, that is, friars of their order, will correct these volumes in the future. If for some reason no benefit can be found from these pages, she quotes Sor Juana as saying, "they should be burned."[33]

At the end of volume 1 of *Noticias de la verdad* another nun, Sor Leonora de San Buenaventura (one of the two nuns from Mexico), included her own declaration of support. In this two-page document, dated October 3, 1630, she states that she has seen and heard the creation of *Noticias de la verdad*, "and it has been written with such haste that you can hardly see the hand of the secretary since the author speaks so quickly." Furthermore, she emphasizes how Sor Jerónima and all the original cofounders have read the work in secrecy and have seen the volumes bound in secret.[34] Indeed, she stresses that no friar, not even Sor Juana's confessor, has read this work. Interestingly, she responds to Montemayor's order to write about each of the founding nuns, claiming that she also "was writing about what happened to me."[35] The possibility that Sor Leonora penned her autobiography is intriguing, but unfortunately it appears that her writings have been lost. The only other information that we have regarding Sor Leonora is that, years later, she would become one of the abbesses of the convent in Manila.[36]

Sor Jerónima herself found great comfort in Sor Juana's *Noticias de la verdad*. For many years she had viewed the Third Order pious laywoman from Toledo Mariana de Jesús as her closest connection to the divine, but now, in the twilight of her life, she saw Sor Juana's potential as a visionary and spiritual leader of the community. In 1629 and in the last pages of her biography Sor Ana repeatedly quotes the abbess as eagerly reading Sor Juana's works. Sor Jerónima also writes a short endorsement in volume 2, which appears to be in her own handwriting.[37]

Sor Jerónima's repeated endorsement of Sor Juana de San Antonio's work was not enough to protect the younger nun from the Inquisition. Sor Juana, despite having served later as abbess on multiple occasions, was accused of heresy during her last years of life. First denounced in 1643 by the convent's own confessor and vicar, Fray Bartolomé de Lajara—who accused her of false revelations and of spreading heretical doctrine though her writings—her case was not actively pursued by the Inquisition until 1658. Then on May 13, 1661, Sor Juana, extremely elderly and frail, was taken into custody and imprisoned in the house of a widow, doña Isabel Esquerra. The Holy Office had begun to collect evidence in the form of testimonies against Sor Juana. They were especially concerned that she was spreading false doctrine to native Kapampangan women who came to visit her in the convent, and there was talk of sending her on a Manila galleon back to Mexico City (the seat of the Inquisition in New Spain) to face trial. Over the next few months, the Dominican friar Francisco de Paula, commissary of the Inquisition in Manila, interviewed eight nuns from the Convent of Santa Clara, including Sor Magdalena de Cristo, the only other living member of the original cofounders.[38] None of the nuns implicated Sor Juana in heretical behavior; instead they all testified that she was a simple woman who only wanted to follow Catholic doctrine. When asked about Sor Juana's papers or notebooks, the nuns stated that they had been burned and did not know what they contained. Further, they all testified that she did not know how to write but instead always used scribes, either nuns or friars. Some of the nuns mentioned María Magdalena de la Cruz by name, others cited Fray Lucas de la Concepción, and one nun said, "When she needed to conduct convent business she would get the first person she could find to do it [write] for her."[39] The case ended abruptly when Sor Juana died on July 15, 1661, while still imprisoned under house arrest. Despite the accusations of the Inquisition, it is notable how the nuns rallied around their former abbess and did not implicate her in heresy.[40]

Sor Luisa de Jesús

Other voices from the nuns in Manila, from both Spain and Asia, are also contained in the last part of Sor Ana's manuscript. Unlike the lengthy mystical text authored by Sor Juana de San Antonio, these final pages shine a light on lesser-known women who might otherwise have been forgotten. For example, we have heard very little about Sor Luisa de Jesús. At this point in the manuscript there are two important texts attributed to Sor Luisa: a dictation of her life story to Sor Ana and an account concerning her relationship to Mariana de Jesús addressed to their shared confessor in Toledo, Luis de la Mesa. It is unclear whether she dictated the latter to Sor Ana or if she wrote it herself, but the subtitle at the beginning of the account indicates that Sor Luisa is the author.[41] Evidently Luis de la Mesa wanted a firsthand account that he could weave into his own biography of Mariana, which he wrote shortly after her death in 1621 but was not published until 1661. Not only do Sor Luisa's two accounts paint a fascinating picture of her life story and her circuitous route to becoming a cofounder of the Manila convent but they also provide some rare glimpses of the life of the nuns in Manila itself. Although I have yet to locate the dates of her birth and death, Sor Ana says she is seventy years old at the time of this account. She does not put a date on the dictated account, but the text written for Luis de la Mesa is dated July 12, 1625. If she dictated her life story after Montemayor's request in 1626, that would put her birth date around 1556—an interesting fact, since it would make her about the same age as Sor Jerónima.

Originally from a small village in Andalusia called Sabiote (near Baeza), Sor Luisa states that she hailed from an Old Christian family and that her parents were from the noble class. Her father died, however, when she was one year old, and her mother arranged a marriage for her at a very young age. She subsequently had a daughter (for whom she in turn arranged a marriage) and later two grandchildren. Widowed and repentant, she decided to leave her hometown and go on a pilgrimage to Rome. She only made it as far as Toledo, however, where she met Mariana de Jesús (1577–1620). Like Mariana, Luisa took the habit as a Third Order Franciscan and changed her name to Luisa de San Francisco. (She later changed it to Luisa de Jesús when she became a nun.) The two women became close friends, and both yearned to become nuns but they were widows and lacked the funds to pay the required dowry. Taking another route into the convent, they became renowned as pious laywomen. Mariana, who outshone her counterpart, practiced extreme penance, distributed alms to the poor, tended to the destitute in local hospitals, and spent long hours in trance-like states, attracting devotees who believed she had a direct connection to God.[42] According to Luisa, "during rapture [*elevada*] she spoke of many great things . . . much of it in Latin."[43] Since they were not cloistered, the two women moved freely throughout Toledo and soon developed a common bond with Sor Jerónima de la Asunción, who used them to help distribute alms outside the convent walls. At first Mariana was going to travel with the nuns to Manila, but the king (influenced by Mesa, who saw her as a potential saint) wrote a letter prohibiting her from becoming one of the cofounders. As her closest advocate, Mesa did not want to see Mariana leave Toledo. Evidently she was also in poor health, because she died a few months after the founders left Castile.

Instead, Luis de la Mesa told Luisa to take Mariana's place. Luisa agreed immediately; most likely she viewed her travel to the Philippines as her only way to profess as a black-veiled nun. Mesa did have some doubts as to Luisa's future as a choir nun, because he asked Mariana if she knew how to read. When she said yes, Mesa responded, "Well, that's good because she should be able to learn Latin." After hearing those words Luisa writes, "Since I left from there [Toledo] I have tried to study Latin."[44] Notably, her advanced age and lack of a convent education separated Sor Luisa from the other nuns in the group. Sor Ana, for example, must have impressed the group with her lengthy manuscript, much of which is sprinkled with Latin. Further, some must have doubted whether such an elderly candidate could carry her weight in Manila. Sor Luisa alludes to these doubts when she writes, "When we arrived in Manila I heard some of the nuns saying that if I were much younger they would find me more dependable." When she heard that critique, she again remembered Mesa's endorsement of her ability to learn Latin. Furthermore, she received encouragement from Sor Jerónima herself, who prayed for her: she was "eager for me to learn it." From that point onward, she writes, "I help out in the choir and because of that I am very happy."[45]

Sor Luisa's account written for Mesa also provides other tidbits about life in Manila. She reiterates the fact that the nuns did not have servants or Third Order friars helping out with mundane tasks. The women took turns weekly in the kitchen and shared other duties. Just as she exalts the penitential acts of her previous spiritual mentor Mariana de Jesús, she also marvels at Sor Jerónima's steely desire to live in extreme poverty. Despite the intense heat in Manila that "causes people to change their clothes twice a day due to sweat and hygiene, Sor Jerónima has not changed [her habit] in two years."[46]

Sor Luisa's short account at the end of Sor Ana's manuscript underscores how some religious women found ways to navigate the strict class system of the Spanish Empire. Her transformation from a penniless widow into a black-veiled nun in Manila makes clear her own adept maneuvering within a society that afforded very few opportunities for women. For years, she and Mariana had tried to become nuns in Toledo, but their lack of youth and their virginity, along with the rigid class system that required a dowry to profess as nuns, made it very difficult for them to enter a convent.[47] Obviously Sor Luisa also had the good fortune to associate herself with Mariana, who clearly outshone Luisa in penitential acts and had made a name for herself as a holy woman in Toledo. On the other hand, perhaps it was her own urgency to become a nun that led Luisa to Mariana. She had few tools to negotiate the system, but through her own agency she understood that extreme piety could lead to devotees and opportunities for advancement. When Mariana was prohibited from leaving Toledo, Luisa accepted her place without question. Later in Manila, as a black-veiled nun at the advanced age of approximately seventy, she learned enough Latin to chant the Divine Office. Her dream of becoming a nun had finally come to fruition.

First Nuns in Manila: A Japanese Novice

After Sor Luisa de Jesús's accounts, Sor Ana's manuscript is transformed into a necrology, offering brief portraits of the first nuns to become nuns and die in Manila. As in other portions of her manuscript Sor Ana inserts her own voice at key moments of her text. In this case she states that there are those who want to know about the first criollas to take the habit in Manila. In an assessment of her writing she states, "I have let the pen run as is my style, full of cobwebs and haste."[48] Although she is nervous that she has written too quickly, she also understands that her writing will provide others with a prism through which to view their nascent community. For the modern reader, her account helps shed added light on life both within the convent and outside the walls of Intramuros.

Interestingly, Sor Ana includes a Japanese novice on her list of the first criollas, although obviously she was not of Spanish descent. Actually this should not come as such a surprise, since Sor Jerónima's evangelistic enterprise sought to include different racial groups within her convent. At the same time, however, she needed to tread lightly, since she had already received criticism from local elites who did not want their daughters to mix with lower social classes. For this reason, the first Japanese novice came from the noble class. Naitō Lucía (?–1629), who later professed as Sor Lucía de San Juan, was born in the royal Japanese city of Kyoto (then called Miyako). Her father, Naitō Tokuan João (1549–1629) was a wealthy feudal lord (*daimyō*) and had been converted to Christianity by Jesuit missionaries. His sister, Naitō Julia (ca. 1566–1627), also converted to Christianity and became a renowned Kirishi-tan (Christian) preacher and founder of the first "convent-like" community for Christian women in Miyako. In 1614 the Japanese shogun Tokugawu Ieyasu expelled Julia's small spiritual community, along with her brother and other noble Christian converts, from Japan to the city of Manila. Due to their ties with Jesuit missionaries, these Japanese exiles were relocated into the sub-urb of San Miguel and not the Dilao, the latter being a domain of the Francis-cans. Julia and her sisters promptly set up a type of *beaterio* in San Miguel, but they essentially enclosed themselves from the outside world and did not accept any new members, not even Julia's niece, Lucía.[49]

In 1628 Sor Jerónima accepted Lucía into the convent and gave her the habit of a novice. According to Sor Ana, the new novice impressed the whole community with her desire to live a life of poverty. She quotes her broken Spanish: "I wish to serve for my Spanish women, I from other nation. . . . I much happy to be nun."[50] Years earlier Fray Sotelo had met Lucía and encour-aged her to become a nun; he had even given her his breviary shortly before he left for Japan. Once in the convent, Sor Lucía de San Juan lived only seven months before she died a premature death. Sor Jerónima honored her final wish and gave her the habit of a black-veiled nun shortly before her death.

Sor Jerónima's Final Words

Sor Ana puts a subtitle on the last part of her manuscript: "Here continues the account of the mother abbess." It comprises the last twenty-three folios of the document, dated April 19 to July 19, 1629. (Sor Jerónima did not die, however, until fifteen months later, on October 22, 1630). Nonetheless, the nuns believed their spiritual leader to be close to death since she suffered from high fevers and debilitating pain. Night after night Sor Ana and her sisters held vigil over the elderly abbess. Between three and six nuns always stayed at her bedside; even during the late hours of night they tried to comfort and warm their spiri-tual leader, who complained of severe chills and pain that she sincerely

believed imitated not only Christ's wounds on the cross but also the martyrdom of Saint John the Baptist. In one vision Sor Jerónima describes how she
saw his beheading and "how they beheaded me and I saw myself without my
own head and with the head of Saint John in my hands that they gave to me."[51]
The martyrdom of Saint John is one of several themes that highlight Sor
Jerónima's connection to supernatural phenomena.

As her scribe, Sor Ana documents Sor Jerónima's final visions and prophesies. Regardless of whether these were born out of miraculous revelations or
delirium from Sor Jerónima's high fevers and malnutrition, Sor Ana holds
them as true. The abbess, who at this point was nothing more than skin and
bones, had been told that she needed to eat meat. This was extremely difficult
for her since throughout her whole adult life she had fasted in order to repli-
cate Christ's suffering. "My daughters," Sor Jerónima addresses the nuns, "I
have suffered terrible hunger in this life . . . but His Majesty has allowed for
this ravenous hunger to be converted into hunger for the Blessed Sacrament."[52]
Sor Jerónima recalls her earlier years in Toledo when she ate only raw wild
herbs or a crust of bread on Thursdays and Sundays. Even in Manila, during
Advent she still insisted on "fasting on bread and water dipped in a little bit of
vinegar or orange juice." Sor Jerónima responds to the nuns' commands that
she take sustenance, saying, "Some of them say I am homicidal to myself [for
not eating]," but she prefers to find nourishment from her spiritual visions.[53]
In fact, the topic of the Virgin Mary's miraculous breast milk becomes a main
focal point of her final reflections. She recalls several visions in which the
Virgin Mary offers the sickly abbess her own breast. In one instance "she put
her nipple in my mouth and I nursed peacefully," and in another she said,
"The Mother of God has nursed me."[54] She also entertains visions of feeding
the Christ Child from her own breasts: "I felt the son of God at my breasts; the
beautiful child nursing very much like any child in his mother's lap."[55]

To the modern reader, unfamiliar with the writings of early modern
nuns, these visions may appear almost sacrilegious. We need to remember,
however, that miraculous occurrences and supernatural phenomena were
commonplace in the psyche of early modern Catholics. Images of nuns offering their breast to the Christ Child or themselves nursing from the Virgin
Mary made up just one of the many colorful discursive threads employed in
the spiritual writings of Catholic nuns. There is even a whole subgenre of art
depicting the nursing Virgin.[56] Further, scholars such as Arenal and Schlau
note how religious women have manipulated images of milk and blood—in
other sections of Sor Ana's manuscript she depicts nuns drinking from

Christ's wounds—to invert traditional female roles and position themselves in a privileged position within the church's hierarchy.[57]

Clearly, now that Sor Jerónima had positioned herself in such a high place within the church hierarchy—she sees herself as the daughter of the Virgin Mary, nursing directly from her breast—she felt emboldened to envision her own role in spreading the Catholic faith. At one point Sor Jerónima urgently shouted, "Help me ask God so that the enemies of the Catholic faith are converted."[58] On the one hand she is worried about the encroachment of Lutherans, that is, the Dutch, who constantly threaten Manila, and on the other, she makes patent her desire to participate in the evangelization of Japan. Surrounded by male missionaries, many of whom saw Manila as a staging ground for martyrdom in Japan, Sor Jerónima also felt imbued with their missionary zeal.[59] Although she could not physically travel to the islands of Nippon, her visions allowed her to express her own version of proselytization. On a more concrete level, under her watch, she had permitted the first Japanese novice to profess in the convent.

Throughout Sor Jerónima's commentary on her own visions she repeatedly refers to Sor Juana de San Antonio's *Noticias* or revelations from God and the Virgin Mary, especially when they bestow favors on her. Whereas in earlier parts of the manuscript she relies on visions from Mother Juana de la Cruz, Sor Luisa de la Ascensión, and Mariana de Jesús, now, during Sor Jerónima's final moments she turns to the younger nun. Perhaps with her imminent death she realized that the convent in Manila needed a new spiritual leader, especially one who could communicate with the spiritual world of saints, Christ, and the Virgin Mary. Thus she transfers authority to Sor Juana de San Antonio, who recently had composed her four-volume opus *Noticias de la verdad*.

This transformation is as much spiritual as it is physical. Up until the last pages of the manuscript, Sor Jerónima insists on wearing her habit and hair shirt. Surrounded by her caring sisters, Sor Ana describes her austere appearance: "And there she is lying on her cot, dressed in her habit and her barbed apparel, and a little piece of wood for her pillow."[60] Although these items inflicted severe pain on Sor Jerónima, in many ways she used them as a shield against the naysayers who attacked her devout faith. Now, at the end of her life, the only way she would let the nuns remove her painful garments was through authorization from Sor Juana de San Antonio. Through one of her revelations Sor Juana explained to the abbess how the founder of their original convent in Toledo, Santa María la Pobre, told her that she should take them off. She further comforted Sor Jerónima with a vision of Saint John the Baptist at her side and an endorsement from Saint Clare of the nuns who kept vigil at her side, especially "my dearest Ana de Cristo." Evidently these words soothed Sor Jerónima, and she finally allowed the nuns to take off her painful garments and replace them with a *camisa de lienzo* (linen shift).

On July 19, 1629, Sor Jerónima, believing her death was near, asked for the last rites of Extreme Unction. She expressed peace with her final decision to remove her harsh instruments of penance, especially because Sor Juana de San Antonio was correct in her revelation "that I would not be harmed by removing the hair shirt that I had worn my whole life."[61] Evidently everyone, including the abbess herself, thought she was about to die, but in fact she lived for another fifteen months. It is unclear, however, why Sor Ana ends her narration here and leaves her final year blank. We can only speculate that she felt these final reflections from the abbess were sufficient to finish her manuscript. On the last page she signs her work: "Sor Ana de Cristo, vicaria [vicaress]."

Sor Jerónima's death shook both the convent and the local community. Quesada, who had been at her side during her final months, preached the funeral sermon.[62] In February 1631, some months after Sor Jerónima's death, an ecclesiastical tribunal was set up to investigate her life and begin gathering testimonies for her beatification case. Sor Ana was the abbess of the Convent of Santa Clara in Manila at the time and wrote a letter endorsing her candidacy. During her lifetime and now after her death, Sor Ana witnessed the growing fervor of Sor Jerónima's devotees. According to one account, hordes of people came out to see Jerónima's dead body. They represented the diverse milieu of cultures and ethnic groups in the Spanish Philippines, highlighting her appeal as a holy woman to many different sectors of society: "In general everyone from this republic—from all the ecclesiastical ranks, secular men and women—went to the convent to ask permission to see the body of the blessed abbess and to praise her as a saint with general applause, not just the Spaniards but the other nations: Indians, Chinese and the Japanese recently converted to the faith."[63] Guards had to be placed next to the corpse so that Sor Jerónima's followers would not try to take pieces of her habit or body as relics. Seeing that this was impossible, her devotees did the next best thing: they touched their rosaries to her body.[64] Much as the sailors had done on the Manila galleon when they asked Sor Jerónima to bless their rosaries, her admirers in Manila now acquired rosary beads touched by a potential saint.[65]

Sor Ana de Cristo as Abbess (1630–1636)

After Sor Jerónima's death, Sor Ana de Cristo took the reins of the convent. Although we do not know this for sure, we can only imagine that Sor Jerónima endorsed her candidacy as the next abbess. Sor Jerónima, like the other nuns from Spain and Mexico, had witnessed the intellectual maturation of Sor Ana, from a semiliterate nun to cofounder of the new convent to author of a lengthy biography. Over the next six years Sor Ana worked tirelessly as abbess until her death in 1636. Drawn to Sor Jerónima's fame of perceived sanctity, postulants began to flood the community. In 1632 Quesada notes that there were fifty-four females in the convent: "twenty-eight nuns (of which twenty-two have taken the habit in Manila), three novices who are in their trial year, and the rest are girls . . . who are waiting to enter the novitiate."[66] By 1635 the total number had risen to sixty-five.[67] Actually, the convent was growing at such a rapid pace that the alms provided by Manila's residents were not enough to sustain all of its members. To remedy the situation, Sor Ana successfully petitioned the king for financial support.[68]

During these years Sor Ana fulfilled Sor Jerónima's dream of expanding the order into China. On October 18, 1633, she sent eight women to Macao to found a new convent of Saint Clare.[69] Among the group were two of the original nuns from Spain: Sor Leonor de San Francisco as abbess and Sor María Magdalena de la Cruz as vicaress (she would later serve as abbess). In addition to the nuns, a noble Kapampangan woman, Marta de San Bernardo, received the habit of novice once on board ship. Just as Sor Jerónima had succeeded in permitting a Japanese novice into the community, Sor Ana also oversaw the first indigenous novice, albeit on the South China Sea.[70] Shortly before Sor Ana's death in 1636, another noble Kapampangan woman, Sor Magdalena de la Concepción, took the veil, but this time in Manila.[71] Nonetheless, these two women appear to be exceptions, since the vast majority of nuns continued to be criollas.

Sor María Magdalena de la Cruz (1575–1653)

Although Sor Ana never wrote specifically about Sor María Magdalena de la Cruz from a biographical angle, it would be remiss not to mention a few details about this exceptional woman. Mariana González de Avila (as she was called before she became a nun) was born in 1575 in the small village of Pinto (near Madrid) to a well-to-do family; her father was a notary of the Inquisition. According to her anonymous biographer, Mariana was born three or four months premature: "at birth everyone thought she was dead: with her ears fixed to her head and her mouth barely formed . . . it was almost sealed shut."[72] The premature baby was kept alive by keeping her warm in untreated wool and by feeding her milk through a straw.[73] Not only did the premature Mariana survive, but she also showed no signs of birth defects, learning to read at the age of three. At a young age she knew she wanted to become a nun, and at age fifteen she entered the Convent of Santa María de la Cruz in Cubas. She first became inspired to travel to the Far East in 1614 (along with Sor Magdalena de Cristo) when Fray Luis Sotelo stopped at her convent with the Japanese embassy on his way to Rome.[74] As a black-veiled nun and with her connection to her famous spiritual predecessor Juana de la Cruz, Sor Magdalena was chosen as vicaress of the initial foundation for Manila. If Sor Jerónima were to die en route, which many people thought possible due to her advanced age, then Sor Magdalena would automatically become her successor. She never did hold that position in Manila, however, and would have to wait until the second foundation in Macao before she finally became an abbess.[75]

Sor Magdalena stayed in Macao until 1644 when, due to power struggles between Franciscans and Jesuits (and within the Santa Clara convent itself)—magnified by political tensions between the division of Spain and Portugal's joint monarchy—three nuns, several friars, and their confessor, Fray Antonio de Santa María, were expelled from China.[76] After this expulsion, Sor María Magdalena's reported life reads more like an adventure novel than the story of a cloistered nun. On their return trip to Manila, due to fierce winds, the ships had to take refuge off the coast of Cochinchina (Vietnam), where it appears the whole crew was captured and sentenced to death. Although the circumstances are somewhat murky, the nuns were eventually pardoned and made it safely back to the Philippines.[77]

At the behest of her confessor, Fray Antonio, Sor María Magdalena wrote a three-volume mystical treatise titled *Floresta franciscana* (The Franciscan grove).[78] She also penned her autobiography, consisting of nineteen chapters, and other mystical treatises.[79] Unfortunately these are all lost, except for several extant copies of *Floresta franciscana*. Those three volumes, annotated and revised by her confessor Fray Antonio, have a total of sixty-two illustrations, describing different biblical scenes such as the creation of Adam and the fall of Lucifer, along with themes important to the Franciscan order, such as the symbolism of Saint Francis and Saint Clare and the glorification of the Immaculate Conception. First as Sor Juana de Antonio's scribe and later as author of her own mystical treatise, Sor Magdalena left her mark as a writer.

Conclusion

The interplay between Sor Jerónima's austere lifestyle—one that gave her currency as a potential saint—and her insistence that the convent in Manila follow the First Rule of Saint Clare ultimately caused a conflict that was not resolved during her lifetime. Ironically, some members of the Discalced Order of Franciscans who sought out Sor Jerónima as a potential saint turned against her when she did not acquiesce to their demands. In essence, Sor Jerónima's vision for her nunnery clashed with the expectations of local families and clerics. Spanish parents of postulants wanted their daughters to have control of their finances, and they did not want them to share power within the convent with mestiza or Filipina novices. It was this complex political landscape that thwarted, or at least considerably slowed, Sor Jerónima's path to sainthood. She challenged the boundaries of race and class acceptable to the Spanish enterprise in the Philippines and paid for it with the bittersweet odor of sanctity. Almost four hundred years later, her case for canonization still continues.[80]

Without ever losing focus on Sor Jerónima as a righteous leader, Sor Ana's manuscript captures the heated conflict that plagued the convent during Sor Jerónima's tumultuous years in Manila. At the end of her manuscript Sor Ana turns her attention to the other nuns who formed part of the foundation of the new convent. As scribe she preserves the voices of her cohort Sor Luisa de Jesús, for example, an ordinary woman who rose to the ranks of a black-veiled nun and who would not have otherwise merited official recording. Further, her position as a nun-widow who took her vows of profession at a very late age adds to findings of current research that exceptional circumstances (nuns usually professed in their late teens and early twenties) did exist within monastic communities.[81] Through Sor Ana's pen we hear a polyphony of voices, in particular the broken Spanish of Sor Lucía de San Juan, the Japanese novice from Kyoto. Likewise, Sor Ana replicates Sor Jerónima's fervent support of Sor Juana de San Antonio as her spiritual successor. She repeatedly notes the veracity of Sor Juana's revelations and endorses her work,

Noticias de la verdad. To some extent Sor Juana did follow in the footsteps of Sor Jerónima. She led the convent as abbess on several occasions and provided spiritual guidance to the nuns and even to local indigenous women from the outlying areas of Manila. Sadly, however, at the end of her life the Inquisition persecuted Sor Juana. Her case is illustrative of the fine line that early modern religious writers walked between sanctity and heresy. It also offers insight into the different levels of intellect and literacy in female convents. Like Sor Ana before leaving Spain, Sor Juana probably knew how to read but did not have any practice or training in putting pen to paper. Unlike Sor Ana, who eventually learned how to write, Sor Juana honed her skills in dictation. This ability served her needs at the time: she dictated her lengthy *Noticias de la verdad*, and even as abbess she used scribes to conduct convent business.

In order to better understand the oral and written tradition cultivated by the Spanish nuns in the Far East, the last chapter of this book returns to our analysis of Sor Ana's manuscript. After contextualizing the tradition of gendered education and literary production in early modern convents, it focuses on Sor Ana's literary style and transformation.

CHAPTER 5

Literacy and Inspirational Role Models

~~∾~~

~~∾~~ THROUGHOUT THE EARLY MODERN CATHOLIC WORLD, FEMALE monastic institutions valued writing as a way to memorialize their members. They turned to members of their own religious orders to write biographies and convent histories. The paths that religious women took to becoming biographers and convent chroniclers could vary, especially regarding their intellectual formation. Recent scholarship on convent education can help us understand the literacy of nuns such as Sor Ana de Cristo and their motivations for taking up the pen.[1] We know that a rudimentary knowledge of reading was a common requirement for profession as a black-veiled nun. Monastic communities cultivated black-veiled nuns as future leaders, as they were the ones who would hold offices as abbesses, vicaresses, treasurers, and novice mistresses, and these positions required basic literacy.[2] Reading formed an important part of prayer for nuns, a necessity to follow the daily routines set forth by each order. Nuanced studies reveal that the definition of literacy was much different in the early modern period from how we understand it today, foremost because it distinguished reading and writing as two separate skills. Furthermore, Anne J. Cruz notes, "Because reading and writing were skills that were learned separately, many women did not learn to write."[3] There was also a strong auditory culture in convents that helped cultivate nuns' intellectual formation. Not only did women religious spend a considerable amount of time listening to sermons, but they also read to each other at mealtimes and during work time, often about the lives of saints.[4] When she was novice mistress in Toledo, for instance, Sor Jerónima read every day to the novices after mass. In general, nuns heard (and some read) passages from the book of hours, breviaries, spiritual treatises, and books of contemplation or meditation by Luis de Granada and Pedro de Alcántara, among others.[5] They found deep inspiration in vidas written by or on female exemplars from the early modern era, such as Catherine of Siena and Teresa of Avila.[6] Through rote and repetition, often by listening to segments from biblical texts, some female monastics learned or at least could repeat phrases of rudimentary Latin. Nuns who did not necessarily know how to write Latin could still quote phrases from the Apostle Paul, John the Baptist, and the book of Psalms. Black-veiled nuns needed to be able to chant the Divine Office in Latin, one of their main occupations.

Ecclesiastical authorities encouraged nuns and other religious women to read and listen to devotional texts. Some confessors provided their penitents with reading material, while others read aloud to unlettered women.[7] Yet they also viewed writing with skepticism because they believed it encouraged immoral behavior.[8] This is not to say that many black-veiled nuns did not know how to write. On the contrary, despite skepticism from church authorities, many nuns did put pen to paper. Saint Teresa of Avila, for example, served as a solid role model for women religious throughout the Iberian Atlantic. Other nuns, such as María de San José Salazar (Teresa of Avila's spiritual daughter) advocated literacy in convents.[9]

A close analysis of Sor Ana's portrayal of Sor Jerónima tells us as much about the biographer as about her subject. Although in an assessment of her own writing, Sor Ana belittles herself as a *ruin sujeto* (wretched creature) and as barely literate, a careful examination of her writing style reveals a learned woman adept in the rhetoric of obedience and humility. Her self-examination speaks to the complex landscape of literacy, writing, and inspirational role models in the early modern world. The purpose of this chapter, therefore, is to examine Sor Ana's writing style and to explore her representation of herself as an author, while she sets out to portray the exemplary life of Sor Jerónima.

Sacred Biographies

It is important to take stock of the other two biographies written about Sor Jerónima during the seventeenth century in order to appreciate Sor Ana's work. These works by Franciscan friars can aid in unraveling meaning or filling in missing facts when Sor Ana's writing is deficient. Ginés de Quesada, who wrote the first biography, knew Sor Jerónima only during the last month and a half of her life. He preached at Sor Jerónima's funeral and was interviewed in the first set of testimonies in her beatification case.[10] Soon thereafter Quesada left for Japan, where he died a martyr in 1634. His manuscript on Jerónima, *Exemplo de todas las virtudes, y vida milagrosa de la venerable madre Gerónima de la Assumpción . . .*, was published posthumously, first in Mexico (1713) and later in Spain (1717).[11] Bartolomé de Letona penned the second biography in Puebla, Mexico, and although he never met Sor Jerónima in person, he did spend time in Manila from 1649–1654, during which, among other items of business, he interviewed her disciples.[12] His work, titled *Perfecta religiosa* (1662), used Sor Jerónima as a model for Poor Clare nuns.

What interests me most here is Quesada's representation of Sor Jerónima, since he interacted with her personally as her confessor in Manila. Placed side by side, Sor Ana's and Quesada's texts share many similarities. Both provide vivid illustrations of Jerónima's renowned status in Toledo years before she embarked on her long journey to the Philippines. Indeed, she was called the "Saint of Toledo" and the "Saint of Santa Isabel." The two biographies also follow the standard pattern of other hagiographical texts. In the strictest definition of the word, hagiography means writing about the life of a saint. From the Middle Ages into the early modern period the term evolved to refer to a much broader type of writing that idealizes the spiritual lives of extremely pious people. In general, a formulaic hagiography underscores the subject's early inclination as a small child to follow Christ, highlights extreme penitential practices, and recounts visions and miraculous occurrences, all the while portraying the subject as an exemplar of Christian life. It does not, however, attempt to re-create a realistic portrayal of events in the modern sense of biography. Due to Counter-Reformation culture and the arrival of the printing press, such texts were standard reading and very common in the early modern period.[13] Nonetheless, as adeptly pointed out by Bilinkoff, we can still learn a great deal from these hagiographies: "In the process of reading about a nun's heroic virtues we may also learn about convent factions, urban politics, family disputes over property, the difficulty of travel, and other fascinating items." Bilinkoff also notes that this style of writing can reveal autobiographical details and insights about the authors themselves, at times producing a type of hybrid text.[14]

Sor Ana's manuscript demonstrates her intimate familiarity with the genre of hagiography. At one point she cites the *Flos Sanctorum* (lives of saints), and her constant references to different saints and their lives corroborate her familiarity with those writings.[15] Likewise, she repeatedly cites passages from the Bible, including the works of St. Paul, the Gospel of St. John, and the book of the Apocalypse (to name a few). She even recalls characters from Greek mythology, quoting Sor Jerónima as saying her strength surpassed that of Hector the Trojan. As previously noted, she might not have *read* all these works, but she probably had *heard* them at her convent in Toledo and later in Manila.

Sor Ana's biography sheds much light on her subject for the obvious reason that she knew Sor Jerónima on an intimate level. The two had met long before they embarked on their epic journey to the Far East, cultivating a much different relationship from that between the nun and her confessor Quesada. Sor Ana had the privilege of asking Sor Jerónima direct questions whenever she had any doubts about her own memory. She even quotes herself as saying, "Madre, when did this happen? How did it occur? Have I forgotten anything?"[16] Toward the end of the manuscript, Sor Ana reemphasizes her personal relationship with Sor Jerónima, reminding her reader that she has spent more than forty years with her mentor.[17] Letona, in his biography, also gives credit to Sor Ana for having known her spiritual sister for more than forty years.[18]

Sor Ana begins the first chapters of her manuscript with a summary of Jerónima's early years in Toledo. Yet much like the male biographers, we need to be careful with all of the dates and facts with which Sor Ana supplies her readers. The most blatant error is in reference to the date of Jerónima's birth: May 9, 1555. This would be the date cited by her biographers all the way into the late twentieth century, but Jerónima's baptismal records clearly indicate that she was born one year later, because she was baptized on May 20, 1556.[19] Sor Ana also explains that her baptism occurred shortly after Jerónima's birth (certainly not a year later, since infants in early modern Spain were generally baptized within days or weeks of their birth). It is important to repeat that Sor Ana and her other biographers did not see themselves as historians but rather as hagiographers. Their main goal was to highlight the saintly essence of their subject, and their version of the truth (one dictated by God) was very different from the way we view it with contemporary eyes.

Sor Ana continues her opening chapters with a description of Jerónima's noble lineage and childhood. Her parents provided her with all advantages common to the noble class, including a rudimentary education. Jerónima and her sisters all learned to read and write by age six, but she was by far the brightest. Sor Ana portrays her subject as extremely intelligent and an avid reader. As a young girl, she would read the life of a saint every night before bedtime. We learn later in her biography that Sor Jerónima continued reading throughout her life; she read every day from one to two in the afternoon, a practice she instilled in the convents of Seville, Cádiz, and later Manila. These details follow the standard formula of a hagiography, making patent her virtuous behavior as a young girl, thus signaling her destiny as a saint. As in other sacred biographies, Sor Ana devotes the vast majority of her text to describing the extreme penitential practices of the nun from Toledo. When Jerónima was very young, even before entering the convent, she would subject her body to harsh corporal punishments, including self-flagellation and constant fasting. From the age of three she started her "disciplinas de sangre" (blood disciplines), and by age six she already wore a hair shirt.

What sets Sor Ana's narrative apart from the male biographers' works is that she subtly inserts her own gendered commentary on Jerónima's life and on the male-dominated world in which they lived. She critiques, for example, certain ingrained traditions, such as favoritism for male offspring. When referring to Jerónima's father, she affirms, "Her father wanted a son as is common among men, as if they had never been born from women."[20] In her critique of Spain's patriarchal society, she affirms that a father's wish for a son does not matter, because the one true Father, God above, does not make such distinctions. She reminds the reader that Christ himself spent nine months in the Virgin's womb. Sor Ana also contends that Jerónima hailed from a long line of wise, saintly virgins, martyrs for the true faith: "There have been many extremely wise women who have converted many people to the holy faith with the wisdom of the Holy Spirit."[21] Sor Ana positions Jerónima among these women and states that if men knew how to appreciate such women, there would be many more.

Sor Ana's Spiritual and Intellectual Formation

Even though Sor Ana wrote a biography of Sor Jerónima, she intersperses details about herself and her own intellectual formation. Unlike Sor Jerónima's story, the information about Sor Ana's life before taking her vows of profession is sparse. The little information that we have about Sor Ana can be gleaned from her own writing and a few brief references about her from male biographers. According to Letona, Ana was born on September 27, 1565, in Getafe (two leagues, or six miles, from Madrid). He describes her parents as *honrados* (honorable) but says that she became an orphan at age seven. She entered the Convent of Santa Isabel de los Reyes in Toledo in 1582 and, after a year's novitiate, she professed in 1583.[22] Sor Ana relates that she was very pleased to have had Sor Jerónima as her novice mistress, since she had heard much about her: their families were neighbors and Sor Ana had been a close friend with Sor Jerónima's sisters. Although Sor Ana does not provide hagiographic details about herself as she does for Jerónima, she does say that she had yearned to be a nun since the age of six.

As novice mistress, Sor Jerónima is portrayed as the ideal role model, teaching her charges the essential virtues of being a nun: "solicitousness, humility, obedience, penance, and great silence."[23] She taught the young women to read in Spanish and most likely to read some elementary Latin.[24] After finishing her novitiate and taking vows as a black-veiled nun, it was Sor Ana's duty to hold certain offices in the convent. This became a problem for her since, in her own words, she knew how to read but she did not know how to write or count. Inhibited by this inadequacy, Sor Ana used this excuse to avoid certain positions, such as discreta (advisor to the abbess) and doorkeeper of the convent. She does mention, however, that she was novice mistress for three years. When one of the former abbesses in Toledo (doña Juana de Toledo) offered to teach her how to write, Sor Ana declined.[25]

It was not until later, on the sea voyage to Manila, that Fray José de Santa María, who was traveling with the nuns, convinced Sor Ana of the importance of learning to write. As a founder of the future convent, she was going to have to hold several important positions, including abbess (a position she later held from 1630 until her death in 1636). She acquiesced and at some point during and after the journey, Fray José taught her how to write and organize her ideas on paper. Later, while writing her manuscript, Sor Ana reflects on this series of events, explaining how she begged the Lord to give her strength as a future leader of the convent.[26]

Apparently Fray José saw great potential in Sor Ana as the future convent chronicler and biographer of Sor Jerónima, otherwise he would not have marked her for such a position. She might not have had much practice in putting quill to paper—thus her statement that she did not know how to write—but it did not take long for her to learn. He and other friars also saw the real possibility of Sor Jerónima's future sainthood, and they wanted to be part of that process.[27] Still, they needed to justify their evangelical mission: in this case, the costly and dangerous endeavor of sending Spanish nuns all the way to Asia. Sor Ana's words formed a crucial part of Sor Jerónima's public relations campaign. Most likely the friars never had any intention of publishing Sor Ana's works, but they could use her notes as the basis of their own biographies—something that occurred with Quesada and later with Letona. This was no secret. The concept of plagiarism did not exist within the genre of hagiography or spiritual biographies. In fact, this is one of the main reasons that Sor Ana's and other religious women's texts were never published. Instead, they served as the main basis for future texts written by confessors and other religious authorities.[28] Male biographers who had access to printing presses saw their own biographical accounts as legitimization of their female subjects as orthodox.[29] In some cases, the original manuscripts became lost over the years and the copies are the only sources remaining. Sor Jerónima herself supposedly was quite a prolific author, yet over the years, with the exception of a few letters, almost all of her works have disappeared: some taken as relics and others lost. Sor Ana, Quesada, and Letona had access to Sor Jerónima's writings, in particular her spiritual autobiography, *Carta de marear en el mar del mundo*, from which they mined information for their biographies, including transcriptions of her poetry.[30]

Later in Sor Ana's manuscript we learn that there were other people and circumstances that inspired her to write her biography of Sor Jerónima. Instead of her confessor or another male authority, it was the abbess in Manila, Madre Leonor de San Francisco (1583–1651), who first ordered that Sor Ana write her account.[31] Why did she wait to reveal these details? Did she do this on purpose, or was this a simple mistake? Did she intentionally leave her introductory remarks vague—referring to holy obedience but not specifying a person or gender? Although we might not have the exact answers to these questions, the section inserted between chapters 40 and 41 provides us with some important clues. The title suggests that someone told Sor Ana to explain when and how she decided to write her biography: "Account of When and How the History of Our Blessed Mother Jerónima de la Asunción Was Begun to Be Written during the First Year of the Mother Leonor de San Francisco's Term as Abbess. Year 1623."[32]

Sor Ana begins this subaccount by narrating how Sor María Magdalena de la Cruz, one of her cofounders from Cubas, Spain, came to her one day in Manila and told her, "Write the vida of our Mother, because that is why you were taught."[33] Sor Ana says she laughed when she heard this. She explains that Sor María Magdalena's request reminded her of another illiterate nun biographer who miraculously wrote the life of Juana de la Cruz (1481–1534), the celebrated visionary nun from Cubas. Years earlier, after reading about this illiterate nun, she felt inspired to write the life story of Sor Jerónima. When the abbess (Sor Leonor de San Francisco) heard about this secret desire, she ordered Sor Ana, under the oath of obedience, to do just that. Interestingly, Sor Ana says that her first drafts about Sor Jerónima were lost at sea, "but they were short and bad, a few scribbles that were poorly written."[34] It was not until 1623, a few years after they reached Manila and Sor Ana was commanded by her spiritual sisters to write the biography, that she seriously took up the task of writing the life story of Sor Jerónima. Soon thereafter, she also received an official mandate from a male prelate, "nuestro Padre Visitador."[35]

This short account sheds much light on Sor Ana as an author and her reasons for writing the biography. In a roundabout manner, we learn that Sor Ana, despite her limitations (she did not know how to write) had always manifested a desire to pen the biography of her beloved Sor Jerónima. We also learn that she was mandated and inspired primarily by two nuns, the current abbess Sor Leonor and Sor María Magdalena, to write the biography. Only later, more as an official stamp of approval, did she receive the order from a male prelate. Unlike some other religious women who penned confessional texts, Sor Ana did not dread or find the writing process agonizing.[36] In general, she embraced the idea of writing Sor Jerónima's biography, but this was also because she felt bolstered by her female spiritual role models, as discussed below.

Female Networks of Support

Historical research on late medieval and early modern convents reveals that networks of literary production, exchange, and reception existed all over Catholic Europe. Scholarship on female monasticism also probes questions of how these women worked together as a collective form of agency.[37] Sor Ana's manuscript speaks to the complex network of support that existed within women's religious communities, a strong tradition that this group of nuns brought with them to the Spanish Pacific. Sor Ana connected with some of these female exemplars (both living and deceased) through oral tradition and written works. She even knew some of them personally or had access to their correspondence. Others she learned about through biographies written by male Franciscan friars, some of whom visited her convent in Toledo.

Two famous role models for the group were Saint Clare of Assisi (1194–1293) and Saint Teresa of Avila (1515–1582). Sor Ana held each of these women in high esteem. She makes countless references to Saint Clare as the founder of their order and ultimate model for humility and poverty. Pedro de Ribadeneira's 1599 edition of *Flos Sanctorum*, common reading for the nuns, had a chapter dedicated to the life of Saint Clare.[38] Sor Ana also recalls the image of Saint Teresa, albeit less frequently. She found inspiration not only in Saint Teresa's writings but also in her reformation of the Carmelite order and her travels related to that task, which correlated with Sor Jerónima's role as reformer of Franciscan convents.[39] Added to her exemplary appeal, Saint Teresa had been canonized in 1622, just shortly after the nuns had arrived in Manila.

Sor Ana also wove other female religious exemplars, mostly from the Franciscan order, into her manuscript. These women, lesser known today, were much revered (and at times vilified) during their lifetimes. One woman in particular, Mariana de Jesús (1577–1620), provided immense pride and inspiration to the group of cofounders. The nuns knew Mariana intimately as a Third Order laywoman living in Toledo, and at one point they even thought she would accompany them on their journey to Manila. Due to her poor health, she stayed behind, and the nuns later learned that she died the same day that they set sail from the port of Cádiz. Like Sor Jerónima, many in Toledo regarded Mariana de Jesús as a possible candidate for sainthood, which in fact was the case. Sor Ana mentions that her beatification case started while they were in Manila.[40] Mariana's confessor, Luis de la Mesa, a great admirer of her pious and penitential lifestyle, wrote a lengthy biography about her.[41] When Mesa prohibited Mariana from leaving Toledo he asked Luisa de Francisco (later called Luisa de Jesús), another Third Order laywoman and a close companion of Mariana, to take her place.

According to Mesa, Mariana was born on February 17, 1577, as Mariana de Rojas in a small village outside Toledo called Escalona. She was a daughter of a *hidalgo* (lower nobility), was married at age fifteen, became a widow after three weeks, and bore a daughter nine months later. Shortly thereafter she married again and became a widow for the second time before consummating the marriage. She then moved to Toledo to live with other family members, where she professed Third Order vows as a Franciscan laywoman. Her fame spread not only because of her humility, poverty, and obedience but also because of her work as a visionary and intercessor for the dead. Many in Toledo venerated her as a type of *santa viva*, or living saint.[42] Sor Ana repeatedly cites Mariana throughout her writing. Mostly she describes how Mariana appeared to Sor Jerónima in visions, urging her to continue with her mission in the Philippines, but she also relates historical anecdotes. In one example she explains how Mariana watched the procession of a large sculpture of the Immaculate Conception that Sor Jerónima had commissioned for the Franciscan Monastery of San Juan de los Reyes in Toledo.[43]

Other Franciscan holy women, also involved in the cult of the Immaculate Conception, loom large in Sor Ana's manuscript. It would be difficult to overstate the importance of Juana de la Cruz (1481–1534) to this group of Spanish nuns, just as it would be difficult to overstate her fame in Spain and in the Americas.[44] Known colloquially as Santa Juana, although she was never canonized, Juana de la Cruz forged a space for herself during her lifetime as a mystic, preacher of sermons, and supporter of the Immaculate Conception.[45] Mother Juana was also abbess of a Third Order Franciscan convent in the village of Cubas, about twenty-eight miles from Toledo. It was not until eighty years after the death of Juana de la Cruz that friars from the Franciscan Order began the first steps in the canonization process, which continues to this day.[46] Allegedly, the Holy Spirit and the Virgin Mary spoke directly through Juana in a series of five- to six-hour visions that took place every Sunday over the course of thirteen years. Important dignitaries, noblemen, and church officials, including Emperor Charles V and the archbishop of Toledo, Cardinal Cisneros, attended these sessions, endorsing her as a true mystic. The seventy-two sermons preached by Mother Juana during her state of ecstatic rapture, known as the *Conorte*, were not published during her lifetime.[47] Evidently she dictated her "semiautobiography," *Vida y fin de la bienaventurada Virgen Santa Juana de la Cruz* (hereafter *Vida y fin*), principally to another nun in her convent, Sor María Evangelista; to this day it remains only as an unpublished manuscript.[48] In an added layer of intrigue, Sor María Evangelista supposedly did not know how to read or write before collaborating on *Vida y fin* but was granted the gift of literacy by divine intervention, thus providing Sor Ana with both a solid role model and an inspiration to write her biography of Sor Jerónima. *Vida y fin* contains two voices: one written in the first person as dictation from Juana, and another in the third person with apparent commentary from Sor Evangelista.[49] The use of scribes was definitely not unique to the case of Juana de la Cruz. Dictation had been the well-established method of choice since the Middle Ages for many religious writers, with examples ranging from Thomas Aquinas to Hildegard of Bingen, and this also continued with the Spanish nuns in the Philippines.[50]

Two of the founding sisters on the journey to Manila hailed from Juana de la Cruz's original convent in Cubas: María Magdalena de Cristo and María Magdalena de la Cruz. The latter, Sor María Magdalena (who told Sor Ana to write the biography), was named vicaress of the future convent in Manila: a prestigious position, putting her second in command to Jerónima. At first glance it might seem odd that Sor Jerónima would have wanted travel companions whom she had never met; yet after reading Sor Ana's manuscript we learn that these women were not selected by chance. Both women brought with them the oral memory of their extraordinary spiritual predecessor, Madre Juana; they would have known her through stories and memories recounted by elderly nuns in their convent.[51] They also brought the textual memory of their holy foremother as documented by her first biographer, Sor María Evangelista, and later by their contemporary, Antonio Daza. Most importantly, as we have seen, they brought with them a sensory reminder of Juana through the touch of her rosary beads.

We are certain that Sor María Magdalena had read *Vida y fin*, because she says so in her testimony regarding Juana's saintly life and miracles as part of the Apostolic Process.[52] Although nuns commonly circulated manuscripts within convents and orders, it appears that Sor Ana did not read *Vida y fin* but instead one of Antonio Daza's published biographies (1610; 1613).[53] We can surmise this because Sor Ana specifically mentions having read *about* the illiterate biographer and not the work by her. Furthermore, Daza speaks about Sor María Evangelista's miraculous literacy in his prologue.

Daza published his first edition of the biography, *Historia, vida y milagros de la bienaventurada virgen Santa Juana de la Cruz*, in 1610 and a revised version because of Inquisitorial censorship in 1613. Among other things, he was required to take the word *saint* out of the title. His biographies became instant bestsellers and were soon translated into French, Italian, German, and English.[54] At one point in her manuscript, Sor Ana makes direct mention of Daza, which is just one of several clues demonstrating her familiarity not only with his biography of Juana de la Cruz but with the man who gained fame as the confessor of Luisa de la Ascensión.[55] Daza's biography would have provided valuable information to Sor Ana. His work also speaks of the miraculous powers attributed to Juana's rosary beads, supposedly elevated to heaven by her guardian angel and blessed by Jesus Christ himself. According to her biographers, Juana de la Cruz distributed the holy beads as relics, and over the years they gained much acclaim for their miraculous powers. The rosaries and any other beads that touched the originals, known as contact relics, had the power to heal the sick, ward off the devil, calm storms, or blow wind into slack sails.[56]

One of the fastest ways to create a following of a would-be saint was through the distribution of rosary beads. A number of seventeenth-century religious women, such as Sor María de Jesús de Agreda (1602–1665), handed out their own beads, claiming they had special curative and protective powers.[57] Sor María de Agreda is best known for her miraculous ability of bilocation, that is, being in two places at the same time. It is said that she would preach to the Native Americans of New Mexico without ever leaving her home convent in Spain. Sor María de Agreda also purportedly had one of Juana's beads, her portrait, and a copy of Daza's 1613 biography. She even underlined certain passages, among them those referencing the power of the rosary beads.[58]

In addition to word of mouth, one of the main reasons that Sor María de Agreda and others coveted Madre Juana's rosary beads is that there circulated a false indulgence—supposedly issued by Gregory XIII (1572–1585)—that verified all of the supernatural powers attributed to the beads.[59] Even though the Inquisition issued an edict in 1605 denouncing the indulgence as false, the devotion to the beads was still firmly entrenched in early modern Catholic society.[60] Sor Ana meticulously documents how the nuns carried several of these rosaries with them on their journey. Not only did the beads endear the nuns to the local peoples, but they also saved them from deadly illnesses and perilous storms.

Juana de la Cruz did not achieve fame for her rosaries alone. Along with her close ally Cardinal Cisneros, she was also one of the original supporters of the doctrine of the Immaculate Conception, a devotional movement based on the belief that the Virgin Mary was conceived and remained free from the stain of original sin (not formally accepted by the Catholic church until 1854). In other words, this purity made her worthy of the miraculous conception of the Son of God. The Spanish nuns found inspiration in this movement, especially since some of their foremothers and female contemporaries were active members of the campaign. In an analysis of this Franciscan movement, we see that several key players had connections to Sor Jerónima and her founding sisters.[61]

Perhaps the most important promoter of the Immaculist Campaign in the early seventeenth century was Sor Luisa de la Ascensión (1565–1636), often referred to as the nun from Carrión, Spain ("la monja de Carrión"). She made a name for herself as a holy woman, and her greatest fame came from her

Figure 15 Sor María de Jesús de Agreda preaching to the Chichimecas of
New Mexico, 1730. Engraving by Antonio de Castro in Alonso de
Benavides's epistolary account "Tanto que se sacó de una carta . . ."
Courtesy of the John Carter Brown Library at Brown University.

founding of a confraternity in defense of the Immaculate Conception of the
Virgin. By 1619 the confraternity had more than eighty thousand members,
including King Philip III, several cardinals, and other powerful leaders, both
religious and secular. Sor Ana, Sor Jerónima, and all the nuns at Santa Isabel
de los Reyes signed the confraternity roster on September 26, 1618. It is unclear
whether Sor Jerónima signed for Sor Ana, since the handwriting in the two
signatures looks quite similar. Many other convents of nuns throughout Spain
also signed this roster. For example, there is an earlier entry from April 16, 1617,

with the signatures of the two founding nuns from the Convent of La Cruz in Cubas (Magdalena de Cristo and Mariá Magdalena de la Cruz).[62] Sor Luisa's confessor, biographer, and staunch supporter was none other than Antonio Daza (he also was an official chronicler of the Franciscan order).[63] The Inquisition persecuted Sor Luisa toward the end of her life, imprisoning her in Salamanca, although her name was cleared posthumously.[64] Her persecution occurred after the death of Sor Jerónima, who had never any reason to doubt the sanctity of the nun from Carrión.

In addition to poetry, a spiritual autobiography and other texts, Sor Luisa wrote hundreds of letters.[65] We know that she communicated by missive with Sor Jerónima because Sor Ana refers to their correspondence in her manuscript and because Sor Jerónima cites her in a letter she wrote to King Philip IV in 1623, after arriving in the Philippines. In that missive, she justifies her reasons for adopting the First Rule of Saint Clare, bolstering her argument by referring to a letter she received from Sor Luisa de la Ascensión while in Mexico City. In the letter Luisa told her to persevere in her mission to found a convent under the First Rule of Saint Clare.[66] Sor Luisa's encouragement through her letters speaks to a network of support between nuns that crossed oceans and continents.

Accepting the notion that Sor Ana felt both humbled and bolstered by her prestigious spiritual sisters can shed light on the reasons why she offers a candid depiction of herself as an author. She starts with her limitations: she is almost sixty, suffers from asthma, and has frequent fevers. Then she emphasizes her strengths: she has direct access to Sor Jerónima and can ask her questions whenever she likes. Foremost, imbued in the rhetoric of humility, is the voice of self-awareness and agency. Sor Ana explains that she might not be the most polished and practiced writer, but at the same time, it is an honor for her to write the life story of her esteemed sister.[67] Through her commentaries, we begin to see that Sor Ana found her own authority through the written word. Though early modern society subordinated her place in society as secondary to her male ecclesiastical counterparts, she was learning to navigate that space.[68]

Sor Ana's Literary Style

Just as Sor Ana's writing style replicates many themes typical of hagiographies, it also employs techniques common to nuns' writing, such as the use of colloquial language and dialogue. Female monastics who did not have formal training in writing or rhetoric often wrote as they spoke. Extremely long, run-on sentences and lack of punctuation can make some of these texts difficult to follow, but thanks to modern editions we are better able to negotiate and contextualize their works. Throughout her manuscript, Sor Ana often reproduces dialogue that she has either been a part of or has heard over the years. She replicates celestial encounters with the Virgin Mary, Christ, and John the Baptist, among other saints. Themes that permeate Franciscan nuns' texts such as visions of Saint Francis, ascetic practices that center on Christ's Holy Wounds, and the cult of the Immaculate Conception are all present in Sor Ana's manuscript. At one point Sor Ana describes dipping her quill into Christ's Holy Wound for divine inspiration.[69] According to Isabelle Poutrin, in order to capture the reader's attention it was necessary to accumulate miraculous episodes, and this type of dialogue was quite common in nuns' visionary writings. Her study helps us understand Sor Ana's lengthy retelling of visions of and dialogues with saints. Poutrin explains that from our modern mind-set this can be tedious and repetitive, but it was not from the perspective of early modern readers. These techniques helped draw the reader into the narrative.[70] Sor Ana explains her own use of repetition. She has no problem repeating details, since they all build on Jerónima's spiritual résumé: "Thus this as well as other things that shall be told twice and more in order not to cut short the account that such magnificent works require and although it may all be the same, sometimes it includes more details than others, and this is why I am moved to do it."[71]

Sor Ana uses dialogue to explore her own literacy and intellectual growth. She prefaces several conversations with Sor Jerónima by contending that she does not know *gramática* (grammar) but then offers her own interpretation of a biblical quote: "Even though I do not know *gramática*, it does not say that, the verse means something else."[72] According to the *Dictionary of the Real Academia* of Spain (1734), the word *gramática* can also mean the study of the Latin language. Indeed, it appears that Sor Ana employs this meaning when she is trying to interpret scripture written in Latin. Sor Ana also explains that Jerónima gives her many verses in Latin, which she reproduces throughout her manuscript and which she then attempts to translate into the Spanish vernacular.[73]

Similarly, at key points throughout her manuscript, Sor Ana assesses her own writing. Although these self-evaluations vary only slightly, they are a window into Sor Ana's psyche. She was wary of crafting a document under the watchful eye of the patriarchal system, one that monitored the writing of early modern women. Yet her work also shows that the power structure marshaled by the church was fluid: it could be negotiated and at times avoided. In the opening lines (preface) of her manuscript, Sor Ana chooses her words carefully. Following a traditional hierarchy of authority, she first pays tribute to God, then to holy obedience that has required her to write the account, and finally to her dear confessor who has also served as her teacher.

In addition to serving the glory of God, Sor Ana articulates her hope that this account will also be of service to those who read it so that "they can see God's miracles."[74] Throughout her introduction she intersperses a rhetoric of humility, referring to herself as *inútil* (useless) and as a *pobre sujeto* (lowly individual) and at the same time combining these derogatory comments with expressions of her disbelief that the Lord would have used her as his holy instrument to write such an important work. Such comments provided a type of rhetorical safety net for Sor Ana, on the one hand because traditional male ecclesiastical authorities would read this and see that she viewed herself as a lowly woman, and on the other because her work was not only sanctioned by her confessor but also inspired and transmitted by the Holy Spirit.[75]

Perhaps it was Sor Ana's reference to Divine Favor that prompted Letona to assert that she had learned to write by divine inspiration. Nonetheless, unless he failed to read (or ignored) the rest of the manuscript, he should have known that her confessor played an important role in Sor Ana's literary education. Instead, it is more likely that Letona was employing the trope of miraculous literacy, a common way of justifying religious women's works and a tradition also embedded in Sor Ana's manuscript.[76] By portraying herself as an agent of Divine Will, she could offset possible criticism that could be leveled against her text.

Sor Ana's expression of self-awareness and agency becomes even sharper in the last chapters of the biography. At one point she elaborates on a deeper level her own motives for writing the work and how she perceives others will respond to it:

> I understand very well that there will be no shortage of people who will say that I have written too much. It is true, but there are also common tastes that do not like fine delicacies, but instead, ordinary and crude. And, in this latter style is how my work will be considered since it does not achieve any expertise. There are those who say: "there is no bad year if you have plenty of bread" and "you can never have enough

of a good thing." The reader, if not too annoyed by the uselessness of the author, can say, "stick to the distaff," and for me, it would be better to do that since I have done it before and it needs less care; however, obedience mandates that I weave tighter threads. This is for the hands of our dear fathers and in particular our Father Fray José de Santa María, who through his myriad titles has many obligations. He was the one who brought us [to Manila] and taught me to write, and for that reason he mandates that I do this. Thus, as father and teacher he will correct the mistakes and imperfections from someone who is not trained in [the art of writing] such an important work.[77]

This lively self-evaluation of her own writing and reasons for taking up the pen not only lets the reader view Sor Ana's perspective on her own use of the word but provides an important prism through which to observe literacy and the production of conventual literature in the early modern period. In the first part of the passage, Sor Ana uses humor, colloquial language, and the rhetoric of humility to assess her own work. She pokes fun at herself, saying that she understands that she is long-winded and might be criticized for this, but that there are all types of tastes and, hopefully, the reader will be able to tolerate her "uselessness." She utilizes a metaphor of spinning wool to describe her role in the production process, comparing her efforts in writing to someone being forced to use a *rueca* (distaff) for the first time. In her case, she has spun a yarn that is long and rustic, but it is the best she has ever done.

Perhaps Sor Ana was playing with the popular belief from her time period that women should stick to the rosary and distaff.[78] This was reinforced by devotional images and paintings of the Virgin at the loom, which became increasingly common throughout Spain and Europe in the early modern period. Indeed, the Virgin at work, spinning and embroidering, was the ultimate archetype for nuns.[79] She does appear to appropriate this misogynistic interpretation that women should stay home praying the rosary and spinning wool and refashions those metaphors to define her own writing. She might have also known the word *distaff* from Proverbs 31:19, which describes the virtues of the ideal wife: "In her hand she holds the distaff and grasps the spindle with her fingers." If that was the case, she borrowed the biblical image of a virtuous woman to describe her writing style. Still, Sor Ana will not take full responsibility for her text, since she returns to the trope of holy obedience, which required her to write the biography. She refers to her audience as "the hands of our dear fathers." She specifies her admiration and debt of gratitude toward her confessor Padre Fray José de Santa María, who accompanied the women all the way to the Philippines and taught her the skill of writing. Sor Ana reminds her reader that he ordered her to write the document and she believes that he will correct all her mistakes. In *Related Lives: Confessors and Their Female Penitents*, Jodi Bilinkoff discusses how this type of positive relationship sometimes developed between nuns and their confessors. Although religious women knew that they needed their confessor's endorsement in the writing process, this did not always have to be a negative experience.[80]

With the friars as her audience and editors, Sor Ana lifts the burden of responsibility off her own shoulders and onto theirs. She purposely weaves this statement into the fabric of her manuscript, omitting mention of Sor María Magdalena and Sor Leonor, who had originally ordered her to write the biography. Like other nuns, she would be wary of seeing her work scrutinized by the Inquisition. By stating that she was writing due to her confessor's command, she protects herself from possible persecution. Yet this does not mean that she did not have her own voice, for that certainly shines through as lively and humorous, as in the long quote above. In the words of Elisa Sampson Vera Tudela, "The idea here is that writing actually empowered nuns, despite the various limits it simultaneously imposed."[81] Sor Ana clearly understands these limitations, but at the same time she feels emboldened to express some of her personal opinions. It must be said, too, that Sor Ana's self-discovery as a writer is not unique among early modern religious women who wrote texts. Asunción Lavrin has noted that it was common for early modern female religious writers who had an inclination to write, whether they were pushed by holy obedience or not, to find their own voice and destiny.[82]

The more that Sor Ana advances in the document, the more she appears to become aware of herself as an author, not just an instrument of obedience to her confessor and other nuns. Without homing in on some of the key quotes about herself, it would be easy to cast Sor Ana into the role of subjugated nun, forced to write by the whim of male prelates. Her own words, however, point to other interpretations. I believe it is for this reason that in different sections of the biography she explores the boundaries of her own concept of literacy and reasons for writing the manuscript. Her musings are not always linear and at times she contradicts herself. In different passages of the biography, she attributes her writing to divine inspiration, to the mandates of her spiritual sisters, and to holy obedience to her confessor, or some combination thereof. All of these players make up the complex landscape of women's literacy in the early modern world and form part of Sor Ana's worldview. Sor Ana understands that writing is not easy, especially with all the other obligations that come along with her position as a black-veiled nun (at the time of writing she was vicaress), not to mention her advanced age and failing health: "I can only write between eight and ten at night when the convent is quiet."[83] This description speaks to her self-awareness as an author and to the many difficulties that writers have been complaining about for centuries. To name only one example, approximately fifty years later Sor Juana Inés de la Cruz, the Mexican nun renowned for her exceptional talent as a poet and playwright, also complained that she did not have enough time to follow her literary pursuits.[84]

Sor Ana's confidence in her own voice begins to gain currency over time. In addition to copying the dialogues relating to Jerónima, she also interjects her own opinions. In chapter 42 the abbess mandates her to document her own spiritual journey to the Philippines. Although she states that she does not want "to bore anyone with my simplicity," she ventures to relate her personal visions, prayers, and hopes for the future. In this section and in others, she prays for sailors, soldiers, captives, and prisoners.[85] She prays for the Franciscan Order and that the Lord will help with the conversion of infidels all over the world. It is her ultimate wish that "Moors" and pagans will be illuminated in the Christian faith. Actually, Sor Ana was not alone in wanting to convert heretics and nonbelievers, since this was a common trope in conventual literature.[86] Yet now, as she begins to explore her own desires and experiences, she is not just writing the biography of Sor Jerónima but also becoming an active participant in the Crown's missionary endeavors.[87] As she reflects on her own literary creation, she comes to the realization that, however small her own contribution might be to converting nonbelievers, her manuscript is important. She hopes that whoever might read her work will "burn with love for God."[88] Ultimately Sor Ana produces a hybrid genre of writing that is as much biographical as it is autobiographical.

Conclusion

The sui generis style of Sor Ana as a writer mirrors her personal transformation. To be sure, she uses all of the tools of her post-Tridentine world. Yet little by little, she begins to find her own voice. I believe that the physical journey of traversing the world's oceans and continents pushed her to explore her worldview and ideas. She becomes creative, interspersing visions, dialogues, and personal anecdotes within her narrative. She begins to develop her own style, not just that of a nun mimicking the themes of her Franciscan Order or the patterns typical of hagiographical writing. She already had the seed planted in her mind, after reading Juana de la Cruz's biography long before in Toledo, that she had the potential to be a writer. Nonetheless, it was not until after the physical and emotional exertion of such a lengthy expedition that she found the impetus to write Sor Jerónima's biography. For Sor Ana, a fifty-five-year-old nun who had spent all of her adult life behind the walls of a cloistered convent, this journey was a type of awakening.

Sor Ana's writing offers the contemporary reader unique insight into the world of travel and adventure across several continents during the early 1600s. It is difficult to imagine that these encounters with the diverse cultural milieu of the early modern world—from the Carib population of Guadalupe, to the Amerindians in Mexico, to the enslaved woman on the Manila galleon, to the native Filipino population—did not change Sor Ana. More likely they even caused her to reflect on her own status as a privileged nun in a tropical city, literally on the other side of the world from her home convent in Toledo. Sor Ana hailed from a long line of religious women authors. She brought this tradition of reading and writing to the Philippines. This is not what sets her work apart from that of her female predecessors. I suggest that the combination of the intellectual journey (her path to literacy) with the physical journey of navigating the Spanish Empire makes her narrative unique. The result is that her writing offers the contemporary reader a gendered perspective on Spain's global empire.

Epilogue

~~&

After a long period of silence and lack of communication because of
the sad circumstances of the horrible war . . . I am writing these
lines with my heart filled with bitterness and pain. . . . The terrible
loss of our ten sisters—seven choir nuns and three from the Third
Order—along with three of our faithful servants; the total destruction of our monastery with its church and vicarage; the complete
loss of more than 300 relics of saints; the irreplaceable archive of the
monastery; the library that contained a collection of old books on
asceticism and mysticism; documents spanning three centuries;
chronicles of the Franciscan order since its foundation. . . . All of
this will give you an idea of the irreparable loss that this community
suffered from the cruel war that occurred on these islands.

—SOR CONCORDIA DE SAN FRANCISCO,
"Carta a la reverenda madre abadesa del convento de monjas
clarisas de Santa Isabel de los Reyes, Toledo, España," April 6, 1945

~~& THERE IS NO SHORTAGE OF HORRIFIC ACCOUNTS OF THE DESTRUC-
tion of World War II. It cannot be denied that these amazing war stories need
to be told, yet as in most of history, women have remained relegated to the
margins. One of those accounts that has been forgotten by many is the shelling and firebombing of the Convent of Santa Clara in Manila during the last
months of World War II, in February 1945. Believing that part of the Japanese
Imperial Army was holed up in the nunnery's walls, the Allied forces relent-
lessly bombed the convent and the vast majority of buildings within
Intramuros. But what the Allies did not know is that the nuns had sought
refuge within their fortress, believing that the thick, solid walls of their

female monastery would save them from the shelling. Instead, the convent became a tomb for many.

We know the intimate details of these events because on April 6, 1946, the mother abbess of the displaced community of Poor Clares, Sor Concordia de San Francisco, composed a letter to the nuns back in Toledo, Spain. Writing from Quezon City, the site of the their future convent, Sor Concordia depicted the suffering that she and her sisters endured between 1941 and 1945. Her six-page, single-spaced missive sheds light on the nuns' life under Japanese occupation and culminates with a detailed account of their escape from the burning walls of their convent on February 23, 1945.[1] Unfortunately, the community suffered many losses (as indicated in the epigraph), not only the loss of thirteen lives, but also of the convent itself and its contents, including the archive. Fortunately for my research, Franciscan prelates had sent copies of many of the convent's documents back to Spain, some during the time of Sor Jerónima and others during the nineteenth century. Nonetheless, as stated in Sor Concordia's letter, the fire destroyed everything that was there, and we do not know what manuscripts and rare books were lost.

This was not the first time that the convent had been leveled to the ground. In 1645 Manila suffered a major earthquake that severely damaged the nunnery, and another hit in 1658 that left it in rubble. On both occasions the nuns were forced to vacate their home until the convent could be repaired and rebuilt in the same location. Over the years natural disasters were not the only events to displace the nuns. In addition to World War II, two other foreign invasions caused the nuns to seek refuge outside of their convent: the British occupation of Manila in 1762–64 during the Seven Years' War and the Spanish-American War in the Philippines of 1898. Although we do not have lengthy accounts of these events (like that of Sor Ana de Cristo's manuscript), we do have nuns' writings from different eras about these historical moments.

On July 16, 1764, the abbess of the convent, Sor Juana de San Antonio (no relation to the cofounder from the 1600s), penned a letter to the viceroy of New Spain, don Joaquín de Montserrat, the Marquis of Cruillas. In her missive, she outlines how the British seized the city of Manila and forced the nuns to abandon their convent. For more than a year they found refuge in a Franciscan monastery outside of the city, and upon their return, "we found the convent quite destroyed."[2] The British had demolished wooden partitions dividing the nuns' cells and had stolen the convent's bells. In her letter to King Charles III of Spain—via the viceroy in Mexico—Sor Juana indicated that it was essential that the monastery receive the Crown's yearly donation.

On March 26, 1765, the king provided a response: he knew of the nuns' travails and promised to send his continued support.[3] The British never managed to take over the entire Philippine archipelago, but their occupation of Manila and the major port of Cavite exposed a chink in Spain's armor, foretelling the unraveling of the Spanish Empire.

It would not be until the end of the nineteenth century, however, that the nuns would document the end of Spanish control of the Philippines. In 1898 Sor Amalia de la Presentación put ink to paper in a text called "Relación de la guerra de los Yankees en Manila" (Account of the war of the Yankees in Manila). Although this topic is beyond the scope of this book, Sor Amalia's fifty-two-page account offers a treasure trove of information for anyone interested in the Spanish-American War in the Philippines. Writing from a first-person perspective, Sor Amalia narrates how the nuns were forced to evacuate Intramuros for fear of native insurgent forces. For several months during the spring of 1898 the nuns lived in a rented house in the area of Sampaloc outside of Manila. They occupied the upper floor of a two-storied building, with the lower floor converted into barracks for Spanish volunteer soldiers. The nuns, obviously loyal to the Spanish Crown, feared the "Yankees" but were much more preoccupied by the "the barbarous violations of the insurgents."[4] Due to the proximity of the insurgents, the nuns were moved back to their convent during the summer of 1898, only to witness the bombing of Manila by the US Navy. In mid-August the "General Yankee" (Brigadier General Arthur MacArthur) marched into the city with his brigade. Later that year, in December 1898, the United States annexed the entire Philippine archipelago from Spain and paid a token $20 million. Sor Amalia's account ends here, but the United States waged war against Tagalog insurgents that would continue until 1902. After the Spanish-American War the United States remained in the archipelago until the Japanese invaded the islands in 1942.

In her letter to the nuns in Toledo, Sor Concordia laments the loss of life within the nunnery itself during World War II. She also explains how she and her spiritual sisters were spared some of the brutal savagery inflicted on the local population. Apparently a young Filipina woman, fluent in Japanese, who lived in front of the convent convinced one of the Japanese commanders to take care of the nuns. During the early years of Japanese occupation, he did help provide the nuns with food and supplies. The "guards" that he stationed in the outer rooms of the convent, however, were one of the reasons that Allied forces bombed the convent, since they believed that it was fully occupied by the Japanese. The situation for the nuns themselves became dire after February 3, 1945, when troops under General Douglas MacArthur liberated thousands of prisoners from the confines of the University of Santo Thomas. Seeking revenge, the Japanese ravaged Manila: they burned houses, shot innocent people on the streets, and rounded up more than a thousand people into Fort of Santiago, where they doused them with gasoline "and dispatched them to the other world."[5] The terrified nuns had wanted to leave their convent months earlier, but their male superiors had ordered them to stay put. They believed that the nuns would be safe from the bombs on the lower levels of the cloister under the stone staircase, and surely the Virgin Mary would take care of them.

Ultimately, the thick walls of their monastery did not save the nuns. On February 23, 1945, the assault on Manila became so intense that the group had to escape the burning wreckage of their convent through broken windows. Separated into two groups, the women were assaulted on all sides: Japanese suicidal "guards" sprayed them with machine-gun fire, relentless artillery rounds destroyed the walls around them, and a massive fire engulfed the walls of their one-time sanctuary. Not all the women and their faithful servants made it out of the building alive. All told, ten nuns and three servants died during those last days of the war. The American troops were surprised to find the nuns of Santa Clara, since they believed that the convent had been evacuated. According to Sor Concordia, the troops quickly gave them food and water and transferred the seriously wounded nuns to the American military hospital. The American military also filmed images of the nuns in part of a newsreel called "Battle for Manila."[6]

After World War II the nuns relocated their community to Quezon City, Philippines. Miraculously, one of the only items salvaged from the rubble of their previous home was the tomb of their founder, Sor Jerónima de la Asunción, and two of her cofounders, most likely Sor Ana de Cristo and Sor María Magdalena de la Cruz.[7] There are currently about twenty-three nuns at the new location on Katipunan Avenue in Quezon City. Behind the chapel they have respectfully displayed the remains of Sor Jerónima and two of her original cofounders. Although the walls of her cloister were destroyed by war, the spirit of Sor Jerónima's foundation remains alive with her successors.

Notes

INTRODUCTION

1. For this study I am defining the Far East as China, Japan, North and South Korea, the Philippines, and other, smaller countries in eastern Asia. Although it was not technically in the Far East according to this definition, in 1610 the Portuguese founded the Augustinian Convent of Santa Monica in Goa, India. On the convent in Goa, see Coates, *Convicts and Orphans*, 167–74.
2. For a review of recent scholarship that depicts the early modern world as the first global era, see Wiesner-Hanks, "Early Modern Gender." On the global early modern world, spanning roughly from 1400 to 1800, see Parker, *Global Interactions*.
3. The folios are labeled 1, 1v, 2, 2v, and so on until the last folio, 228.
4. Huerta, *Estado geográfico*, 41.
5. All quotes from Sor Ana de Cristo come from the manuscript *Historia de nuestra santa madre Jerónima de la Asunción*, located at the Archivo del Monasterio de Santa Isabel de los Reyes in Toledo, Spain (hereafter Sor Ana, AMSIRT), fol. 195. All English translations of the manuscript are mine.
6. Donahue, "Wondrous Words," 108–16.
7. Congregatio Causis Sanctorum, *Manilen, Beatificationis et Canonizationis*. Ruano is also the author of *Jerónima de la Asunción*.
8. Quesada, *Exemplo de todas las virtudes*; Letona, *Perfecta religiosa*.

CHAPTER 1

1. Sor Ana, AMSIRT, fol. 80.
2. Ibid.
3. Canabal Rodríguez, "Los conventos."
4. Martínez Caviró, *El Monasterio*.
5. Kagan, *Urban Images*, 200.
6. On *The Burial of the Count of Orgaz*, see Schroth, "Burial."

7. Martínez Caviró, "El arte mudéjar"; Villegas Díaz, "Santa Isabel de los Reyes"; Canabal Rodríguez, "Los conventos," 474–79; and Moreno Nieto, *Toledo oculto*, 109.

8. Sor Ana named this street and church when interviewed in 1631, a year after Jerónima's death. "Proceso ejecutado," Archivio Segreto Vaticano, Vatican City, (hereafter ASV), fol. 30v.

9. Sor Ana, AMSIRT, fol. 6v.

10. "Carta de dote de doña Ieronima Yáñez: Y en la religión llamada sor Gerónima de la Assumpción," August 8, 1571, AMSIRT.

11. "Proceso ejecutado," ASV, fol. 31v.

12. Sor Ana, AMSIRT, fol. 16. Some of Sor Jerónima's physical symptoms are reminiscent of modern-day eating disorders. On fasting and religious women, see Bell, *Holy Anorexia*; and Bynum, *Holy Feast*.

13. Saint Clare wrote the First Rule in 1253 and the modified Second Rule was legislated by Pope Urban IV in 1261. For a discussion of strict observant reforms of the Franciscan order in Spain, see Roest, *Order and Disorder*, 202–8.

14. Alison Weber's recent edited collection on devout laywomen emphasizes the myriad of experiences of religious laywomen who lived outside the cloister. Weber, *Devout Laywomen*.

15. *Canons and Decrees*, 220–21 (twenty-fifth session, December 3–4, 1563, chapter 5).

16. The first female convent in Mexico City was the Convento de Nuestra Señora de la Concepción. On Mexico as a stepping stone to Asia, see Morales, "De la utopía."

17. In vague terms Sor Ana records that several foundations fell through. The only one that she names was the discalced Convent of Corpus Christi, but I have been unable to find more information about what happened to that convent. See Sor Ana, AMSIRT, fol. 21, 21v, 31v, and 106v; and Quesada, *Exemplo de todas las virtudes*, 207.

18. Sor Ana, AMSIRT, fol. 21v.

19. Sor Ana says he was visiting a family member; AMSIRT, fol. 33v. Quesada says a cousin; *Exemplo de todas las virtudes*, 339. Ruano says a sister; *Jerónima de la Asunción*, 26.

20. Sor Ana describes their visit to the convent in Toledo: AMSIRT, fol. 54–54v. See also Letona, *Perfecta religiosa*, 39r; Ruano, *Jerónima de la Asunción*, 27; and Sánchez Fuertes, "La madre," 382–83.

21. On Sotelo's important role in the Japanese embassy, see Barrón Soto, "La participación."

22. Sor Ana, AMSIRT, fol. 115.

23. Ibid., fol. 23v.

24. Sales Colín, "El colegio."

25. The excerpt and translation is from Cruz, "Servir a Dios," 201. Cruz consulted the will of Pedro de Chaves and Ana de Vera, August 27, 1612, Manila, in Archivo Franciscano Ibero-Oriental, Madrid, Spain (hereafter AFIO), 47.

26. Santiago, "First Filipino capellanías," 423.

27. On the diverse reasons for convent patronage, see Atienza López, *Tiempos de conventos*, 266–74.

28. Moreno Nieto, *Toledo oculto*, 109.

29. Cruz, "Servir a Dios," 202; AFIO, 47.

30. Weber, "Saint Teresa's Problematic Patrons."

31. Sor Ana, AMSIRT, fol. 70.

32. See Feros, *Kingship and Favoritism*, 249; and Sánchez, *Empress*, 14. Tanya J. Tiffany notes that Velázquez later held these positions under King Philip IV; *Diego Velázquez's Early Paintings*, 54.

33. On the powerful women of the Mendoza family, see Nader, *Power and Gender*.

34. Sor Ana, AMSIRT, fol. 21v.

35. Ibid., fol. 23, 114v.

36. Magdalena Sánchez notes that Queen Margaret "could use her affectionate relationship with Philip III, her private access to him, and their blood ties to sway his opinion on given matters." *Empress*, 49.

37. The examples are numerous but, to name a few, Philip III sought out the Augustinian nun Mariana de San José for political and spiritual advice, and Philip IV carried on a long correspondence with the Franciscan nun Sor María de Jesús de Agreda (1602–1665). See Sánchez, *Empress*, 24; and *María de Jesús de Ágreda*.

38. Sánchez, *Empress*, 5.

39. Isabella Clara Eugenia of Austria (the daughter of King Philip II) became a Franciscan tertiary in 1621. Although not a nun, Empress María of Austria (Philip III's aunt) lived with the Discalced Franciscans in Madrid until her death in 1603. Her daughter Margaret of the Cross, on the other hand, entered that convent as a nun in 1588 and remained there until she died in 1633. According to Stephen Haliczer, "But it was Margaret of the Cross, of all the pious and mystical women of his kingdom, who was able to exert the greatest influence over Philip III." *Between Exaltation and Infamy*, 242; see also Sánchez, "Pious and Political Images," 91; Sánchez, *Empress*, 78–80; and Sánchez, "Where the Palace and Convent Met."

40. Sánchez, *Empress*, 13.

41. Sor Ana, AMSIRT, fol. 34v.

42. Ibid., fol. 23.

43. On these painted wooden sculptures, see Bray, *Sacred Made Real*, 15–71, 91–102; and McKim-Smith, "Spanish Polychrome Sculpture."

44. Most likely she sent alms to the Hospital de la Misericordia and the Hospital de San Nicolás. Sor Luisa de Jesús describes how she and Mariana de Jesús worked at these hospitals in an account within Sor Ana's manuscript, AMSIRT, fol. 196 and 204v.

45. On gift exchange in the context of the Descalzas Reales, see Sánchez, "Where the Palace and Convent Met," 75–77.

46. Arenal and Schlau, *Untold Sisters*, 8.

47. Sor Ana, AMSIRT, fols. 49–50. See also Martínez Caviró, *El Monasterio*, 48.

48. On the Immaculist movement and debate in Seville, see Stratton, *Immaculate Conception*, 3 and 73–87; Bray, *Sacred Made Real*, 53, 91; Cuadriello, "Theopolitical Visualization," 133–34; and Tiffany, *Diego Velázquez's Early Paintings*, 28–29.

49. The work was commissioned between 1616 and 1617. The artist who created this sculpture remains unknown. For a discussion of San Juan de los Reyes and the debates with Dominicans on the Immaculate Conception, see Martínez Caviró, *El Monasterio*, 38–48.

50. See Webster, "Shameless Beauty"; and Webster, *Art and Ritual*, 118–21.

51. Sor Ana, AMSIRT, fol. 49.

52. Cuadriello, "Theopolitical Visualization," 123.

53. For the definitive study on de los Ríos, see Crossley, *Hernando de los Ríos Coronel*.

54. Nueva Segovia was a new diocese in the north of Luzon, originally based in Lal-lo but now in Vigan.

55. Sor Ana, AMSIRT, fol. 55.

56. He carried his own letter with him that stated the details of the will and also mentioned another donation of stone houses by doña María de Jesús. See Archivo General de Indias, Seville, Spain (hereafter AGI), Filipinas, 5, N.213. The letter is also transcribed in Sánchez Fuertes, "Los Monasterios," 78–79.

57. For the map of Luzon, see AGI, Filipinas, 6.

58. See Crossley, *Hernando de los Ríos Coronel*, chaps. 5 and 8 and pages 187–89.

59. Ruano, *Jerónima de la Asunción*, 29; Sánchez Fuertes, "Impresos Franciscanos," 317–19.

60. Sánchez Fuertes, "Los Monasterios," 53.

61. Sor Ana, AMSIRT, fol. 55. The exact dates for these permissions are somewhat confusing. According to Ruano, on February 29, 1620, Fray José de Santa María had his permission to take the nuns in Spanish fleet to New Spain; *Jerónima de la Asunción*, 80; AGI, Filipinas, 5, N.213. There is also a petition from Santa María apparently dated March 23, 1620, asking to take the nuns (see AGI, Filipinas, 85, N.40) but already on March 9, 1620, a royal decree had been issued to the Audiencia of Manila giving a license to found a nunnery there (AGI, Indiferente, 450, L.A6, fols. 37–37v). Sánchez Fuertes also reviews these dates and documents; "Los Monasterios," 53, 78–79.

62. Sor Ana, AMSIRT, fol. 55r.

63. The role of Hernando de los Ríos is discussed at length in the article I coauthored with John Newsome Crossley; Crossley and Owens, "First Nunnery."

64. Sor Ana, AMSIRT, fol. 81v.

65. The names and information regarding the other friar and servants are discussed in the next chapter.

66. Sor Ana, AMSIRT, fol. 66v. The convent was founded by doña María Suárez de Toledo (1437–1507), who was known as María la Pobre. Canabal Rodríguez, "Los conventos," 475.

67. Sor Ana, AMSIRT, fol. 79v.

68. The exact date of his death is unknown, although it appears to be in either 1623 or 1624. See "Memorial de Juan Gómez, testamentario de Fernando de los Ríos Coronel," AGI, Filipinas, 5, N.303.

69. Cómez Ramos, "Las casas."

70. Sor Ana often uses the term *imagen* (image) for sculptures, although at times also for paintings. Here most likely she was referring to a large sculpture of the Immaculate Conception. It is unclear if this "large room" was different from the convent choir. Sor Ana, AMSIRT, fol. 81v.

71. Sor Ana, AMSIRT, fol. 81v.

72. According to Colleen R. Baade, at least eight nun musicians were granted dowry waivers at the Convent of Santa Isabel de los Reyes in Toledo between 1600 and 1800; "Two Centuries," 4. See also, Baade, "Music: Convents."

73. Sor Ana, AMSIRT, fol. 82.

74. Ibid., fol. 82v.

75. In another curious instance, Sor Margarita de Cristo (from the convent in Cubas) swallowed some of Sor Jerónima's saliva to cure her sore throat. Ibid., fol. 82v.

76. For studies on the elaborate celebrations of Corpus Christi in the Americas, see Merrim, *Spectacular City*; and Dean, *Inka Bodies*. For an analysis of Sor Jerónima's visit to the Convent of Santa Clara during Corpus Christi, see Tiffany, "Portrait."

77. This quote comes from Mindy Nancarrow Taggard's study of nuns' experiences with printed portrait images, but I believe it can be applied in general to the reception of religious visions like that of Sor Jerónima. See Nancarrow Taggard, "17th-Century Spanish *Vida*," 35.

78. Sor Ana, AMSIRT, fol. 83v.

79. Brigstocke and Vélez, *En torno a Velázquez*, 78–81; Tiffany, *Diego Velázquez's Early Paintings*, 57, 171–72n42.

80. This was the first known canvas that he signed and dated (1620).

81. At that time the nuns at Santa Isabel handed over the painting to the Prado for the Exposición Franciscana, and Velázquez's signature was discovered during restoration. For a more complete discussion of this event, see Tiffany, *Diego Velázquez's Early Paintings*, 168n51.

82. For this and other examples, see ibid., 56–57.

83. The engraving included in Quesada's biography was by José Mota. On the engraving, see Donahue-Wallace, "Abused and Battered," 133–34.

84. The phrase above her head is "BONVUM ESTS PRESTOLARI CVM SILENTIO SALVTARE DEI," Lam. 3:26. For a translation, see Tiffany, *Diego Velázquez's Early Paintings*, 51. The phrase on the banderole is "SATIABOR DVM GLORIFICATVS FVERIT," Ps. 16:15; Tiffany, *Diego Velázquez's Early Paintings*, 51. The banderole was removed from one of the paintings when the Prado restored it. At the bottom of the portrait is a short description of the mission to the Philippines with the names of the Spanish nuns who accompanied Sor Jerónima. See Bray, *Sacred Made Real*, 122–25.

85. Herbert González Zymla has uncovered account ledgers from the Sevillian Convent of Santa Clara indicating a payment of 400 reales for "gastos extraordinarios" that he believes could have been used to pay Velázquez. "La fundación e historia," 221.

86. Tiffany, *Diego Velázquez's Early Paintings*, 57–58.

87. Balbina Martínez Caviró describes an altarpiece (in the chapel of the Hurtado de Mendoza) in Santa Isabel of Saint John the Baptist painted by Juan Sánchez Cotán (1560–1627). "El arte en los conventos," 514.

88. On the pedagogical possibilities of these images, see Sánchez Lora, *Mujeres*, 265. In her study on Carmelite nuns, Mindy Nancarrow Taggard lists some of these books: Francisco de Osuna's *Abecedario espiritual*, Juan de Avila's *Audi fili*, Luis de Granada's *Guía de pecadores*, and Pedro de Alcántara's *Tratado de oración y meditación*. See Nancarrow Taggard, "Picturing Intimacy," 105.

89. Sor Ana, AMSIRT, fol. 40. Quesada also discusses this painting in *Exemplo de todas las virtudes*, 660–61.

90. Revenga Domínguez, "El arte de la pintura."

91. Kasl, "Painters, Polychromy."

92. Sor Ana, AMSIRT, fol. 49.

93. Nancarrow Taggard, "Art and Alienation," 27.

94. In general, religious communities placed a high value on art (if not on the artists themselves). See Tiffany's reference to Pacheco, who received commissions from the Convent of Santa Clara in Seville; *Diego Velázquez's Early Paintings*, 58. In reference to early modern Italian convents Marilyn R. Dunn has noted, "The decorative enterprises of female convents were financed both by the patrimony of the religious community and by significant contributions from individual nuns who enjoyed private incomes from their families." Dunn, "Spiritual Philanthropists," 156. For an overview of conventual art in New Spain (the images of nun's shields and portraits of crowned nuns), see Perry, "Convents, Art, and Creole Identity."

95. Nancarrow Taggard, "Picturing Intimacy," 99–111; and Arenal and Schlau, *Untold Sisters*, 131–50.

96. Nancarrow Taggard, "Art and Alienation," 27.

97. For a recent study on early modern Hispanic women playwrights and their works, see Romero-Díaz and Vollendorf, *Women Playwrights*. On conventual theater in New Spain, see Lavrin, *Brides of Christ*, 327–31.

98. Normally a loa is a short introductory piece, used to praise important dignitaries or authorities before a longer play. In this case it appears to be a standalone work.

99. Arenal and Schlau, *Untold Sisters*, 13 and 148.

100. Felipe IV's first wife, Isabel de Borbón (1602–1644), was a great aficionado of theater and even acted in some plays held at court. See Romero-Díaz and Vollendorf, *Women Playwrights*, 14.

101. Sor Ana, AMSIRT, fols. 84–84v.

102. Arenal and Schlau cite the example of the two sisters Cecilia del Nacimiento and María de San Alberto, who composed theatrical productions set to music. *Untold Sisters*, 149.

103. Sor Ana, AMSIRT, fol. 85.

104. In the context of New Spain, Asunción Lavrin writes, "Those sisters with special abilities in music or singing were lovingly remembered in conventual chronicles." *Brides of Christ*, 159.

105. Sor Ana, AMSIRT, fol. 84v.

106. Lavrin, *Brides of Christ*, 24-25.

CHAPTER 2

1. On the reasons that Spain chose Acapulco as its base for the Manila galleons, see Sales Colín, *El movimiento*, 37-42, 52-62; and Phelan, *Hispanization*, 42-43.

2. For a discussion of the papal bulls, see Arias and Marrero-Fente, introduction, x-xi.

3. See O'Flanagan, *Port Cities*, 25, 47-49; and Schurz, *Manila Galleon*, 403-4.

4. See Burkholder, "Empire Beyond Compare," 131; and Lane, *Pillaging the Empire*, 18.

5. Herbert González Zymla identifies the second friar as Fray Francisco de San Bernardino, although it is unclear why his name was Fray Francisco de Granada on the passenger list; "La fundación e historia," 223. On the two male servants, see AGI, Contratación, 5374, N.6, June 15, 1620.

6. Sánchez Fuertes, "Los Monasterios," 53, 54.

7. González Zymla, "La fundación e historia," 222. He lists the original location of the document in the AGI, Contratación, 5538, but I have been unable to locate the source.

8. Ibid., 222n67.

9. In reference to white linen, Sor Ana explains that the nuns in Seville helped them sew the "ropa blanca" (household linens) for the journey since Sor Jerónima did not let them bring anything from Toledo. AMSIRT, fol. 82.

10. AGI, Contratación, 551. For a recent transcription of this document, see Sánchez Fuertes, "Los Monasterios," 86-87.

11. Pérez-Mallaína, *Spain's Men of the Sea*, 134; and Phillips, *Six Galleons*, 165.

12. Meléndez's main cargo consisted of wine to be sold in the New World; see González Zymla, "La fundación e historia," 223n. Sor Ana mentions that a Diego Meléndez from Seville (most likely the same person) helped them on their route from Veracruz to the capital; AMSIRT, fol. 86v.

13. Gónzalez Zymla, "La fundación e historia," 222. In 1634 General Juan de Benavides was sentenced to death for losing most of the fleet of New Spain and merchandise to the Dutch in 1628. Dominguez Ortiz, *Sociedad y mentalidad*, 51-70. Pérez-Mallaína, *El hombre frente al mar*, 123-24.

14. Gónzalez Zymla, "La fundación e historia," 224.

15. Sor Ana, AMSIRT, fols. 85–85v.

16. During the time period between 1580 and 1640 when the same Habsburg monarchs jointly ruled Spain and Portugal (although their empires remained officially separate), Portuguese mariners were quite common on Spanish ships. See Phillips, "Organization of Oceanic Empires."

17. For a recent study on secular women's experiences on Spanish ships, see Poska, *Gendered Crossings*, 59–84.

18. Phillips, *Six Galleons*, 153.

19. On this group of Capuchin nuns and their shipboard experiences, see Alba González, "Presencia de América en Toledo," 50.

20. Pérez-Mallaína, *Spain's Men of the Sea*, 135, 136; and Phillips, *Six Galleons*, 155–56.

21. Alba González, "Presencia de América en Toledo," part I, 54. All translations are mine.

22. Ibid., part I, 57–58.

23. Ibid., part I, 61–62.

24. Poole, *Our Lady of Guadalupe*, 23.

25. Boucher, "Frontier Era," 211.

26. Sor Ana, AMSIRT, fol. 85v.

27. Quesada, *Exemplo de todas las virtudes*, 391–92.

28. Sor Ana, AMSIRT, fol. 85v.

29. On the Spanish view of natives as children, see Elliott, *Empires of the Atlantic World*, 72.

30. Sor Ana, AMSIRT, fol. 85v.

31. Parker, *Global Interactions*, 163. See also Phillips, *Six Galleons*, 80.

32. Sor Ana, AMSIRT, fol. 86.

33. Gage, *Thomas Gage's Travels*, 25.

34. On deforestation in the Caribbean, see Parker, *Global Interactions*, 180, 165. It was after the signing of a peace treaty in 1660 with the Caribs that most of the remaining wilderness areas of Martinique and Guadeloupe were deforested. See Boucher, "Frontier Era," 212.

35. The term *doctrinero* was first applied to friars and then later to parish priests, who "indoctrinated" Amerindians in the Christian faith. See Elliott, *Empires of the Atlantic World*, 69; and Nesvig, "Indian Question," 66.

36. Burkholder, "Empire Beyond Compare," 127. Linda A. Curcio-Nagy cites the pre-Conquest population in the central valley of Mexico at twenty-five million. "Faith and Morals," 161.

37. Burkholder, "Empire Beyond Compare," 128.

38. See David Tavárez, *Invisible War*, 62–101. See also Lockhart, *Nahuas*, 201–60.

39. Wheat, *Atlantic Africa*, 221.

40. In one estimate, the African population of Mexico City was as high as 20 percent. See Curcio-Nagy, "Faith and Morals," 163–64. The first African slaves were brought to Mexico in 1520. See Burkholder, "Empire Beyond Compare," 124.

41. Curcio-Nagy, "Faith and Morals," 166.

42. Diego Panes was commissioned by Viceroy Matías de Gálvez y Gallardo to map the routes from Veracruz to Mexico (1783). For Panes's detailed description and maps of these routes, see *Descripción de los caminos*; and Vargas Matías, "El Camino Real de Veracruz."

43. Sor Ana, AMSIRT, fol. 87.

44. Ibid., fols. 87–87v.

45. Ibid., fol. 88.

46. Ibid., fol. 88v.

47. Ibid., fol. 89.

48. Friars or monks were part of the mendicant clergy, also known as regulars, who took vows of poverty and belonged to a religious community, such as Franciscans, Augustinians, or Dominicans. Many of them served as missionaries in the New World. Diocesan or secular clergy were not part of a religious order and instead answered to the bishop of their particular diocese.

49. Sor Ana, AMSIRT, fol. 89.

50. See Lundberg, "El clero indígena"; Morales, *Ethnic and Social Background*, 38–53; and Po-Chia Hsia, *World of Catholic Renewal*, 192.

51. We do know that Franciscan friars made use of native converts to help in the instruction of others. For an early example from the first half of the sixteenth century, see Lopes Don, *Bonfires of Culture*, 87; and Curcio-Nagy, "Faith and Morals," 156–57.

52. Losa, *La vida*. On López and Losa, see Bilinkoff, "Francisco Losa and Gregorio López."

53. "She gave them a good warning about this by citing examples of many people who had lost themselves and caused others to lose their haciendas and souls." Sor Ana, AMSIRT, fols. 88, 88v.

54. Villa-Flores, "On Divine Persecution," 242–43.

55. See Gerhard, *Guide to the Historical Geography*, 377.

56. According to Stafford Poole, "By the 1570's Guadalupe had become the principal point of entrance into Mexico City, and it was customary for important figures, such as arriving viceroys and archbishops, to tarry there while being met by reception committees from the city." *Our Lady of Guadalupe*, 50.

57. Sor Ana, AMSIRT, fols. 89–89v.

58. Much has been written on the history of the cult of Our Lady of Guadalupe. Among other works, see Lafaye, *Quetzalcoatl and Guadalupe*; Poole, *Our Lady of Guadalupe*; Brading, *Mexican Phoenix*; Watson Marrón, *El templo*; and Matovina, "Origins of the Guadalupe Tradition."

59. The Mexican scholar Arturo Rocha has compiled a facsimile edition of this text and other documents relating to the shrine of the Virgin of Guadalupe in the sixteenth century. Rocha, *Monumenta guadalupensia mexicana*.

60. This modernized quote is taken from Poole, *Our Lady of Guadalupe*, 69–70. For a full version of Philip's account, see Hakluyt, *Principal Navigations*, 6: 296–336. For the facsimile version from 1598, see Rocha, *Monumenta guadalupensia mexicana*, 76–85. Philip's account describes events occurring between 1567 and 1582.

61. The Chapel of the Pocito is aptly named for the well housed in the chapel; the water source was originally hot springs, renowned among the local indigenous populations for their healing powers. Later, during the sixteenth and seventeenth centuries, pilgrims drank the salty waters in hopes of miraculous cures. The springs were covered with a basic structure some time between 1648 and 1649, but it was not until the end of the eighteenth century that the Mexican architect Francisco Guerrero y Torres built the lavish baroque chapel that stands on the spot today. García Lascuráin, *Plano topográfico*, 32–33.

62. According to Brading, "As a Protestant, Philips was more impressed by a silver statue recently donated by a wealthy silver miner, Alonso de Villaseca, than by the simple painting of the Virgin which adorned the sanctuary." *Mexican Phoenix*, 2.

63. Fuchs, "English *Pícaro*," 61–62.

64. The Crown's Christianizing mission and the nexus between conversion and colonization are discussed in Rafael, *Contracting Colonialism*, 17–22.

65. Fray Bernardino de Sahagún's work, written between 1570 and 1582, directly cites the shrine of Guadalupe as occupying the same location as the previous Aztec temple dedicated to Tonantzin, mother of the gods. Sahagún, *Historia de las cosas*, 704–5.

66. For a discussion of the tensions between Franciscans and Dominicans regarding the Virgin of Guadalupe and her relationship to Tonantzin, see Zires, "Los mitos."

67. On Sor Ana's male counterparts, see Morales, "Native Encounter." Motolinía was one of the first Franciscan friars to arrive in Mexico (1524). He was part of the famous group known as the Twelve Apostles because they had walked barefoot all the way from Veracruz to the capital.

68. Poole, *Our Lady of Guadalupe*, 132. Matovina discusses the indigenous population living at Tepeyac, contradicting Stafford Poole's argument for the lack of indigenous devotion to the Guadalupe cult in Poole's more recent book, *The Guadalupan Controversies in Mexico*. See also Matovina, "Origins of the Guadalupe Tradition," 260.

69. Watson Marrón, *El templo*, 74–78.

70. Sor Ana, AMSIRT, fol. 89.

71. For a brief description of Mexico City, see Burkholder, "Empire Beyond Compare," 113; and for a longer study, see Merrim, *Spectacular City*, 13–47.

72. Gage, *Thomas Gage's Travels*, 71.

73. This was due to the lack of charitable donations and the harsh physical conditions of the damp location. See Muriel, *Conventos de monjas*, 212; and Amerlinck de Corsi and Ramos Medina, *Conventos de monjas*, 95.

74. "Memorial de fray José de Santa María al duque de Lerma para que se conceda licencia para fundar en Manila un monasterio de monjas," 1612, transcription of letter in Sánchez Fuertes, "Los Monasterios," 77–78.

75. Letona provides a list of the eight abbesses who served the Convent of Santa Clara in Manila before 1662, including Sor Leonora de San Buenaventura. The nurse María de los Angeles is not on the list. See Perfecta religiosa, n.p.

76. According to Angela Muñoz Fernández, it was common for religious communities to have one main devotional painting during the seventeenth century. She also explains that the Virgin Mary was commonly referred to with general titles such as la Concepción, la Esperanza, la Misericordia, la Asunción, and la Natividad. Muñoz Fernández, Acciones e intenciones, 61.

77. Sor Ana, AMSIRT, fol. 90v.

78. Quesada, Exemplo de todas las virtudes, 317.

79. Van Deusen, Global Indios, 8.

80. For a discussion of the beads and the sources, see Bieñko de Peralta, "Los impresos novohispanos," 221.

81. Sor Ana, AMSIRT, fol. 90.

82. On the China Poblana, see Myers, Neither Saints nor Sinners, 44–68; and Seijas, Asian Slaves, 8–31. For an Afro-Peruvian example of a donada, see van Deusen, Souls of Purgatory.

83. Sor Ana, AMSIRT, fol. 91.

84. See Lavrin, Brides of Christ, 32–33; Muriel, Conventos de monjas, 188; and Vetancurt, "Menologio Franciscano," 362–65.

85. Sor Ana, AMSIRT, fol. 91v.

86. Letona says that they left Mexico City on Ash Wednesday, which would have been February 24, 1621; Perfecta religiosa, book 1, 41v. Antonio de la Llave says it took them seventeen days to travel from the capital to the coast; Crónica de la provincia, fol. 1277. If this is true, and they left on February 24, they would have arrived in Acapulco on March 12. This corroborates Sor Ana's later statement that they spent a little less than a month in Acapulco, with a departure on April 6, 1621; AMSIRT, fol. 93v.

87. The road was also called the Camino de Acapulco or the Camino de Asia. For a description of the China Road and the port of Acapulco during the colonial period, see Schurz, Manila Galleon, 371–87; and Serrera, "El camino de China."

88. For a published transcription of this account, see Herrera y Montemayor, "Viaje," 2; my translation.

89. Daza mentions these materials in his description of Juana's miraculous beads. Historia, vida y milagros, chapter 10, 42v.

90. Sor Ana, AMSIRT, fol. 92.

91. On medicinal powers attributed to coral in medieval times, see Lev and Amar, Practical Materia Medica, 153–55.

92. See, for example, Cara Feinberg, "The Placebo Phenomenon," *Harvard Magazine*, January–February 2013, http://harvardmagazine.com/2013/01/the-placebo-phenomenon.

93. Sor Ana, AMSIRT, fol. 93.

94. Pita thread (*hilo de pita*) is generally made from the inner part of the agave plant. For this definition of pita, see the online version of the *Real Academia Española Diccionario de Autoridades*, vol. 5, 1737, http://web.frl.es/DA.html.

95. Sor Ana, AMSIRT, fol. 92v.

96. For a discussion on the metaphor of Mexico as a spring-like paradise in Creole texts, see More, *Baroque Sovereignty*, 66–67.

97. Jorge Cañizares-Esguerra has also studied the trope of Spanish American nuns as flowers in God's garden. *Puritan Conquistadors*, 141, 200.

98. See Slack, "*Chinos* in New Spain"; Barceló Quintal, "Acapulco, frontera comercial"; and Schurz, *Manila Galleon*, 374, 381.

99. Sor Ana states they set sail on Holy Tuesday, which was April 6, 1620. Letona sets the date as April 1, 1620; *Perfecta religiosa*, 41. Archival research at the AGI reveals that Sor Ana was correct: "Pago a Diego de Rivera, maestre de la nao San Andrés que vino de Nueva España en 1621. Salió de Acapulco el 6 de abril de 1621 y llegó a Cavite el 26 de octubre," AGI, Cont. 1212. See chapter 3 for more information on this ship and a possible companion vessel.

100. See Crossley, *Hernando de los Ríos Coronel*, 81.

101. Sor Ana writes, "We were there for close to a month"; AMSIRT, fol. 93v. But Quesada and Letona both say they spent ten days in Acapulco. Quesada, *Exemplo de todas las virtudes*, 399; and Letona, *Perfecta religiosa*, book 1, 41v.

102. Quesada notes, "Well, there are very few men of moderate means (from what I have seen in New Spain and on these Islands) that do not venerate her holy image; all of them trying to obtain one of her original or touched beads." *Exemplo de todas las virtudes*, 550.

CHAPTER 3

1. In this quote he was referring to the return trip eastward from Manila to Acapulco. Gemelli Careri, *Voyage*, 131.

2. The Spaniards first called these islands the Ladrones but then changed the name to the Marianas in 1668 to commemorate Queen Mariana, the widow of Philip IV of Spain. Magellan first sighted the archipelago, which includes the island of Guam, in 1521.

3. For a concise overview of the perils of the Manila galleon route, see Williams, "Tapping the Orient."

4. Barceló Quintal notes that people in New Spain used the terms "Galeón de Manila" or "Nao de China," while those who lived in Manila referred to the ships as the "Galeón de Acapulco." Barceló Quintal, "Acapulco, frontera comercial," 368.

5. For an assessment of the currents and winds that affected the Manila galleons, see García et al., "Atmospheric Circulation Changes."

6. According to William J. McCarthy, "Vessels became the colony's most important product until the expansion of sugar and tobacco production in the late eighteenth century." See McCarthy, "Yards at Cavite," 155.

7. Most of the goods came from China and India, but some also came from many other places, such as the Philippines itself, Ceylon, India, Burma, Japan, Cambodia, Siam, and the Moluccas. See Buschmann, Slack, and Tuelle, *Navigating the Spanish Lake*, 26; Gasch-Tomás, "Asian Silk"; Barceló Quintal, "Acapulco, frontera comercial," 362; and Yuste López, *El comercio de la Nueva España*, 25–27, 71.

8. See Seijas, *Asian Slaves*, 1; and Slack, "*Chinos* in New Spain."

9. On the goods transported to Manila, see Sales Colín, "Las cargazones"; and Yuste López, *El comercio de la Nueva España*, 71. On the silver trade, see Flynn and Giraldez, "Born with a 'Silver Spoon.'"

10. Tatiana Seijas's *Asian Slaves* is a notable exception. Research on the Manila galleons is also somewhat limited. The classic study of the Manila galleon route is Schurz, *Manila Galleon*; early essays on the galleons have been compiled in Flynn, Giraldez, and Sobredo, *European Entry into the Pacific*; and for the most recent full-length study, see Giraldez, *Age of Trade*.

11. According to Quesada, there was only one ship on that voyage, the *nao San Andrés*. It was commandeered by the *general* of the armada, don Jerónimo de Valenzuela. *Exemplo de todas las virtudes*, 399. See also Sor Ana, AMSIRT, fol. 93v; and AGI, Cont-1212.

12. This imaginary longitude was fixed by a series of papal bulls in 1493–1494. In short, Spain gained rights to new lands discovered west of the line and Portugal those to the east.

13. Schurz, *Manila Galleon*, 20.

14. Urdaneta is famous for finding the *tornaviaje*, or eastern return route to Acapulco.

15. See Crossley, *Hernando de los Ríos Coronel*, 8; García et al., "Atmospheric Circulation," 2437–38; and Schurz, *Manila Galleon*, 280–83.

16. For example, the Dominican friar Domingo Fernández Navarrete describes how in 1647 his galleon landed at Lampon, on the eastern coast of Luzon. From there it was an arduous four-day overland journey to Manila. Fernández Navarrete, *Travels*, 48.

17. Sor Ana, AMSIRT, fol. 93v.

18. Giraldez, *Age of Trade*, 132.

19. Sor Ana, AMSIRT, fol. 93v.

20. Ibid., fol. 95v.

21. These were the latrines for the Atlantic runs, but it appears the Manila galleons had a similar setup. See Giraldez, *Age of Trade*, 121; and Pérez-Mallaína, *Spain's Men of the Sea*, 140.

22. Sor Ana, AMSIRT, fol. 93v.

23. For an overview of these naval positions, see Phillips, *Six Galleons*, 119–29; and Giraldez, *Age of Trade*, 137–39. Archival documents from the AGI also refer to Valenzuela as "general de la armada" and Rivera as "maestre": "Parece que parte en 1621 una armada a Filipinas a cargo del general don Gerónimo de Valenzuela," AGI, Cont-904; and "Pago a Diego de Rivera, maestre de la nao San Andrés que vino de Nueva España en 1621. Salió de Acapulco el 6 de abril de 1621 y llegó a Cavite el 26 de octubre," AGI, Cont-1212.

24. The viceroy of New Spain made the decision to allow the nuns and Franciscan friars to travel that year. Sor Ana, AMSIRT, fol. 91. Huerta specifies twenty-four Franciscan friars. *Estado geográfico*, 36.

25. Quesada, *Exemplo de todas las virtudes*, 399.

26. Giraldez, *Age of Trade*, 139.

27. On the sacralization of space, see Coster and Spicer, *Sacred Space*. For a study on French "floating convents," see Keller-Lapp, "Floating Cloisters."

28. See Pérez-Mallaína, *Spain's Men of the Sea*, 182–83; and Haring, *Trade and Navigation*, 219.

29. For information on epidemics and immunity in colonial Philippines, see Newson, *Conquest and Pestilence*, 20–23; on epidemics in Spanish America, see Pérez-Mallaína, *Spain's Men of the Sea*, 182–83; on diseases introduced into the Portuguese seaborne empire, see Russell-Wood, *World on the Move*, 119–22; and on the ravaging effects of smallpox and other epidemics in North America, see Steele, *English Atlantic*, 253–59.

30. Allen, *European Slave Trading*, 52.

31. For definitions of amoebic and bacillary dysentery, see Kiple, *Cambridge Historical Dictionary*, 19–21, 43–44.

32. Fernández Navarrete, *Travels*, 38.

33. Giraldez, *Age of Trade*, 134.

34. Some exceptions to this rule did exist. Tatiana Seijas has unearthed documents regarding the lucrative business of keeping bodies on the return trip back to Mexico to be buried in hallowed ground in Acapulco. *Asian Slaves*, 80.

35. Gemelli Careri, *Voyage*, 163.

36. Phillips, *Six Galleons*, 186–87.

37. Sor Ana, AMSIRT, fol. 94.

38. Breast cancer was quite common in early modern convents of nuns. See Owens, "Cloister as Therapeutic Space."

39. María Rosa, *Journey*, 64.

40. Much has been written on the good death. For a case of traveling nuns, see Owens, "Nun's Account"; and for mendicant friars, see Lavrin, "Los espacios de la muerte."

41. On healing in Mexican convents, see Salazar Simarro and Owens, "Cloistered Women in Health Care."

42. Sor Ana, AMSIRT, fol. 94.

43. Ibid., fol. 94v.

44. Ibid.

45. The medicinal qualities of coral are discussed in the previous chapter.

46. Sor Ana, AMSIRT, fol. 94v. Fire on board ships was a perennial problem and greatly feared.

47. Equating the image of a black man with the devil was common in nuns' writings. See Weber, "Saint Teresa, Demonologist," 175.

48. Sor Ana, AMSIRT, fol. 95.

49. Davidson, "Negro Slave Control," 241.

50. On the calculation of African slaves brought to Spanish America, see Wheat, *Atlantic Africa*, 12. See also the Trans-Atlantic Slave Trade Database, http://slave voyages.org/assessment/estimates. For an overview of numbers of Africans and persons of African descent in New Spain, see Bennett, *Africans in Colonial Mexico*, 1; and Bennett, *Colonial Blackness*, 4–5.

51. Seijas, *Asian Slaves*, 84–89.

52. Pérez-Mallaína, *Spain's Men of the Sea*, 38–40; Klein and Vinson, *African Slavery*, 14; and Kirk and Rivett, introduction, 19–20.

53. Crossley, *Hernando de los Ríos Coronel*, 176; Seijas, *Asian Slaves*, 84, 85; and AGI Filipinas, 27, N.121.F.698 (1621).

54. Pérez-Mallaína, *Spain's Men of the Sea*, 164–66.

55. According to de los Ríos, "Many sailors—and even others, who should furnish a good example—take slave women and keep them as concubines. He [de los Ríos] knew a certain prominent official who carried with him fifteen of these women; and some were delivered of children by him, while others were pregnant, which made a great scandal." Quoted from Hernando de los Ríos Coronel, "Reforms needed in Filipinas," in Blair and Robertson, *Philippine Islands*, vol. 18. See also Seijas, *Asian Slaves*, 79; Crossley, *Hernando de los Ríos Coronel*, 81, 82, 155; Giraldez, *Age of Trade*, 135.

56. Seijas, *Asian Slaves*, 79.

57. Catarina de San Juan later gained her freedom in Mexico and made a name for herself as a popular saint. Ibid., 15.

58. Sor Ana, AMSIRT, fol. 94v.

59. Williams, "Tapping the Orient," 46; Giraldez, *Age of Trade*, 152; and Schurz, *Manila Galleon*, 335.

60. See McCarthy, "Yards at Cavite," 156; and Williams, "Tapping the Orient," 46–47.

61. Giraldez, *Age of Trade*, 140–42.

62. For a description of weather-related wrecks, see ibid., 128–31.

63. According to Giuseppe Marcocci, oceanic travel created a space ripe for religious conversion and repentance among sailors. "Saltwater Conversion," 246.

64. Sor Ana, AMSIRT, fol. 95. The belief in the power of Juana de la Cruz's rosary beads continued at least into the next century. For instance, when a group of Capuchin nuns left Spain in 1710 to travel to Lima, Peru, the mother abbess describes how she

tossed some "authentic beads from Saint Juana" into the sea to obtain favorable weather. María Rosa, *Journey*, 101.

65. Sor Ana, AMSIRT, fol. 95.

66. Pope Urban VII beatified the Nagasaki martyrs as a group in 1627, and they were canonized in 1862. See Conover, "Saintly Biography"; and Ellis, *They Need Nothing*, 39–46. See also Gil, *Hidalgos y samurais*, 69–78.

67. Breen and Williams, introduction, 1.

68. Japanese Christians in Manila settled in a district called Dilao. According to de los Ríos, in 1619 there was a population of two thousand Japanese living in Manila. Cited in Giraldez, *Age of Trade*, 106.

69. See Barrón Soto, "La participación"; Ellis, *They Need Nothing*, 47–53; and Gil, *Hidalgos y samurais*, 384–425.

70. On August 25, 1624, Sotelo was burned at the stake in Ōmura, north of Nagasaki; and Quesada, who had been hung by his feet from gallows, died after five days, on June 7, 1634, in Osaka.

71. Quesada, *Exemplo de todas las virtudes*, 404. For departure and arrival dates, see "Pago a Diego de Rivera, maestre de la nao San Andrés que vino de Nueva España en 1621. Salió de Acapulco el 6 de abril de 1621 y llegó a Cavite el 26 de octubre," AGI, Cont-1212.

72. For maps of religious parishes on Luzon, see Phelan, *Hispanization*, 174–76. See also Costa, "Episcopal Jurisdiction," 44; and "Philip II to Damariñas," Aranjuez, April 27, 1594, in Blair and Robertson, *Philippine Islands*, vol. 9.

73. Most scholars attribute this first bilingual catechism to the Franciscan Juan de Plasencia. Plasencia, *Doctrina christiana*. See Sánchez Fuertes, "Impresos Franciscanos," 311–16.

74. Phelan, "Prebaptismal Instruction," 36–37.

75. Giraldez, *Age of Trade*, 78.

76. See Rafael, *Contracting Colonialism*, on the intricate links between language and conversion in Tagalog colonial society. Rafael also comments in depth on the Tagalog social structure (138–46).

77. On the Spaniards' justification for native tribute and labor, see ibid., 156–60; Phelan, *Hispanization*, 93–104; and Ellis, *They Need Nothing*, 142.

78. Horacio de la Costa notes, "During the decade 1624–1634, for instance, there were only sixty lay Spaniards in the islands who resided outside the cities of Manila and Cebu." "Episcopal Jurisdiction," 55.

79. Sor Ana, AMSIRT, fol. 95v. The Portuguese also commonly used slave labor to carry hammocks. In the case of Brazil, "A hammock (*rede*) or litter of fibre or cotton net could be slung from a single bamboo borne on the shoulders of two slaves and with a cloth thrown over the pole to conceal the occupant." Russell-Wood, *World on the Move*, 52. The Chinese tradition of the sedan chair was also present in Manila. The early Spanish chronicler Antonio de Morga describes the arrival of three Chinese dignitaries in 1603: "They went straight in chairs carried

on men's shoulders, very curiously made of ivory and fine woods and gilding, to the royal buildings of the High Court." *Philippine Islands*, 217.

80. On domestic labor in the Philippines, the Jesuit Alonso Sánchez wrote in 1603 that natives "act as bearers and oarsmen for *encomenderos* and missionaries, for there are no pack animals here, and so they must perforce be our beasts of burden." Quoted in Giraldez, *Age of Trade*, 77. See also Newson, *Conquest and Pestilence*, 171.

81. The Negritos (sometimes referred to as Zambales) were of Australoid descent and arrived on the Philippine archipelago some five to six thousand years ago. They mostly lived in the highlands but were notorious for conducting headhunting raids on Pampangans, who in turn helped the Spaniards in retaliatory and punitive expeditions. See Newson, *Conquest and Pestilence*, 55, 171–72.

82. By labeling the Negritos of Luzon and the *moros* (Muslims) of the south as infidels, the Spaniards justified their enslavement. See Seijas, *Asian Slaves*, 47, 48; and Phelan, *Hispanization*, 17, 94, 140–43.

83. For a detailed discussion on the Spaniards' justification for slavery in the Philippines, including the lucrative business of buying and selling human chattel in local and foreign markets, see Seijas, *Asian Slaves*, 32–49.

84. Sor Ana, AMSIRT, fol. 96.

85. Rafael, *Contracting Colonialism*, 161.

86. Spaniards allowed the indigenous elite to keep their slaves up until the early 1700s. Seijas, *Asian Slaves*, 46.

87. See Brewer, *Shamanism, Catholicism and Gender Relations*, 120–21.

88. Sor Ana, AMSIRT, fol. 96.

89. Ibid.

90. The convent as such did not exist when the nuns arrived in Manila, but since Sor Ana was writing her narration in retrospect (sometime between 1623 and 1626), she added this to her description.

91. Marcocci, "Saltwater Conversion," 238.

92. For this quote and examples of African women's resistance to slavery in New Spain, see McKnight, "Blasphemy as Resistance," esp. 235. For a more general overview of resistance and rebellion, see Klein and Vinson, *African Slavery*, 165–92.

93. On translation of Christian doctrine and conversion of Tagalog natives, see Rafael, *Contracting Colonialism*, 23–54.

CHAPTER 4

1. Sor Ana, AMSIRT, fol. 96v.

2. Quesada, *Exemplo de todas las virtudes*, 417–18.

3. Phelan, *Hispanization*, 32.

4. For the years 1565–1570 Newson puts the population of Manila at forty-three thousand. *Conquest and Pestilence*, 256. Tatiana Seijas estimates the population

to be about forty thousand. Seijas also notes, "By the 1620s, the city had 8,000 indigenous slaves and 2,000 foreign slaves, in addition to an untold number of Muslim slaves." *Asian Slaves*, 34–35.

5. For a description of the founding of the city and the previous local rulers (Rajamora and Rajamatanda), see Morga, *Philippine Islands*, 18, 19.

6. Irving, *Colonial Counterpoint*, 19.

7. For a firsthand account of this trade, see Bobadilla, "Relation of the Filipinas Islands" (1640). According to Bobadilla, "There are twenty thousand Sangleys or Chinese, who practice all the arts needed in a community; and every year they pay nine escudos and six reals of tribute," n.p.

8. Irving, *Colonial Counterpoint*, 37.

9. Seijas, *Asian Slaves*, 37.

10. Dissension within convents was not uncommon. For a fascinating case of conflict among nuns and with their prelates in Mexico, see Chowning, *Rebellious Nuns*.

11. Sor Ana, AMSIRT, fol. 96v.

12. Sor Ana names the first novice as doña Ana Enríquez. AMSIRT, fol. 97v.

13. "Patente de fray Diego de Otalora, comisario de la Nueva España, a sor Jerónima de la Asunción," February 23, 1621, Biblioteca Nacional de Antropología e Historia de México, Fondo Franciscano, Mexico City, vol. 100, fols. 65v–66v.

14. Sor Ana, AMSIRT, fols. 101v–102. Most likely Sor Ana was referring to Saint Benedict the Moor (1526–1589), but it is unclear who the second Franciscan was. Perhaps she was referring more generally to Saint Augustine of Hippo (354–430), although he was the founder of the Augustinians.

15. Sánchez Fuertes, "La madre," 381.

16. Sor Ana, AMSIRT, fol. 100.

17. Ibid. Captain Méndez also donated 7,000 *ducados* to help with construction of the convent and church. For more information on Méndez and other donors, see Sánchez Fuertes, "Los Monasterios," 59–62, 93–94.

18. For an overview of Sor Jerónima's battles with the provincial Fray Juan Bautista and subsequent religious and secular authorities in Manila, see Quesada, *Exemplo de todas las virtudes*, 411–45. See also Sánchez Fuertes, "Los Monasterios," 55–68; and Sánchez Fuertes, "La madre," 387–96.

19. For example, on August 1, 1623, Sor Jerónima wrote a letter to the king of Spain asking for his support in these desires to follow the First Rule. In her missive she also specifically mentions the lack of support from the new provincial, Fray Juan Bautista, who "does not like the established norms and prefers that we should have properties against what is prescribed in the First Rule of Saint Clare." English version of letter quoted from Ruano, *Jerónima de la Asunción*, 85; AGI, Filipinas, 85, N.54. A copy of Sor Jerónima's letter to the Real Audiencia of Manila (1623) can be found in Sor Ana's manuscript, AMSIRT, fols. 157–58. I have not located Sor Jerónima's letters to Venido and Montemayor, but we know from their responses that she wrote to them.

20. "Patente de Fray Juan Venido," June 18, 1624, Biblioteca Nacional de Antropología e Historia de México, Fondo Franciscano, Mexico City, vol. 100, fols. 62–63. For an English translation of another letter from Venido, dated July 18, 1624, see Ruano, *Jerónima de la Asunción*, 88–90.

21. See Díaz, *Indigenous*.

22. For an English translation of the letter, see Ruano, *Jerónima de la Asunción*, 95–96; AGI, Filipinas, 85, N.62.

23. Fray Alonso Montemayor held the position of commissary general of New Spain from 1622 to 1627. In that role he was directly responsible for the Franciscan Order in New Spain, New Mexico, the Philippines, and Japan. The only other authority higher than him was the commissary general of Indies (Fray Juan Venido), who was in charge of all the religious orders in the New World. For his four letters to the nuns, see Sor Ana, AMSIRT, fols. 152–56v.

24. See Congregatio Causis Sanctorum, *Manilen, Beatificationis et Canonizationis*, 43–45, for a transcription of Venido's patent (July 18, 1624). For an English translation, see Ruano, *Jerónima de la Asunción*, 88–90.

25. On an interesting side note, during archival research in Mexico, I found another letter from Montemayor addressed to the then-abbess, Sor Leonor de San Francisco, dated March 8, 1625, in which he also ordered the observance of the First Order of Saint Clare. This letter was not included in Sor Ana's manuscript. "Patente de Fray Alonso Montemayor," Biblioteca Nacional de Antropología e Historia de México, Fondo Franciscano, Mexico City, vol. 100, fols. 66v–68.

26. Sor Ana, AMSIRT, fol. 153v. Discretas are normally advisors to the abbess, although in this case it appears some of them had turned against Sor Jerónima.

27. On this rhetorical strategy, see Díaz, "Establishment of Feminine Paradigms," 61.

28. Montemayor calls Sor Jerónima's work "Avisos para acertar a navegar en el mar de la religión," but it has also been titled *Carta de marear en el mar del mundo*. I use the English translation of the title from Tiffany, *Diego Velázquez's Early Paintings*, 54.

29. The complete set of four volumes is located in the Archive of the Monastery of Santa Isabel in Toledo, Spain. Juana de San Antonio, *Noticias de la verdad*.

30. Sor Juana names her parents as Miguel Jiménez and Isabel Gallega. Ibid., vol. 1, fol. 1.

31. Sor Ana states in the prologue to her manuscript (written in 1623) that Sor Juana de San Antonio had been Sor Jerónima's familiar for fifteen years—pointing to her status as a lay woman integrated into the monastic "family" of the Convent of Santa Isabel. Sor Ana, AMSIRT, fol. vii. According to María del Mar Graña Cid, it is sometimes difficult to distinguish between the categories of servants, donadas, and familiares because they all formed part of the servant class in female convents. See Graña Cid, "La familia de fuera," 319. The Colegio de Silíceo, officially known as the Colegio de Doncellas Vírgenes de Nuestra Señora de los Remedios, was a charitable institution that had been established in 1551 for local women (they did not

necessarily have to be of noble blood) and was concerned with their moral and Christian education. For more information on this *colegio*, see Howe, *Education and Women*, 107–9.

32. Sor María Magdalena de la Cruz, prologue to Juana de San Antonio, *Noticias de la verdad*, vol. 1, n.p.

33. Sor María Magdalena de la Cruz, prologue, in ibid., second page.

34. Ibid., fol. 470.

35. Ibid., fols. 470–70v.

36. Triviño identifies Sor Leonora de San Buenaventura as abbess at the time of her declaration (October 3, 1630), but this does not make sense, since Sor Jerónima was still alive at the time (she died a few weeks later, on October 22) and Sor Ana de Cristo would become the next abbess upon her death. Triviño, *Escritoras clarisas*, 125.

37. "Esta relación enbió del convento de Manila a V. Rma. y berdaderos trasladados de las noticias de la madre Juana de San Antonio, y así lo firmo de mi nombre. Sor Jerónima de la Asunción, abadesa." Volume 2, which contains this small quote with Sor Jerónima's signature, is located in the Biblioteca Nacional in Madrid. It is the only volume of the work in their collection. Biblioteca Nacional de España, Madrid, MSS/19256 Juana de San Antonio, OSC, *Revelaciones*, fol. 1023v. The complete four-volume set is located in the Archivo del Monasterio de Santa Isabel de los Reyes, but it does not contain a signature from Sor Jerónima.

38. When interviewed for the case Sor Magdalena de Cristo cites her own age as "66 or 67." That would put her birth year around 1594. "Proceso y causa criminal contra la M. Sor Juana de San Antonio, Religiosa de Sta. Clara," 1668, Archivo General de la Nación, Mexico City (hereafter AGN), Inquisición, vol. 603, fol. 136.

39. Ibid., fol. 136v.

40. For a detailed analysis of the trial, interrogation questions, and testimonies, see Cruz, "Servir a Dios," 247–73.

41. "Comienza una breve relación que la madre Luisa de Jesús religiosa del convento de Santa Clara de Manila hace a su confesor Luis de la Mesa tocante a cosas de lo que le pasaron con la venerable madre María [Mariana] de Jesús," in Sor Ana, AMSIRT, fols. 196–206v. The dictation to Sor Ana of her life story is in fols. 180v–189v.

42. Sor Luisa mentions two of the hospitals by name: La Misericordia and San Nicolás.

43. Sor Luisa de Jesús in Sor Ana, AMSIRT, fol. 196v.

44. Ibid., fol. 206.

45. Ibid.

46. Ibid.

47. On qualifications for professing and exceptions, see Lavrin, *Brides of Christ*, 21–25.

48. Sor Ana, AMSIRT, fol. 214v.

49. For more information on Naitō Julia and the beaterio of San Miguel, see Ward, *Women Religious Leaders*, 60–104.

50. "Yo pienso servir para mis españolas, yo otra nación . . . yo mucho contento de ser monja." Sor Ana, AMSIRT, fol. 213v.

51. Ibid., fol. 217v.

52. Ibid.

53. Ibid., fol. 218.

54. Ibid., fols. 226, 227v.

55. Ibid., fol. 220v.

56. For information on maternal imagery in religious writing and art, see Sperling, *Medieval and Renaissance Lactations*; Fondaras, "Our Mother"; Bray, *Sacred Made Real*, 102; and Bynum, *Holy Feast*, 269–76.

57. Arenal and Schlau, *Untold Sisters*, 203. One of the most notable writers to depict maternal imagery, especially the mystical benefits of Mary's breast milk, was the Mexican nun María Anna Agueda de San Ignacio (1695–1756). See Eich, *Other Mexican Muse*; and Arenal and Schlau, *Untold Sisters*, 353–55.

58. Sor Ana, AMSIRT, fol. 219.

59. For a firsthand account of Franciscan missionaries and martyrs in Japan, see San Francisco, *Vida clandestina*.

60. Sor Ana, AMSIRT, fol. 220v.

61. Ibid., fol. 228.

62. Quesada, "Sermón predicado," AFIO, 396/10.

63. "Proceso ejecutado," ASV, fols. 24v, 25.

64. Ibid., fols. 25, 25v.

65. Following much the same protocol as in the case of Juana de la Cruz, the nuns (including Sor Ana and Sor María Magdalena), friars such as Quesada and anyone else who had some sort of relationship with Jerónima were interviewed in the convent parlor of Saint Clare using a twenty-eight-question inquiry. These interviews and other related documents (among them short testimonies by local indigenous people claiming an assortment of miracles, mostly from touching fragments of Jerónima's habit) can be found in "Proceso ejecutado," ASV.

66. Quesada, *Exemplo de todas las virtudes*, 419.

67. Cruz, "Servir a Dios," 236.

68. "Petition of the abbess," June 30, 1636, AGI, Filipinas, 85, N.86. See Blair and Robertson's English translation of her letter (also signed by other nuns) and the Crown's response in *Philippine Islands*, vol. 26. For an analysis of the letter, see Cruz, "Servir a Dios," 236–40.

69. There were six nuns, Sor Leonor de San Francisco and Sor María Magdalena de la Cruz (original cofounders from Spain) and Sor Melchora de la Trinidad, Sor Clara de San Francisco, Sor Margarita de la Concepción, and Sor Juana de la Concepción (nuns who had professed in Manila), as well as two pious women (one of whom was the future novice Marta de San Bernardo). Anonymous, *Entrada de la seraphica religion de nuestro P. S. Francisco en las islas Philipinas* (originally published in 1649); translated English edition, "Entrance of the Seraphic Order of Our

Father St. Francis into the Philippine Islands," in Blair and Robertson, *Philippine Islands*, vol. 35.

70. "The novitiate habit was given on the ship to Marta de San Bernardo, a Pampanga Indian woman whom the father provincial refused to allow to receive the habit in the convent of Manila, because of that fact." Sánchez Fuertes, "Los Monasterios," 74.

71. Martínez, *Compendio historico*, book 1, 319.

72. "Resumen de la vida de la venerable María Magdalena . . ." Biblioteca Nacional de España, MSS/11014, Fondo Antiguo, fols. 338–338v.

73. According to Carol L. Wagner, MD, professor of neonatal medicine at the Medical University of South Carolina, the description of baby Mariana is consistent with the physical appearance of an infant born three months premature. She notes, "Three months premature would be 28 weeks of gestation. If the mother had a stressful pregnancy, then the infant would have been stressed and the lungs more mature than expected. The wool would have given the immature skin oils and warmth and feeding through a straw would have been the only way to deliver—I assume expressed breast milk? It is a plausible scenario." Email correspondence with author, February 2, 2016.

74. See chapter 3 for more information on the Japanese embassy.

75. For more on Sor María Magdalena de la Cruz, see Triviño, *Escritoras clarisas*, 104–12; and Barbeito Carneiro, *Mujeres*, 353–59.

76. Three of the original founding nuns—Sor María Magdalena de la Cruz, Sor Clara de San Francisco, and Sor Margarita de la Concepción—two women, and one girl (who appear to have been siblings) returned to Manila. Sor Leonor de San Francisco stayed in Macao. For a description of this tumultuous period at the convent in Macao, see Penalva, *Mulheres em Macau*, 71–113; Martínez, *Compendio histórico*, 298–99; and Alberts, *Conflict and Conversion*, 160–62.

77. Their chaplain and escort, Fray Antonio de Santa María, wrote a colorful account of their imprisonment for the nuns back in Macao. For a transcription, see Penalva, *Mulheres em Macau*, 151–68. The original, which I have not consulted, is located in Rome at the Archivum Romanum Societatis Iesu, Jap-Sin 68. See also Alberts, *Conflict and Conversion*, 162–67.

78. Sor María Magdalena de la Cruz, *Floresta franciscana*.

79. Huerta, *Estado geográfico*, 42, 43.

80. On November 16, 2004, the "Congregation of the Cause of Saints" held a special meeting to discuss the possible beatification of Sor Jerónima. At the end of the meeting seven of the nine consultants voted to continue the process, but only if the information in the documentation regarding her case could be clarified and contextualized. In essence, it appears that the consultants were asking for a new positio. Congregation of the Cause of Saints, Report and votes of the special meeting held on 16 November 2004, Vatican City State (translated from Latin/Italian original).

81. On nun-widows, see Lavrin, *Brides of Christ*, 23, 24.

CHAPTER 5

1. For a whole collection of chapters devoted to conventual literacy, see Cruz and Hernández, *Women's Literacy*.
2. Lavrin, *Brides of Christ*, 310–11.
3. A. Cruz, introduction, 1–2.
4. Stephen Haliczer explains that it was common for a nun to read aloud about the life of a saint while other nuns sewed. *Between Exaltation and Infamy*, 39.
5. Bilinkoff, *Related Lives*, 96–110; A. Cruz, "Reading over Men's Shoulders," 44. On the types of texts novices were encouraged to read, see Lavrin, "La educación," 81–83.
6. Bilinkoff, *Related Lives*, 104–6.
7. Ibid., 100.
8. A. Cruz, introduction, 1–2.
9. See Weber, introduction, 9–26.
10. Ginés de Quesada, "Sermón predicado en las honras o exequias que el vigilantísimo cabildo de esta ciudad, celebró en la muerte de la V. M. Gerónima de la Asunción abadesa del Convento de las Descalzas de Sta. Clara de Manila," AFIO, 396/10; "Proceso ejecutado," ASV, fols. 412–412v.
11. For more information on Quesada, see Sánchez Maurandi, "Fr. Ginés de Quesada."
12. Letona's first order of business was to set up a new province of Franciscans under the observant branch of the order. This angered the already established discalced branch, and in 1654 he was expelled from the islands. See Sánchez Fuertes, "Impresos Franciscanos," 487.
13. In the words of Jodi Bilinkoff, "Hagiography is by no means a peculiarly medieval genre; arguably it reached its apogee in the early modern period, when the printing press hugely expanded the availability of texts and when a resurgent Catholic Church encouraged the cult of saints in reaction to the Reformation." Introduction, xiv. See also Bilinkoff, *Related Lives*, 3.
14. Bilinkoff, *Related Lives*, 9, 10.
15. There were multiple authors and editions of the *Flos Sanctorum*. On the *Flos Sanctorum*, see Baranda Leturio, *Cortejo a lo prohibido*, 30. See the discussion later in this chapter.
16. Sor Ana, AMSIRT, fol. 69.
17. Ibid., fol. 113v.
18. Letona, *Perfecta religiosa*, prologue.
19. Libro de Bautismos de San Bartolomé, 1548–1577, Archive of the Parroquia de San Andrés de Toledo, Spain; Sor Ana, AMSIRT, fol. 2.
20. Sor Ana, AMSIRT, fol. 1v.
21. Ibid.

22. Letona, *Perfecta religiosa*, book 1, 76.

23. Sor Ana, AMSIRT, fol. 22.

24. According to Domingo Martínez, before entering the convent, Sor Ana did not know how to read or write, but after her yearlong novitiate she learned to "read in Latin with admiration." *Compendio histórico*, 241.

25. Sor Ana, AMSIRT, fols. 76–76v.

26. Ibid., fol. 76v.

27. According to Stephen Haliczer, "Probably the most important motivation for authors to take up the task of writing a biography was the desire to broadcast the achievements of the exemplary members of their own religious order." *Between Exaltation and Infamy*, 99–100.

28. To name another example, among many, we can turn to the Mexican nun Sor Sebastiana Josefa de la Santísima Trinidad (ca. 1700–1757). Over the course of her life she wrote more than sixty letters to her confessor José Eugenio Valdés. He used those letters to form basis of his hagiography of the nun (often quoting verbatim whole sections of the letters), which he published in 1756. Sampson Vera Tudela, "Illustrating Sainthood," 87–88. See also Bilinkoff, *Related Lives*, 75.

29. Bilinkoff, *Related Lives*, 5.

30. María Victoria Triviño transcribes several sections from Jerónima's autobiography (taken from Quesada) in *Escritoras clarisas*, 46–53. Letona, *Perfecta religiosa*, 50v–51v.

31. Madre Leonor was abbess in Manila from 1623 to 1626.

32. Sor Ana, AMSIRT, fol. 68v–69v.

33. Ibid., fol. 68v.

34. Ibid., fol. 69.

35. Ibid.

36. On anxiety of authorship and nuns, see Arenal and Schlau, *Untold Sisters*, 14.

37. See Winston-Allen, *Convent Chronicles*, 169–204. For a transatlantic example, see Kirk, *Convent Life*, 143–75.

38. Castro Brunetto, "Evolución de la iconografía clariana," 1:121.

39. On Teresa's missionary inclination and effect on others, see Wilson, "From *Mujercilla* to *Conquistadora*."

40. "Mariana de Jesús, ven. vidua. mon. prof. III Ord. Saec. S. Frco. (Escalona 17 feb. 1577, Toledo 8 jul. 1629). Toletan. Decr. Causae Int. 1692. Cfr. Index ac Status Causarum, 1988, p. 233," Cited in Congregatio Causis Sanctorum, *Manilen, Beatificationis et Canonizationis*, 690n8.

41. Mesa, *Vida, favores, y mercedes*. See also Haliczer, *Between Exaltation and Infamy*, 66, 271, 275.

42. On Mariana de Jesús and the tradition of living saints, see Morte Acín, "Tradiciones y pervivencia medievales."

43. Sor Ana, AMSIRT, fol. 133. That sculpture has now been returned to the Convent of Santa Isabel de los Reyes and sits on the main altarpiece. See Martínez Caviró, *El Monasterio*, 48. See figure 6.

44. For an overview on this subject in Spanish, see Owens, "El legado."

45. Much has been written about Juana de la Cruz: Surtz, *The Guitar of God*; Juana Inés de la Cruz, *El Conhorte*; Pablo Maroto, "La 'Santa Juana'"; Boon, "Mother Juana de la Cruz"; and Juana Inés de la Cruz, *Mother Juana de la Cruz*.

46. The process was closed in 1731 but reopened in 1985. Juana Inés de la Cruz, *El Conhorte*, 68.

47. There are two extant manuscripts, one in the Biblioteca del Real Monasterio de San Lorenzo de El Escorial (MS. J-II-18) and the other in the Vatican (SS. Ritum. Proc. 3074). For a study of the manuscripts and their authorship, see Juana Inés de la Cruz, *El Conhorte*, 69–80. It is generally believed that Sor María Evangelista served as Juana's scribe for the majority of these sermons. Other amanuenses were also involved. For an English translation of select sermons, see Juana Inés de la Cruz, *Mother Juana de la Cruz*.

48. The manuscript is located in the Real Biblioteca del Monasterio, El Escorial, K-III-13.

49. For more information on the choice of referring to this work as a "semiautobiography," see Jessica A. Boon, introduction, in Juana Inés de la Cruz, *Mother Juana de la Cruz*, 14–17.

50. On the use of scribes, see Boon, "Mother Juana de la Cruz," 128, 135–36; and Pablo Maroto, "La 'Santa Juana,'" 587.

51. Sor María Magdalena de la Cruz from the convent in Cubas was one of the eighty-seven witnesses to be interviewed as part of the Apostolic Process for Juana de la Cruz, which was conducted between 1614 and 1616. Juana Inés de la Cruz, *El Conhorte*, 131–39.

52. El Proceso Toledano, fol. 44, quoted in ibid., 25.

53. For this study I am using Daza's edition from 1613, *Historia, vida y milagros*. There was another biography written by Fray Pedro Navarro, but it was not published until 1622, after the nuns had already left Spain. Navarro, *Favores*.

54. Surtz, *Guitar of God*, 1.

55. Sor Ana begins this chapter by listing all of the important figures (including Daza) linked to Sor Jerónima and the founding of the future convent in Manila. Sor Ana, *AMSIRT*, fol. 69v.

56. Montgomery, "Contact Relics."

57. Morte Acín, "Tradiciones y pervivencia medievales," 317–20; and Haliczer, *Between Exaltation and Infamy*, 225.

58. Juana Inés de la Cruz, *El Conhorte*, 125–26.

59. Haliczer, *Between Exaltation and Infamy*, 269.

60. Juana Inés de la Cruz, *El Conhorte*, 37. In the first edition of his biography of Juana de la Cruz (1610) Daza accepted the veracity of the indulgences, even saying that Jesus Christ himself endorsed them, but in the second edition (1613) he modified those chapters, specifically by rejecting the indulgences as false. He also added a chapter on the miracles stemming from the virtue of the rosary beads. See ibid., 38.

61. For example, Daza, *Libro de la purísima concepción*.

62. "Firmas de los miembros de los conventos y monasterios pertenecientes a la Hermandad," Biblioteca Nacional de España, Madrid, Ms. 8540. This is also part of the digitized collection that I consulted for this study, pages 47 and 86. A special thanks to Jane Tar for alerting me to the whereabouts of this book and the signatures.

63. Daza's biography of Luisa de la Ascensión remains in manuscript form: "Vida y otras cosas de la M. Luisa de la Ascensión, tan admirables como verdaderas," sixteen chapters, Archivo Histórico Nacional, Madrid, Inquisición, Leg.3.704, cited in Triviño, *Escritoras clarisas*, 70.

64. For the definitive work on Sor Luisa, see García Barriúso, *La monja de Carrión*. García Barriúso also has a shorter article, "La monja de Carrión."

65. Triviño, *Escritoras clarisas*, 68–73.

66. AGI, Filipinas, 85, N.54. For a Spanish transcription, see González Zymla, "La fundación e historia," 233–34n130. For an English translation of the letter, see Ruano, *Jerónima de la Asunción*, 84–86.

67. Sor Ana, AMSIRT, fol. 69.

68. On agency and gender as related to women religious, see Lundberg, *Mission and Ecstasy*, 27–28.

69. Sor Ana, AMSIRT, fol. 139–39v.

70. Poutrin, "Para qué servían," 152–54.

71. Sor Ana, AMSIRT, fol. 132.

72. Ibid., fol. 66v.

73. Ibid., fol. 132v.

74. Ibid., fol. i.

75. Much has been written about nuns' writing and the rhetoric of humility. For a key example, see Weber, *Teresa of Avila*.

76. On miraculous literacy, see Donahue, "Wondrous Words," 111–12.

77. Sor Ana, AMSIRT, fols. 135v–136.

78. This mentality is reflected in Jesuit Pedro Navarro's recorded reaction to the Inquisition's list of prohibited books (el Indice de 1559): "We live in a time where it is preached that women take up the distaff and the rosary"; cited in Andrés Martín, *Historia de la mística*, 315–16. See also, Andrés Martín, *La teología española*, 626.

79. On the motif of spinning in religious art, see Moffit, "Mary as 'Prophetic Seamstress'"; and Hamburger, *Nuns as Artists*, 186–87.

80. Bilinkoff, *Related Lives*, 28.

81. Sampson Vera Tudela also notes, "We should resist the temptation to idealize the cloister as a parallel or separate feminine sphere, however." "Illustrating Sainthood," 94.

82. Lavrin, "Erudición, devoción," 70.

83. Sor Ana, AMSIRT, fol. 139v.

84. Sor Juana Inés de la Cruz describes these interruptions in her famous autobiographical letter "Respuesta a Sor Filotea de la Cruz." Juana Inés de la Cruz, *The Answer/La respuesta*, 59.

85. Sor Ana, AMSIRT, fols. 73v–77v.
86. Lavrin, "Erudición, devoción," 83. Later in the manuscript Sor Ana quotes Sor Jerónima as also wanting to convert pagans and Moors. Sor Ana, AMSIRT, 134–34v.
87. I agree with Lundberg's definition of mission and that contemplative religious women did have a missionary role. He writes, "I understand mission much more inclusively as acts made by a person perceived to be in favour of the salvation of others." *Mission and Ecstasy*, 16.
88. Sor Ana, AMSIRT, fol. 140.

EPILOGUE

1. Concordia de San Francisco, "Carta." Sor Concordia wrote a series of letters back to the nuns and friars in Spain about their trials during World War II, many of which are housed in the AFIO. Other nuns also documented these events.
2. AGN, GD68MARINA, Manila, July 16, 1764, vol. 19, exp. 63, fol. 357.
3. AGN, GD68MARINA, Manila, March 26, 1765, vol. 19, exp. 63, fol. 358.
4. Amalia de la Presentación, "Relación," fol. 29.
5. Concordia de San Francisco, "Carta," 3.
6. See "Battle for Manila Newsreel 1945," https://www.youtube.com/watch?v=OcDtiaxwykk. I believe a short image of the nuns appears at the end of this clip.
7. Huerta indicates that the three nuns had been buried together. *Estado geográfico*, 41, 42.

Glossary

⁓ℓ

almiranta Second ship in a Spanish fleet.

Audiencia High court.

beata Religious laywoman who lived an ascetic lifestyle.

beaterio House for beatas.

black-veiled nun Also called choir nuns, the highest echelon within a convent hierarchy; nuns who dedicated their time to praying the Divine Office.

calced A term used to refer to less strict orders of nuns (as opposed to discalced).

capitana Flagship in a Spanish fleet; sometimes the nuns referred to Sor Jerónima as their capitana.

chinos Generic term to refer to people of Asian descent living in the Philippines or New Spain.

criollo/a Person of Spanish descent born abroad.

discalced Literally, "barefoot"; a strict order of nuns and friars who embraced poverty and lived off of alms; Sor Ana and Quesada (among others from this time period) used this word interchangeably with the First Rule of Saint Clare.

discretas Female advisors to the abbess.

doctrina Segregated parish of converted indigenous peoples; could also be used to indicate a document used for religious instruction.

donada Servant class within a convent; a donada was sometimes "donated" by a family member or even by a former slave owner to a convent. Some woman chose to become donadas, especially indigenous women and women of African descent, because they did not meet other requirements to profess as nuns. Often these women were revered for their piety.

encomienda Grants of rights to indigenous labor and tribute.

familiar Term used specifically within the Franciscan order in Spain to denote the servant class within a convent.

fogón A communal cooking stove on a ship.

galleon A large sailing vessel used by the Spanish fleet, especially on the Manila galleon route.

guardian Friar in charge of a monastery.

Intramuros Walled area within Manila, populated with Spaniards and their descendants.

Manila galleon route Generic term used to describe the sailing route between Manila and Acapulco.

mestizo/a Person of mixed indigenous and European descent.

mulatto/a Person of mixed African and European descent.

Negritos Indigenous people from the mountainous areas of Luzon.

negro/a Person of African descent or from sub-Saharan Africa.

Parian Neighborhood outside Intramuros, populated with Sangleys.

positio Papers for the process of beatification.

Sangley Chinese merchant population living in Manila.

sor Derived from the Latin word *soror*, meaning "sister"; title used to address nuns; this is the term most commonly used in Sor Ana's manuscript, although she does sometimes refer to Jerónima and some of the other nuns as "madre."

Third Order vows Vows that a pious layman or woman took to live a religious lifestyle—combining daily prayer and penance—without actually becoming a friar or nun.

tornera Nun in charge of the torno.

torno Literally "turn"; a revolving door used to pass goods and messages in and out of enclosed convents.

vicaria Vicaress; office held within a female convent; second in charge after the abbess.

vida Spiritual autobiography.

white-veiled nun Lay sisters, also called *legas*, below black-veiled nuns in a convent hierarchy; nuns who could not afford to pay a dowry and divided their time between prayer and convent chores.

zambo Person of African and indigenous descent.

Bibliography

SELECTED PRIMARY ARCHIVAL SOURCES

Archivo del Monasterio de Santa Isabel de los Reyes (AMSIRT), Toledo, Spain.
Archivo Franciscano Ibero-Oriental (AFIO), Madrid, Spain.
Archivo General de Indias (AGI), Seville, Spain.
Archivo General de la Nación (AGN), Mexico City, Mexico.
Archivio Segreto Vaticano (ASV), Vatican City.
Biblioteca Nacional de Antropología e Historia de México, Fondo Franciscano, Mexico City, Mexico.
Biblioteca Nacional de España, Madrid, Spain.

Amalia de la Presentación, Sor. "Relación de la guerra de los Yankees en Manila. Año de 1898." AFIO, 99/33, fols. 1–52.
Ana de Cristo, Sor. *Historia de nuestra santa madre Jerónima de la Asunción*. 1623–29. AMSIRT.
Concordia de San Francisco, Sor. "Carta a la reverenda madre abadesa del convento de monjas clarisas de Santa Isabel de los Reyes, Toledo, España." April 6, 1945. AFIO, 492/6–6.
"Firmas de los miembros de los conventos y monasterios pertenecientes a la Hermandad." Biblioteca Nacional de España, Madrid. Mss. 8540.
Juana de San Antonio, Sor. *Noticias de la verdad y luz de los divinos atributos*. 4 vols. 1629. AMSIRT.
Llave, Antonio de la. *Crónica de la provincia*. Vol. 3. 1625. AFIO, B 063.
María Magdalena de la Cruz, Sor. *Floresta franciscana de ilustraciones celestiales cogida al hilo de la oración en la aurora de María . . .* 3 vols. 1640–1647. AFIO, 387/1, 387/2, 387/3.
"Proceso ejecutado por autoridad ordinaria en la audiencia arzobispal de esta ciudad de Manila sobre la ejemplar vida y milagros de la venerable Madre Gerónima de la Asumpción." ASV, Congr. Riti, Processus 1654, Vol. 1.

"Proceso y causa criminal contra la madre sor Juana de San Antonio, religiosa de Santa Clara en las islas Filipinas." 1668. AGN, Mexico City, Inquisición, Tomo 603, No. 3, fols. 122–42.

Quesada, Ginés de. "Sermón predicado en las honras o exequias que el vigilantísimo cabildo de esta ciudad, celebró en la muerte de la V. M. Gerónima de la Asunción abadesa del convento de las Descalzas de Sta. Clara de Manila." AFIO, 396/10.

"Resumen de la vida de la venerable María Magdalena [sic] de Pinto, una de las fundadoras del convento de Santa Clara de Manila, y de el de Macao, ilustre autora de tres libros de la *Floresta Franciscana*." Biblioteca Nacional de España, Madrid. Mss/ 11014, Fondo Antiguo, fols. 335–358v.

Sánchez Maurandi, A. "Fr. Ginés de Quesada. Gloria franciscano-muleño." Murcia, 1927. 1–48. AFIO 126/16.

PRIMARY PRINTED SOURCES

Anonymous. "Entrance of the Seraphic Order of Our Father St. Francis into the Philippine Islands." In *The Philippine Islands*, edited and translated by Emma Helen Blair and James Alexander Robertson, 35: 278. Cleveland, OH: A. H. Clark Company, 1903–1909.

Blair, Emma Helen, and James Alexander Robertson, eds. and trans. *The Philippine Islands, 1493–1898*. 1617–1620. Cleveland, OH: A. H. Clark, 1903–1909. http://www. gutenberg.org.

Bobadilla, Diego de. "Relation of the Filipinas Islands" (1640). In *The Philippine Islands, 1493–1898*, edited and translated by Emma Helen Blair and James Alexander Robertson, 29: n.p. Cleveland, OH: A. H. Clark, 1903–1909.

Congregatio Causis Sanctorum. *Manilen, Beatificationis et Canonizationis Ven. Servae Dei Sororis Hieronymae ab Assumptione (in saec. H. Yañez), Fundatricis et primae Abbatissae Monasterii Monialium Excalceatarum S. Clarae Ordinis S. Francisci . . . Positio super Vita et Virtutibus.* Rome, 1991.

Daza, Antonio. *Historia, vida y milagros, éxtasis y revelaciones de la bienaventurada virgen sor Juana de la Cruz.* Madrid: Luis Sánchez, 1613.

———. *Libro de la purísima concepción de la madre de Dios . . .* Madrid: Viuda de Luis Sánchez, 1628.

Fernández Navarrete, Domingo. *The Travels and Controversies of Friar Domingo Navarrete, 1618–1686.* Vol. 1. Edited and translated by J. S. Cummins. Cambridge: Cambridge University Press, 1962.

Gage, Thomas. *Thomas Gage's Travels in the New World.* Edited by J. Eric S. Thompson. 1648. Reprint, Westport, CT: Greenwood Press, 1981.

Gemelli Careri, Giovanni Francesco. *A Voyage to the Philippines.* 1699. Reprint, Manila: Filipiniana Book Guild, 1963.

Hakluyt, Richard, collector. *The Principal Navigations, Voyages, Traffiques and Discoveries of the English Nation*. 1599. Edited by Edmund Goldsmid. Vol. 6. Reprint, London: J. M. Dent and Sons, 1927.

Herrera y Montemayor, Juan de. "Viaje que Juan de Herrera y Montemayor hizo en el año 1617." In *Relaciones de viajes (Siglo XVI, XVII y XVIII)*, edited by Rubén Vargas Ugarte, 1–117. Lima: Biblioteca Histórica Peruana, 1947.

Huerta, Félix de. *Estado geográfico, topográfico, estadístico, histórico-religioso de la Provincia de San Gregorio . . .* Manila: Imprenta de M. Sánchez, 1865.

Juana Inés de la Cruz, Sor. *The Answer/La respuesta*. Edited and translated by Electa Arenal and Amanda Powell. New York: Feminist Press, 1994.

———. *El Conhorte: Sermones de una mujer: La Santa Juana (1481–1534)*. Vol. 1. Edited by Inocente García de Andrés. Madrid: Fundación Universitaria Española, 1999.

———. *Mother Juana de la Cruz, 1481–1534: Visionary Sermons*. Edited by Jessica A. Boon and Ronald E. Surtz. Translated by Ronald E. Surtz and Nora Weinerth. Tucson, AZ: ACMRS and ITER, 2016.

Letona, Bartolomé de. *Perfecta religiosa*. Puebla: Viuda de Juan de Borja, 1662.

Losa, Francisco. *La vida que hizo el siervo de dios Gregorio Lopez, en algunas lugares de esta Nueva España . . .* Mexico City: Juan Ruiz, 1613.

María de Jesús de Ágreda, Sor. *María de Jesús de Ágreda: Correspondencia con Felipe IV, religión y razón de estado*. Edited by Consolación Baranda Leturio. Madrid: Castalia, 1991.

María Rosa, Madre. *Journey of Five Capuchin Nuns*. Edited and translated by Sarah E. Owens. Toronto: CRRS & ITER, 2009.

Martínez, Domingo. *Compendio histórico de la apostólica provincia de San Gregorio de Philipinas de religiosos menores descalzos . . .* Madrid: Viuda de Manuel Fernández, 1756.

Mesa, Luis de. *Vida, favores, y mercedes que nuestro Señor hizo a la venerable hermana Mariana de Jesús, de la tercera orden de San Francisco, natural de la villa de Escalona, que vivió y murió en Toledo*. Madrid: 1661.

Morga, Antonio de. *The Philippine Islands, Moluccas, Siam, Cambodia, Japan and China at the Close of the Sixteenth Century*. Edited and translated by Henry E. J. Stanley. 1609. Reprint, Farnham, UK: Ashgate, 2010.

Navarro, Pedro. *Favores de el rey de el cielo hechos a su esposa la santa Juana de la Cruz, religiosa de la orden tercera de N. P. S. Francisco: Con anotaciones theologicas y morales a la historia de su vida*. Madrid: Thomas Iunti, 1622.

Panes, Diego. *Descripción de los caminos que desde la plaza de Veracruz se dirigen a México por distintos rumbos*. Facsimile ed. Madrid: Banco Santander, 1992.

Plasencia, Juan de. *Doctrina christiana en lengua española*. Manila: Impresa con licencia en S. Gabriel, de la orden de S. Domingo, 1593.

Quesada, Ginés de. *Exemplo de todas las virtudes, y vida milagrosa de la venerable madre Gerónima de la Assumpción, abadesa, y fundadora del Real Convento de la Concepción de la Virgen Nuestra Señora, de monjas descalzas de nuestra Madre Santa*

Clara de la ciudad de Manila. Mexico City: Viuda de Miguel de la Rivera, 1713. In Congregatio Causis Sanctorum, *Manilen, Beatificationis et Canonizationis Ven. Servae Dei Sororis Hieronymae ab Assumptione*. Rome, 1991. Also published in Madrid by Antonio de Marín, 1717.

Rocha, Arturo. *Monumenta guadalupensia mexicana: Colección facsimilar de documentos guadalupanos del siglo XVI custodiados en México y el mundo, acompañados de paleografías, comentarios y notas*. Mexico City: Insigne y Nacional Basílica de Santa María de Guadalupe/Grupo Estrella Blanca, 2010.

Sahagún, Fray Bernardino de. *Historia de las cosas de la Nueva España*. Edited by Angel María Garibay K. Mexico City: Porrúa, 1992.

San Francisco, Diego de. *Vida clandestina de un misionero en Japón*. 1625. Edited by Cayetano Sánchez Fuertes. Reprint, Seville: Punto Rojo Libros, 2014.

Vargas Ugarte, Rubén, ed. *Relaciones de viajes (siglo XVI, XVII y XVIII)*. Lima: Biblioteca Histórica Peruana, 1947.

Vetancurt, Augustín de. "Menologio Franciscano." In *Teatro Mexicano*. 1696. Reprint, Mexico: Imprenta de I. Escalante, 1871.

SECONDARY SOURCES

Alba González, Emilia. *Fundación del Convento de San Felipe de Jesús de Clarisas Capuchinas en Nueva España*. Mexico City: Ediciones Dabar, 2002.

———. "Presencia de América en Toledo: Aportación cultural y social." PhD diss., Universidad Complutense de Madrid, 1998. http://dialnet.unirioja.es.

Alberts, Tara. *Conflict and Conversion: Catholicism in Southeast Asia, 1500–1700*. Oxford: Oxford University Press, 2013.

Allen, Richard B. *European Slave Trading in the Indian Ocean, 1500–1850*. Athens: Ohio University Press, 2014.

Amerlinck de Corsi, María Concepción, and Manuel Ramos Medina, eds. *Conventos de monjas: Fundaciones en el México virreinal*. Mexico City: Grupo Condumex, 1995.

Andrés Martín, Melquíades. *Historia de la mística de la Edad de Oro en España y América*. Madrid: Biblioteca de Autores Cristianos, 1994.

———. *La teología española en el siglo XVI*. Madrid: Biblioteca de Autores Cristianos, 1976.

Arenal, Electa, and Stacey Schlau, eds. *Untold Sisters: Hispanic Nuns in Their Own Works*. Albuquerque: University of New Mexico Press, 1989.

Arias, Santa, and Raúl Marrero-Fente. Introduction to *Coloniality, Religion, and the Law in the Early Iberian World*, edited by Santa Arias and Marrero-Fente, ix–xxiv. Nashville: Vanderbilt University Press, 2014.

Atienza López, Angela. *Tiempos de conventos: Una historia social de las fundaciones en la España moderna*. Madrid: Marcia Pons Historia, 2008.

Baade, Colleen R. "Music: Convents." In *Lexikon of the Hispanic Baroque: Transatlantic Exchange and Transformation*, edited by Evonne Levy and Kenneth Mills, 240–42. Austin: University of Texas Press, 2013.

———. "Two Centuries of Nun Musicians in Spain's Imperial City." *TRANS-Revista Transcultural de Música/Transcultural Music Review* 15 (2011): 1–22.

Baranda Leturio, Nieves. *Cortejo a lo prohibido: Lectoras y escritoras en la España moderna*. Madrid: Arco, 2005.

Barbeito Carneiro, María Isabel. *Mujeres y literatura del siglo de oro: Espacios profanos y espacios conventuales*. Madrid: SAFEKAT, 2007.

Barceló Quintal, Raquel Ofelia. "Acapulco, frontera comercial del reino español (1565–1815)." In *Fronteras del mundo hispánico: Filipinas en el contexto de las regiones liminares novohispanas*, edited by Marta María Manchado López and Miguel Luque Talaván, 361–84. Córdoba, Spain: Universidad de Córdoba, 2011.

Barrón Soto, María Cristina E. "La participación de fray Luis Sotelo y los japoneses de la Misión Hasekura." *México y la Cuenca del Pacífico* 17, no. 50 (May 2014): 43–65.

Bell, Rudolph M. *Holy Anorexia*. Chicago: University of Chicago Press, 1985.

Bennett, Herman L., ed. *Africans in Colonial Mexico: Absolutism, Christianity, and Afro-Creole Consciousness, 1570–1640*. Bloomington: Indiana University Press, 2003.

———. *Colonial Blackness: A History of Afro-Mexico*. Bloomington: Indiana University Press, 2009.

Bieñko de Peralta, Doris. "Los impresos novohispanos sobre religiosas clarisas españolas en el siglo XVII." In *Monacato femenino franciscano en Hispanoamérica y España*, edited by Mina Ramírez Montes, 213–22. Querétaro: Poder Ejecutivo del Estado de Querétaro, 2012.

Bilinkoff, Jodi. "Francisco Losa and Gregorio López: Spiritual Friendship and Identity Formation." In *Colonial Saints: Discovering the Holy in the Americas*, edited by Allan Greer and Jodi Bilinkoff, 115–28. New York: Routledge, 2003.

———. Introduction to *Colonial Saints: Discovering the Holy in the Americas*, edited by Allan Greer and Jodi Bilinkoff, xiii–xxii. New York: Routledge, 2003.

———. *Related Lives: Confessors and Their Female Penitents*. Ithaca, NY: Cornell University Press, 2005.

Boon, Jessica A. "Mother Juana de la Cruz: Marian Visions and Female Preaching." In *A New Companion to Hispanic Mysticism*, edited by Hilaire Kallendorf, 127–48. Leiden, Netherlands: Brill, 2010.

Boucher, Philip P. "The 'Frontier Era' of the French Caribbean, 1620s–1690s." In *Negotiated Empires: Centers and Peripheries in the Americas, 1500–1820*, edited by Christine Daniels and Michael V. Kennedy, 205–34. New York: Routledge, 2002.

Brading, D. A. *Mexican Phoenix: Our Lady of Guadalupe, Image and Tradition Across Five Centuries*. Cambridge: Cambridge University Press, 2001.

Bray, Xavier, ed. *The Sacred Made Real: Spanish Painting and Sculpture, 1600–1700*. London: National Gallery Company; New Haven, CT: Yale University Press, 2009. Exhibition catalog.

Breen, John, and Mark Williams. Introduction to *Japan and Christianity: Impacts and Responses*, edited by John Breen and Mark Williams, 1–7. London: Macmillan, 1996.

Brewer, Carolyn. *Shamanism, Catholicism and Gender Relations in Colonial Philippines, 1521–1685*. Aldershot, UK: Ashgate, 2004.

Brigstocke, Hugh, and Zahira Vélez, eds. *En torno a Velázquez: The Apelles Collection*. Oviedo, Spain: Museo de Bellas Artes de Asturias, 1999. Exhibition catalog.

Burkholder, Mark A. "An Empire Beyond Compare." In *The Oxford History of Mexico*, edited by Michael C. Meyer and William H. Beezley, 113–49. New York: Oxford University Press, 2000.

Buschmann, Rainer F., Edward R. Slack, and James B. Tuelle. *Navigating the Spanish Lake: The Pacific in the Iberian World, 1521–1898*. Honolulu: University of Hawai'i Press, 2014.

Bynum, Caroline Walker. *Holy Feast and Holy Fast: The Religious Significance of Food to Medieval Women*. Berkeley: University of California Press, 1987.

Canabal Rodríguez, Laura. "Los conventos de clarisas en Toledo (siglos XIV, XV y XVI)." *Archivo Ibero-Americano* 54, no. 213–14 (1994): 473–83.

Cañizares-Esguerra, Jorge. *Puritan Conquistadors: Iberianizing the Atlantic, 1550–1700*. Stanford, CA: Stanford University Press, 2006.

Castro Brunetto, Carlos Javier. "Evolución de la iconografía clariana en el mundo iberoamericano." In *I Congreso Internacional del Monacato Femenino en España, Portugal y América*, 1:121–28. Leon, Spain: Ediciones Lancia, 1992.

Chowning, Margaret. *Rebellious Nuns: The Troubled History of a Mexican Convent, 1752–1863*. Oxford: Oxford University Press, 2006.

Coates, Timothy J. *Convicts and Orphans: Forced State-Sponsored Colonizers in the Portuguese Empire, 1550–1755*. Stanford, CA: Stanford University Press, 2001.

Cómez Ramos, Rafael. "Las casas del infante don Fadrique y el convento de Santa Clara en Sevilla." *Historia, Instituciones, Documentos* 34 (2007): 95–116.

Conover, Cornelius. "Saintly Biography and the Cult of San Felipe de Jesús in Mexico City, 1597–1697." *The Americas* 67, no. 4 (April 2011): 441–66.

Costa, Horacio de la. "Episcopal Jurisdiction in the Philippines during the Spanish Regime." In *Studies in Philippine Church History*, edited by Gerald H. Anderson, 44–64. Ithaca, NY: Cornell University Press, 1969.

Coster, Will, and Andrew Spicer, eds. *Sacred Space in Early Modern Europe*. Cambridge: Cambridge University Press, 2005.

Crossley, John Newsome. *Hernando de los Ríos Coronel and the Spanish Philippines in the Golden Age*. Farnham, UK: Ashgate, 2011.

Crossley, John Newsome, and Sarah E. Owens. "The First Nunnery in Manila: The Role of Hernando de los Ríos Coronel." *Catholic Historical Review* 102, no. 3 (Summer 2016): 469–91.

Cruz, Anne J. Introduction to *Women's Literacy in Early Modern Spain and the New World*, edited by Anne J. Cruz and Rosilie Hernández, 1–16. Burlington, VT: Ashgate, 2011.

———. "Reading over Men's Shoulders: Noblewomen's Libraries and Reading Practices."
In *Women's Literacy in Early Modern Spain and the New World*, edited by Anne J.
Cruz and Rosilie Hernández, 41–58. Burlington, VT: Ashgate, 2011.

Cruz, Anne J., and Rosilie Hernández, eds. *Women's Literacy in Early Modern Spain and
the New World*. Burlington, VT: Ashgate, 2011.

Cruz, Reginald D. "Servir a Dios en Recogimiento: Religious Life as Woman's Space in
the Archdiocese of Manila (1590–1700)." PhD diss., University of the Philippines,
2009.

Cuadriello, Jaime. "The Theopolitical Visualization of the Virgin of the Immaculate
Conception." In *Sacred Spain: Art and Belief in the Spanish World*, edited by Ronda
Kasl, 121–45. Indianapolis: Indianapolis Museum of Art; New Haven, CT: Yale Uni-
versity Press, 2010.

Curcio-Nagy, Linda A. "Faith and Morals in Colonial Mexico." In *The Oxford History of
Mexico*, edited by Michael C. Meyer and William H. Beezley, 151–82. New York:
Oxford University Press, 2000.

Davidson, David M. "Negro Slave Control and Resistance in Colonial Mexico, 1519–
1650." *Hispanic American Historical Review* 46, no. 3 (August 1966): 235–53.

Dean, Carolyn. *Inka Bodies and the Body of Christ: Corpus Christi in Colonial Cuzco,
Peru*. Durham, NC: Duke University Press, 1999.

Díaz, Mónica. "The Establishment of Feminine Paradigms: Translators, Traitors, Nuns."
In *The Cambridge History of Latin American Women's Literature*, edited by Ileana
Rodríguez and Mónica Szurmuk, 52–65. Cambridge: Cambridge University Press,
2015.

———. *Indigenous Writings from the Convent: Negotiating Ethnic Autonomy in Colonial
Mexico*. Tucson: University of Arizona Press, 2010.

Dominguez Ortiz, Antonio. *Sociedad y mentalidad en la Sevilla del Antiguo regimen*.
Seville: Servicio de Publicaciones del Ayuntamiento de Sevilla, 1979.

Donahue, Darcy. "Wondrous Words: Miraculous Literacy and Real Literacy in the Con-
vents of Early Modern Spain." In *Women's Literacy in Early Modern Spain and the
New World*, edited by Anne J. Cruz and Rosilie Hernández, 106–22. Burlington,
VT: Ashgate, 2011.

Donahue-Wallace, K. "Abused and Battered: Printed Images and the Female Body in
Viceregal Spain." In *Women and Art in Early Modern Latin America*, edited by
Kellen Kee McIntyre and Richard E. Phillips, 125–47. Leiden, Netherlands: Brill,
2007.

Dunn, Marilyn R. "Spiritual Philanthropists: Women as Convent Patrons in Seicento
Rome." In *Women and Art in Early Modern Europe: Patrons, Collectors, and Con-
noisseurs*, edited by Cynthia Lawrence, 154–88. University Park: Pennsylvania State
University Press, 1997.

Durán López, Fernando. "Religious Autobiography." In *A New Companion to Hispanic
Mysticism*, edited by Hilaire Kallendorf, 15–38. Leiden, Netherlands: Brill, 2010.

Eich, Jennifer. *The Other Mexican Muse: Sor María Anna Agueda de San Ignacio, 1695–
1756*. New Orleans: University Press of the South, 2004.

Elliott, J. H. *Empires of the Atlantic World: Britain and Spain in America, 1492–1830*. New Haven, CT: Yale University Press, 2006.

Ellis, Robert Richmond. *They Need Nothing: Hispanic-Asian Encounters of the Colonial Period*. Toronto: University of Toronto Press, 2012.

Feros, Antonio. *Kingship and Favoritism in the Spain of Philip III, 1598–1621*. Cambridge: Cambridge University Press, 2000.

Flynn, Dennis O., and Arturo Giraldez. "Born with a 'Silver Spoon': The Origin of World Trade in 1571." *Journal of World History* 6, no. 2 (1995): 201–21.

Flynn, Dennis O., Arturo Giraldez, and James Sobredo, eds. *European Entry into the Pacific: Spain and the Acapulco-Manila Galleons*. Aldershot, UK: Ashgate, 2001.

Fondaras, Antonia K. "'Our Mother the Holy Wisdom of God': Nursing in Botticelli's Bardi Altarpiece." *Storia dell'Arte* 111 (2005): 7–34.

Fuchs, Barbara. "An English *Pícaro* in New Spain: Miles Philips and the Framing of National Identity." *CR: The New Centennial Review* 2, no. 1 (Spring 2002): 55–68.

García, Rolando R., Henry F. Díaz, Ricardo García Herrera, Jon Eischeid, María del Rosario Prieto, Emiliano Hernández, Luis Gimeno, Francisco Rubio Durán, and Ana María Bascary. "Atmospheric Circulation Changes in the Tropical Pacific Inferred from the Voyages of the Manila Galleons in the Sixteenth–Eighteenth Centuries," *Bulletin of the American Meteorological Society* 82, no. 11 (November 2001): 2435–55.

García Barriúso, Patrocinio. *La monja de Carrión: Sor Luisa de la Ascensión Colmenares Cabezón*. Madrid: Ediciones Monte Casino, 1986.

———. "La monja de Carrión Sor Luisa de la Ascensión y Sor María de Jesús, la monja de Agreda." *Verdad y Vida* (Franciscanos Españoles) 49, no. 193–96 (1991): 547–52.

García Lascuráin, Ana Rita Valero de, ed. *Plano topográfico de la Villa de Nuestra Señora de Guadalupe y sus alrededores en 1691*. Mexico City: Centro de Investigaciones y Estudios Superiores en Antropología Social (CIESAS), 2004.

Gasch-Tomás, José Luis. "Asian Silk, Porcelain and Material Culture in the Definition of Mexican and Andalusian Elites, c. 1565–1630." In *Global Goods and the Spanish Empire, 1492–1824: Circulation, Resistance and Diversity*, edited by Bethany Aram and Bartolomé Yun-Casilla, 153–73. London: Palgrave Macmillan, 2014.

Gerhard, Peter. *A Guide to the Historical Geography of New Spain*. Cambridge: Cambridge University Press, 1972.

Gil, Juan. *Hidalgos y samurais: España y Japón en los siglos XVI y XVII*. Madrid: Alianza Editorial, 1991.

Giraldez, Arturo. *The Age of Trade: The Manila Galleons and the Dawn of the Global Economy*. Lanham, MD: Rowman and Littlefield, 2015.

González Zymla, Herbert. "La fundación e historia del convento de monjas franciscanas de Manila: Una frontera espiritual y artística del imperio español." In *Fronteras del mundo hispánico: Filipinas en el contexto de las regiones liminares novohispanas*, edited by Marta María Manchado López and Miguel Luque Talaván, 207–40. Córdoba, Spain: Universidad de Córdoba, 2011.

Graña Cid, María del Mar. "'La familia de fuera': Aproximación a las clientelas de los monasterios de clarisas (Córdoba, siglos XIII–XVI)" *Archivo Ibero-Americano* 265–66, no. 70 (2010): 317–43.

Haliczer, Stephen. *Between Exaltation and Infamy: Female Mystics in the Golden Age of Spain.* Oxford: Oxford University Press, 2002.

Hamburger, Jeffery F. *Nuns as Artists: The Visual Culture of a Medieval Convent.* Berkeley: University of California Press, 1997.

Haring, Clarence Henry. *Trade and Navigation Between Spain and the Indies in the Time of the Hapsburgs.* Cambridge, MA: Harvard University Press, 1918.

Howe, Elizabeth Teresa. *Education and Women in the Early Modern Hispanic World.* Burlington, VT: Ashgate, 2013.

Irving, D. R. M. *Colonial Counterpoint: Music in Early Modern Manila.* Oxford: Oxford University Press, 2010.

Kagan, Richard L. *Urban Images of the Hispanic World, 1493–1793.* New Haven, CT: Yale University Press, 2000.

Kasl, Ronda. "Painters, Polychromy and the Perfection of Images." In *Spanish Polychrome Sculpture 1500–1800 in United States Collections*, edited by Suzanne L. Stratton, 33–35. New York: Schneidereith and Sons, 1994.

Keller-Lapp, Heidi M. "Floating Cloisters and Femmes Fortes: Ursuline Missionaries in Ancien Régime France and Its Colonies." PhD diss., University of California, San Diego, 2005.

Kiple, Kenneth F., ed. *The Cambridge Historical Dictionary of Disease.* New York: Cambridge University Press, 2003.

Kirk, Stephanie L. *Convent Life in Colonial Mexico: A Tale of Two Communities.* Gainesville: University Press of Florida, 2007.

Kirk, Stephanie L., and Sarah Rivett. Introduction to *Religious Transformations in the Early Modern Americas*, edited by Stephanie Kirk and Sarah Rivett, 1–22. Philadelphia: University of Pennsylvania Press, 2014.

Klein, Herbert S., and Ben Vinson III. *African Slavery in Latin America and the Caribbean.* New York: Oxford University Press, 2007.

Lafaye, Jacques. *Quetzalcoatl and Guadalupe: The Formation of Mexican National Consciousness, 1531–1813.* Translated by Benjamin Keen. Chicago: University of Chicago Press, 1976.

Lane, Kris E. *Pillaging the Empire: Piracy in the Americas, 1500–1750.* Armonk, NY: M. E. Sharpe, 1998.

Lavrin, Asunción. *Brides of Christ: Conventual Life in Colonial Mexico.* Stanford, CA: Stanford University Press, 2008.

———. "La educación de una novicia capuchina." *Hispanófila* 171 (June 2014): 77–93.

———. "Erudición, devoción y creatividad tras las rejas conventuales." In *Las letras en la celda: Cultura escrita de los conventos femeninos en la España moderna*, edited by Nieves Baranda Leturio and María Carmen Marín Pina, 65–88. Madrid: Iberoamericana/Vervuert, 2014.

————. "Los espacios de la muerte." In *Espacios en la historia: Invención y transformación de los espacios sociales*, edited by Pilar Gonzalbo Aizpuru, 49–73. Mexico City: El Colegio de Mexico, 2014.

Lehfeldt, Elizabeth A. *Religious Women in Golden Age Spain: The Permeable Cloister.* Burlington, VT: Ashgate, 2005.

Lev, Efraim, and Zohar Amar. *Practical Materia Medica of the Medieval Eastern Mediterranean According to the Cairo Genizah.* Leiden, Netherlands: Brill, 2008.

Lockhart, James. *The Nahuas after the Conquest.* Stanford, CA: Stanford University Press, 1992.

Lopes Don, Patricia. *Bonfires of Culture: Franciscans, Indigenous Leaders, and the Inquisition in Early Mexico, 1524–1540.* Norman: University of Oklahoma Press, 2010.

Lundberg, Magnus. "El clero indígena en Hispanoamérica: De la legislación a la implementación y práctica eclesiástica." *Estudios de Historia Novohispana* 38 (January–June 2008): 39–62.

————. *Mission and Ecstasy: Contemplative Women and Salvation in Colonial Spanish America and the Philippines.* Uppsala: Swedish Institute of Mission Research, 2015.

Marcocci, Giuseppe. "Saltwater Conversion: Trans-oceanic Sailing and Religious Transformation in the Iberian World." In *Space and Conversion in Global Perspective*, edited by Giuseppe Marcocci, Wietse de Boer, Aliocha Maldavsky, and Ilaria Pavan, Intersections, vol. 35, 235–59. Leiden, Netherlands: Brill, 2014.

Martínez Caviró, Balbina M. "El arte en los conventos de Toledo." In *I Congreso Internacional del Monacato Femenino en España, Portugal y América, 1492–1992*, 2:495–521. León, Spain: Universidad de León, 1993.

————. "El arte mudéjar en el convento toledano de Santa Isabel." *Al-Andalus* 36 (1971): 177–95.

————. *El Monasterio de San Juan de los Reyes.* Toledo: Iberdrola, 2002.

Matovina, Timothy. "The Origins of the Guadalupe Tradition in Mexico." *Catholic Historical Review* 100, no. 2 (Spring 2014): 243–70.

McCarthy, William J. "The Yards at Cavite: Shipbuilding in Early Colonial Philippines." *International Journal of Maritime History* 7, no. 2 (December 1995): 149–62.

McKim-Smith, Gridley. "Spanish Polychrome Sculpture and Its Critical Misfortunes." In *Spanish Polychrome Sculpture 1500–1800 in United States Collections*, edited by Suzanne L. Stratton, 13–31. New York: Schneidereith and Sons, 1994.

McKnight, Kathryn Joy. "Blasphemy as Resistance: An African Slave Woman before the Mexican Inquisition." In *Women in the Inquisition: Spain and the New World*, edited by Mary E. Giles, 229–53. Baltimore: Johns Hopkins University Press, 1999.

Merrim, Stephanie. *The Spectacular City, Mexico, and Colonial Hispanic Literary Culture.* Austin: University of Texas Press, 2011.

Moffit, John F. "Mary as 'Prophetic Seamstress' in Siglo de Oro Sevillian Painting." In *Wallraf-Richartz-Jahrbuch*, edited by Peter Wallman, 141–61. Cologne: Dumont Buchverlag, 1993.

Montgomery, Scott. "Contact Relics." In *Encyclopedia of Medieval Pilgrimage*, edited by Larissa J. Taylor, Leigh Ann Craig, John B. Friedman, Kathy Gower, Thomas Izbicki, and Rita Tekippe. Brill Online Reference Works. http://brillonline.nl/entries/encyclopedia-of-medieval-pilgrimage/contact-relics-SIM_00235.

Morales, Francisco. "De la utopía a la locura: El Asia en la mente de los franciscanos de Nueva España del siglo XVI al XIX." In *Ordenes religiosas entre América y Asia: Ideas para una historia misionera de los espacios coloniales*, edited by Elisabetta Corsi, 57–83. Mexico City, 2008.

———. *Ethnic and Social Background of the Franciscan Friars in Seventeenth-Century Mexico*. Washington, DC: Academy of American Franciscan History, 1973.

———. "The Native Encounter with Christianity: Franciscans and Nahuas in Sixteenth-Century Mexico." *The Americas* 65, no. 2 (October 2008): 137–59.

More, Anna. *Baroque Sovereignty: Carlos de Sigüenza y Góngora and the Creole Archive of Colonial Mexico*. Philadelphia: University of Pennsylvania Press, 2013.

Moreno Nieto, Luis. *Toledo oculto: Los conventos*. Toledo: Imprenta Serrano, 1999.

Morte Acín, Ana. "Tradiciones y pervivencia medievales en los modelos de santidad femenina en la edad moderna: Curaciones milagrosas y mediación." *Medievalia* 18, no. 2 (2015): 297–323.

Muñoz Fernández, Angela. *Acciones e intenciones de mujeres: Vida religiosa de las madrileñas (ss. XV–XVI)*. Madrid: Horas y HORAS, 1995.

Muriel, Josefina. *Conventos de monjas en la Nueva España*. 1946. Reprint, Mexico City: Editorial Jus, 1995.

Myers, Kathleen Ann. *Neither Saints nor Sinners: Writing the Lives of Women in Spanish America*. Oxford: Oxford University Press, 2003.

Nader, Helen, ed. *Power and Gender in Renaissance Spain: Eight Women of the Mendoza Family, 1450–1650*. Urbana: University of Illinois Press, 2004.

Nancarrow Taggard, Mindy. "Art and Alienation in Early Modern Spanish Convents." *South Atlantic Modern Language Association* 65, no. 1 (Winter 2000): 24–40.

———. "Picturing Intimacy in a Spanish Golden Age Convent." *Oxford Art Journal* 23, no. 1 (2000): 99–111.

———. "The 17th-Century Spanish *Vida*: Producing Sanctity with Words and Images." *Women's Art Journal* 25, no. 1 (Spring–Summer 2004): 32–38.

Nesvig, Martin Austin. "The 'Indian Question' and the Case of Tlatelolco." In *Local Religion in Colonial Mexico*, edited by Martin Austin Nesvig, 63–89. Albuquerque: University of New Mexico Press, 2006.

Newson, Linda A. *Conquest and Pestilence in the Early Spanish Philippines*. Honolulu: University of Hawai'i Press, 2009.

O'Flanagan, Patrick. *Port Cities of Atlantic Iberia, c. 1500–1900*. Aldershot, UK: Ashgate, 2008.

Owens, Sarah E. "The Cloister as Therapeutic Space: Breast Cancer Narratives in the Early Modern World." *Literature and Medicine* 30, no. 2 (Fall 2012): 295–314.

————. "Crossing Mexico (1620–1621): Franciscan Nuns and Their Journey to the Philippines." *The Americas* 72, no. 4 (October 2015): 583–606.

————. "A Nun's Account of Death and Dying in a Foreign Land." *Magistra* 16, no. 1 (Summer 2010): 12–37.

————. "El legado del rosario milagroso en los escritos de viaje de sor Ana de Cristo hacia Filipinas." *Boletín de Monumentos Históricos/Tercera Época* 30 (January–April 2014): 22–35.

————. "Monjas españolas en Filipinas: La formación de lectura y escritura de sor Ana de Cristo." In *Las letras en la celda: Cultura escrita de los conventos femeninos en la España moderna*, edited by Nieves Baranda Leturio and María Carmen Marín Pina, 379–92. Madrid: Iberoamericana/Vervuert, 2014.

Pablo Maroto, Daniel de. "La 'Santa Juana,' mística franciscana del siglo XVI español: Significación histórica." *Revista de espiritualidad* 60 (2001): 577–601.

Parker, Charles H. *Global Interactions in the Early Modern Age, 1400–1800.* Cambridge: Cambridge University Press, 2010.

Penalva, Elsa. *Mulheres em Macau: Donas honradas, mulheres libres e escravas (séculos XVI e XVII).* Lisbon: Centro de História de Além-Mar/Centro Científico e Cultural de Macau, 2011.

Pérez, Lorenzo. "Mártires de Japón en el año de 1622." *Archivo Iberoamericano* 18 (1922): 145–73.

Pérez-Mallaína, Pablo Emilio. *El hombre frente al mar: Naufragios en la Carrera de India durante los siglos XVI y XVII.* Seville, Spain: University of Seville, 1996.

————. *Spain's Men of the Sea: Daily Life on the Indies Fleets in the Sixteenth Century.* Translated by Carla Rahn Phillips. Baltimore: Johns Hopkins University Press, 1998.

Perry, Elizabeth. "Convents, Art, and Creole Identity in Late Viceregal New Spain." In *Women and Art in Early Modern Latin America*, edited by Kellen Kee McIntyre and Richard E. Phillips, 321–41. Leiden, Netherlands: Brill, 2007.

Phelan, John Leddy. *The Hispanization of the Philippines: Spanish Aims and Filipino Responses, 1565–1700.* 1967. Reprint, Madison: University of Wisconsin Press, 2011.

————. "Prebaptismal Instruction and the Administration of Baptism in the Philippines during the Sixteenth Century." In *Studies in Philippine Church History*, edited by Gerald H. Anderson, 22–43. Ithaca, NY: Cornell University Press, 1969.

Phillips, Carla Rahn. "The Organization of Oceanic Empires. The Iberian World in the Habsburg Period." In *Seascapes: Maritime Histories, Littoral Cultures, and Transoceanic Exchanges*, edited by Jerry H. Bentley, Renate Bridenthal, and Kären Wigen, 71–86. Honolulu: University of Hawai'i Press, 2007.

————. *Six Galleons for the King of Spain: Imperial Defense in the Early Seventeenth Century.* Baltimore: Johns Hopkins University Press, 1986.

Po-Chia Hsia, Ronnie. *The World of Catholic Renewal, 1540–1770.* Cambridge: Cambridge University Press, 2005.

Poole, Stafford. *The Guadalupan Controversies in Mexico*. Stanford, CA: Stanford University Press, 2006.

———. *Our Lady of Guadalupe: The Origins and Sources of a Mexican National Symbol, 1531–1797*. Tucson: University of Arizona Press, 1997.

Poska, Allyson M. *Gendered Crossings: Women and Migration in the Spanish Empire*. Albuquerque: University of New Mexico Press, 2016.

Poutrin, Isabelle. "¿Para qué servían los libros de revelaciones de mujeres? Deleites místicos, movilización católica y entretenimiento devote en la España barroca." In *Las letras en la celda: Cultura escrita de los conventos femeninos en la España moderna*, edited by Nieves Baranda Leturio and María Carmen Marín Pina, 147–58. Madrid: Iberoamericana/Vervuert, 2014.

Rafael, Vicente L. *Contracting Colonialism: Translation and Christian Conversion in Tagalog Society Under Early Spanish Rule*. 1993. Reprint, Durham, NC: Duke University Press, 2005.

Revenga Domínguez, Paula. "El arte de la pintura y la cuestión corporative en el Toledo del siglo XVII." *Anales de Historia del Arte* 10 (2000): 149–67.

Roest, Bert. *Order and Disorder: The Poor Clares Between Foundation and Reform*. Leiden, Netherlands: Brill, 2013

Romero-Díaz, Nieves, and Lisa Vollendorf, eds. *Women Playwrights of Early Modern Spain: Feliciana Enríquez de Guzmán, Ana Caro Mallén, and Sor Marcela de San Félix*. Translated by Harley Erdman. Tucson, AZ: Iter and ACMRS, 2016.

Ruano, Pedro. *Jerónima de la Asunción: Poor Clares' First Woman Missionary to the Philippines*. Quezon City, Philippines: Monasterio de Santa Clara, 1991.

Rubial García, Antonio. "Icons of Devotion: The Appropriation and Use of Saints in New Spain." In *Local Religion in Colonial Mexico*, edited by Martin Austin Nesvig, 37–61. Albuquerque: University of New Mexico Press, 2006.

Russell-Wood, A. J. R. *A World on the Move: The Portuguese in Africa, Asia, and America, 1415–1808*. New York: St. Martin's Press, 1993.

Salazar Simarro, Nuria, and Sarah E. Owens. "Cloistered Women in Health Care: The Convent of Jesús María, Mexico City." In *Women of the Iberian Atlantic*, edited by Sarah E. Owens and Jane E. Mangan, 128–47. Baton Rouge: Louisiana State University Press, 2012.

Sales Colín, Ostwald. "Las cargazones del galeón de la Carrera de Poniente: Primera mitad del siglo XVII." *Revista de Historia Económica/Journal of Iberian and Latin American Economic History* 18, no. 3 (December 2000): 629–61.

———. "El colegio para mujeres de Santa Potenciana de Filipinas, siglo XVII." In *El monacato femenino en el imperio español*, edited by Manuel Ramos Medina, 115–24. Mexico City: Condumex, 1995.

———. *El movimiento portuario de Acapulco: El protagonismo de Nueva España en la relación con Filipinas, 1587–1648*. Mexico City: Plaza y Valdés, 2000.

Sampson Vera Tudela, Elisa. "Illustrating Sainthood: The Construction of Eighteenth-Century Spanish American Hagiography." In *Eve's Enlightenment: Women's*

Experience in Spain and Spanish America, 1726–1839, edited by Catherine M. Jaffe and Elizabeth Franklin Lewis, 84–100. Baton Rouge: Louisiana State University Press, 2009.

Sánchez, Magdalena S. *The Empress, the Queen, and the Nun: Women and Power at the Court of Philip III of Spain*. Baltimore: Johns Hopkins University Press, 1998.

———. "Pious and Political Images of a Habsburg Woman at the Court of Philip III (1598–1621)." In *Spanish Women in the Golden Age: Images and Realities*, edited by Magdalena S. Sánchez and Alain Saint-Saëns, 91–107. Westport, CT: Praeger, 1996.

———. "Where the Palace and Convent Met: The Descalzas Reales in Madrid." *Sixteenth Century Journal* 46, no. 1 (Spring 2015): 53–82.

Sánchez Fuertes, Cayetano. "Impresos Franciscanos Hispano-Filipinos 1593–1699." Parts 1 and 2. *Philippiniana Sacra* 50, no. 150 (May–August 2015): 295–334; 50, no. 151 (September–December 2015): 473–514.

———. "La madre Jerónima de la Asunción y su fundación del Monasterio de Santa Clara de Manila: Incidencias y consecuencias." *Verdad y Vida* 52 (1994): 379–400.

———. "Los Monasterios de Santa Clara de Manila y Macao: Nuevos documentos para su historia." *Archivum Franciscanum Historicum* 105 (2012): 51–104.

Sánchez Lora, José Luis. *Mujeres, conventos y formas de la religiosidad barroca*. Madrid: Fundación Universitaria Española, 1988.

Santiago, Luciano P. "The First Filipino Capellanías (1605–1699)." *Philippiniana Sacra* 22, no. 66 (1987): 421–34.

Schroeder, Rev. H. J., ed. *Canons and Decrees of the Council of Trent*. 1941. Reprint, London: B. Herder, 1960.

Schroth, Sarah. "Burial of the Count of Orgaz." *Studies in the History of Art* 11 (1982): 1–17.

Schurz, William Lytle. *The Manila Galleon*. 1939. Reprint, New York: E. P. Dutton, 1959.

Seijas, Tatiana. *Asian Slaves in Colonial Mexico: From Chinos to Indians*. New York: Cambridge University Press, 2014.

Serrera, Ramón María. "El camino de China." In *Filipinas puerta de Oriente: De Legazpi a Malaspina*, edited by Alfredo J. Morales, 111–29. Barcelona: Lunwerg/Sociedad Estatal para la Acción Cultural Exterior, 2003.

Slack, Edward R., Jr. "The *Chinos* in New Spain: A Corrective Lens for a Distorted Image." *Journal of World History* 20, no. 1 (2009): 35–67.

Sperling, Jutta Gisela, ed. *Medieval and Renaissance Lactations: Images, Rhetorics, Practices*. Burlington, VT: Ashgate, 2013.

Steele, Ian K. *The English Atlantic, 1675–1740: An Exploration of Communication and Community*. Oxford: Oxford University Press, 1986.

Stratton, Suzanne L. *The Immaculate Conception in Spanish Art*. New York: Cambridge University Press, 1994.

Surtz, Ronald E. *The Guitar of God: Gender, Power, and Authority in the Visionary World of Mother Juana de la Cruz (1481–1534)*. Philadelphia: University of Pennsylvania Press, 1990.

Tavárez, David. *The Invisible War: Indigenous Devotions, Discipline, and Dissent in Colonial Mexico*. Stanford, CA: Stanford University Press, 2011.

Tiffany, Tanya J. *Diego Velázquez's Early Painting and the Culture of Seventeenth-Century Seville*. University Park: Penn State University Press, 2012.

———. "The Portrait of Madre Jerónima de la Fuente and the Convent of Santa Clara in Seville." In *El joven Velázquez: A propósito de la educación de la Virgen de Yale*, proceedings from the Simposio Internacional Celebrado en el Espacio Santa Clara de Sevilla, October 15–17, 2014, 292–311. Seville: ICAS, 2015.

Triviño, María Victoria, ed. *Escritoras clarisas españolas*. Madrid: Biblioteca de Autores Cristianos, 1992.

Van Deusen, Nancy E. *Global Indios: The Indigenous Struggle for Justice in Sixteenth-Century Spain*. Durham, NC: Duke University Press, 2015.

———. ed. and trans. *The Souls of Purgatory: The Spiritual Diary of a Seventeenth-Century Afro-Peruvian Mystic, Ursula de Jesús*. Albuquerque: University of New Mexico Press, 2004.

Vargas Matías, Sergio Arturo. "El Camino Real de Veracruz: Pasado, presente y futuro." M.A. thesis, Universidad Anáhuac, 2011. http://aprendeenlinea.udea.edu.co/revistas/index.php/folios/article/viewFile/12769/11508.

Villa-Flores, Javier. "On Divine Persecution: Blasphemy and Gambling." In *Religion in New Spain*, edited by Susan Schroeder and Stafford Poole, 238–62. Albuquerque: University of New Mexico Press, 2007.

Villegas Díaz, Luis Rafael. "Santa Isabel de los Reyes (Toledo) en el siglo XVII: Datos para su historia." *Archivo Ibero-Americano* 54, no. 213–14 (1994): 511–44.

Ward, Haruko Nawata. *Women Religious Leaders in Japan's Christian Century, 1549–1650*. Farnham, UK: Ashgate, 2009.

Watson Marrón, Gustavo. *El templo que unió a Nueva España: Historia del santuario y colegiata de Guadalupe, extramuros de México, en el siglo XVIII*. Mexico City: Porrúa, 2012.

Weber, Alison, ed. *Devout Laywomen in the Early Modern World*. London: Routledge, 2016.

———. Introduction to *Book for the Hour of Recreation*, by María de San José Salazar, 1–26. Chicago: University of Chicago Press, 2002.

———. "Saint Teresa, Demonologist." In *Culture and Control in Counter-Reformation Spain*, edited by Anne J. Cruz and Mary Elizabeth Perry, 171–95. Minneapolis: University of Minnesota Press, 1992.

———. "Saint Teresa's Problematic Patrons." *Journal of Medieval and Early Modern Studies* 29, no. 2 (1999): 357–79.

———. *Teresa of Avila and the Rhetoric of Femininity*. Princeton, NJ: Princeton University Press, 1990.

Webster, Susan Verdi. *Art and Ritual in Golden Age Spain: Sevillian Confraternities and the Processional Sculpture of Holy Week*. Princeton, NJ: Princeton University Press, 1998.

————. "Shameless Beauty and Worldly Splendor: On the Spanish Practice of Adorning the Virgin." In *The Miraculous Image in the Late Middle Ages and Renaissance*, edited by Eric Thunø and Gerhard Wolf, 249–71. Rome: L'Erma di Bretschneider, 2004.

Wheat, David. *Atlantic Africa and the Spanish Caribbean, 1570–1640*. Chapel Hill: University of North Carolina Press, 2016.

Wiesner-Hanks, Merry E. "Early Modern Gender and the Global Turn." In *Mapping Gendered Routes and Spaces in the Early Modern World*, edited by Merry E. Wiesner-Hanks, 55–74. Burlington, VT: Ashgate, 2015.

Williams, John Hoyt. "Tapping the Orient: Voyages of the Manila Galleons." *Oceans* 15 (1982): 44–49.

Wilson, Christopher C. "From *Mujercilla* to *Conquistadora*: St. Teresa of Ávila's Missionary Identity in Mexican Colonial Art." In *Women and Art in Early Modern Latin America*, edited by Kellen Kee McIntyre and Richard E. Phillips, 419–41. Leiden: Brill, 2007.

Winston-Allen, Anne. *Convent Chronicles: Women Writing About Women and Reform in the Late Middle Ages*. University Park: Pennsylvania State University Press, 2004.

Yuste López, Carmen. *El comercio de la Nueva España con Filipinas, 1590–1785*. Mexico City: INAH, 1984.

Zires, Margarita. "Los mitos de la Virgen de Guadalupe." *Mexican Studies/Estudios Mexicanos* 10, no. 2 (Summer 1994): 281–313.

Index